www.ingramcontent.com/pod-product-compliance
Lightning Source LLC
Chambersburg PA
CBHW060757100426
42813CB00004B/852

Recollections of Abraham Lincoln 1847-1865

by Ward Hill Lamon

Edited by Dorothy Lamon Teillard

CHAPTER I.

EARLY ACQUAINTANCE.

When Mr. Lincoln was nominated for the Presidency in 1860, a campaign book-maker asked him to give the prominent features of his life. He replied in the language of Gray's "Elegy," that his life presented nothing but

"The short and simple annals of the poor."

He had, however, a few months previously, written for his friend Jesse W. Fell the following:--

I was born Feb. 12, 1809, in Harden County, Kentucky. My parents were both born in Virginia, of undistinguished families--second families, perhaps I should say. My mother, who died in my tenth year, was of a family of the name of Hanks, some of whom now reside in Adams, some others in Macon counties, Illinois--My paternal grandfather, Abraham Lincoln, emigrated from Rockingham County, Virginia, to Kentucky, about 1781 or 2, where, a year or two later, he was killed by indians,--not in battle, but by stealth, when he was laboring to open a farm in the forest--His ancestors, who were quakers, went to Virginia from Berks County, Pennsylvania--An effort to identify them with the New England family of the same name ended in nothing more definite, than a similarity of Christian names in both families, such as Enoch, Levi, Mordecai, Solomon, Abraham, and the like--

My father, at the death of his father, was but six years of age; and he grew up, literally without education--He removed from Kentucky to what is now Spencer county, Indiana, in my eighth year--We reached our new home about the time the State came into the Union--It was a wild region, with many bears and other wild animals still in the woods--There I grew up--There were some schools, so called; but no qualification was ever required of a teacher, beyond "readin, writin, and cipherin" to the Rule of Three--If a straggler supposed to understand latin happened to sojourn in the neighborhood, he was looked upon as a wizzard--There was absolutely nothing to excite ambition for education. Of course when I came of age I did not know much--Still, somehow, I could read, write, and cipher to the Rule of Three; but that was all--I have not been to school since--The little advance I now have upon this store of education, I have picked up from time to time under the pressure of necessity--

I was raised to farm work, which I continued till I was twenty two--At twenty one I came to Illinois, and passed the first year in Macon county--Then I got to New-Salem at that time in Sangamon, now in Menard county, where I remained a year as a sort of Clerk in a store--Then came the Black Hawk war; and I was elected a Captain of Volunteers--a success which gave me more pleasure than any I have had since--I went the campaign, was elected, ran for the Legislature the same year (1832) and was beaten--the only time I ever have been beaten by the people--The next, and three succeeding biennial elections, I was elected to the Legislature--I was not a candidate afterwards. During this Legislative period I had studied law, and removed to Springfield to practice it--In 1846 I was once elected to the lower House of Congress--Was not a candidate for re-election--From 1849 to 1854, both inclusive, practiced law more assiduously than ever before--Always a whig in politics; and generally on the whig electoral tickets, making active canvasses--I was losing interest in politics, when the repeal of the Missouri Compromise aroused me again--What I have done since then is pretty well known--

If any personal description of me is thought desirable, it may be said, I am, in height, six feet, four inches, nearly; lean in flesh, weighing, on an average, one hundred and eighty pounds; dark complexion, with coarse black hair, and grey eyes--No other marks or brands recollected--

Yours very truly A. LINCOLN.

J. W. Fell, Esq. WASHINGTON, D. C., March 20, 1872.

We the undersigned hereby certify that the foregoing statement is in the hand-writing of Abraham Lincoln.

DAVID DAVIS. LYMAN TRUMBULL. CHARLES SUMNER.[E]

[E] The circumstances under which the original preceding sketch was written are explained in the following letter:--

NATIONAL HOTEL, WASHINGTON, D. C., Feb. 19, 1872.

COLONEL WARD H. LAMON:

DEAR SIR,--In compliance with your request, I place in your hands a copy of a manuscript in my possession written by Abraham Lincoln, giving a brief account of his early history, and the commencement of that political career which terminated in his election to the presidency.

It may not be inappropriate to say, that some time preceding the writing of the enclosed, finding, in Pennsylvania and elsewhere, a laudable curiosity in the public mind to know more about the early history of Mr. Lincoln, and looking, too, to the possibilities of his being an available candidate for the presidency in 1860, I had on several occasions requested of him this information, and that it was not without some hesitation he placed in my hands even this very modest account of himself, which he did in the month of December, 1859.

To this were added, by myself, other facts bearing upon his legislative and political history, and the whole forwarded to a friend residing in my native county (Chester, Pa.),--the Hon. Joseph J. Lewis, former commissioner of internal revenue,--who made them the basis of an ably-written and somewhat elaborate memoir of the late president, which appeared in the Pennsylvania and other papers of the country in January, 1860, and which contributed to prepare the way for the subsequent nomination at Chicago the following June.

Believing this brief and unpretending narrative, written by himself in his own peculiar vein,--and in justice to him I should add, without the remotest expectation of its ever appearing in public,--with the attending circumstances, may be of interest to the numerous admirers of that historic and truly great man, I place it at your disposal.

I am truly yours, JESSE W. FELL.

Were I to say in this polite age that Abraham Lincoln was born in a condition of life most humble and obscure, and that he was surrounded by circumstances most unfavorable to culture and to the development of that nobility and purity which his wonderful character afterward displayed, it would shock the fastidious and super-fine sensibilities of the average reader, would be regarded as prima facie evidence of felonious intent, and would subject me to the charge of being inspired by an antagonistic animus. In justice to the truth of history, however, it must be acknowledged that such are the facts concerning this great man, regarding whom nothing should be concealed from public scrutiny, either in the surroundings of his birth, his youth, his manhood, or his private and public life and character. Let all the facts concerning him be known, and he will appear brighter and purer by the test.

It may well be said of him that he is probably the only man, dead or living, whose true and faithful life could be written and leave the subject more ennobled by the minuti?of the record. His faults are but "the shadows which his virtues cast." It is my purpose in these recollections to give the reader a closer view of the great war President than is afforded by current biographies, which deal mainly with the outward phases of his life; and in carrying out this purpose I will endeavor to present that many-sided man in those relations where his distinguishing traits manifest themselves most strongly.

With the grandeur of his figure in history, with his genius and his achievements as the model statesman and chief magistrate, all men are now familiar; but there yet remain to be sketched many phases of his inner life. Many of the incidents related in these sketches came to my knowledge through my long-continued association with him both in his private and public life; therefore, if the Ego shall seem at times pushed forward to undue prominence, it will be because of its convenience, or rather necessity, certainly not from any motive of self-adulation.

My personal acquaintance with Mr. Lincoln dates back to the autumn of 1847. In that year, attracted by glowing accounts of material growth and progress in that part of the West, I left my home in what was then Berkeley County, Virginia, and settled at Danville, Vermillion County, Illinois. That county and Sangamon, including Springfield, the new capital of the State, were embraced in the Eighth Judicial Circuit, which at that early day consisted of fourteen counties. It was then the custom of lawyers, like their brethren of England, "to ride the circuit." By that circumstance the people came in contact with all the lawyers in the circuit, and were enabled to note their distinguishing traits. I soon learned that the man most celebrated, even in those pioneer days, for oddity, originality, wit, ability, and eloquence in that region of the State was Abraham Lincoln. My great curiosity to see him was gratified soon after I took up my residence at Danville.

I was introduced to Mr. Lincoln by the Hon. John T. Stuart, for some years his partner at Springfield. After a comical survey of my fashionable toggery,--my swallow-tail coat, white neck-cloth, and ruffled shirt (an astonishing outfit for a young limb of the law in that settlement),--Mr. Lincoln said: "And so you are a cousin of our friend John J. Brown; he told me you were coming. Going to try your hand at the law, are you? I should know at a glance that you were a Virginian; but I don't think you would succeed at splitting rails. That was my occupation at your age, and I don't think I have taken as much pleasure in anything else from that day to this."

I assured him, perhaps as a sort of defence against the eloquent condemnation implied in my fashionable clawhammer, that I had done a deal of hard manual labor in my time. Much amused at this solemn declaration, Mr. Lincoln said: "Oh, yes; you Virginians shed barrels of perspiration while standing off at a distance and superintending the work your slaves do for you. It is different with us. Here it is every fellow for himself, or he doesn't get there."

Mr. Lincoln soon learned, however, that my detestation of slave labor was quite as pronounced as his own, and from that hour we were friends. Until the day of his death it was my pleasure and good fortune to retain his confidence unshaken, as he retained my affection unbroken.

I was his local partner, first at Danville, and afterward at Bloomington. We rode the circuit together, traveling by buggy in the dry seasons and on horse-back in bad weather, there being no railroads then in that part of the State. Mr. Lincoln had defeated that redoubtable champion of pioneer Methodism, the Rev. Peter Cartwright, in the last race for Congress. Cartwright was an oddity in his way, quite as original as Lincoln himself. He was a foeman worthy of Spartan steel, and Mr. Lincoln's fame was greatly enhanced by his victory over the famous preacher. Whenever it was known that Lincoln was to make a speech or argue a case, there was a general rush and a crowded house. It mattered little what subject he was discussing,--Lincoln was subject enough for the people. It was Lincoln they wanted to hear and see; and his progress round the circuit was marked by a constantly recurring series of ovations.

Mr. Lincoln was from the beginning of his circuit-riding the light and life of the court. The most trivial circumstance furnished a back-ground for his wit. The following incident, which illustrates his love of a joke, occurred in the early days of our acquaintance. I, being at the time on the infant side of twenty-one, took particular pleasure in athletic sports. One day when we were attending the circuit court which met at Bloomington, Ill., I was wrestling near the court house with some one who had challenged me to a trial, and in the scuffle made a large rent in the rear of my trousers. Before I had time to make any change, I was called into court to take up a case. The evidence was finished. I, being the Prosecuting Attorney at the time, got up to address the jury. Having on a somewhat short coat, my misfortune was rather apparent. One of the lawyers, for a joke, started a subscription paper which was passed from one member of the bar to another as they sat by a long table fronting the bench, to buy a pair of pantaloons for Lamon,--"he being," the paper said, "a poor but worthy young man." Several put down their names with some ludicrous subscription, and finally the paper was laid by some one in front of Mr. Lincoln, he being engaged in writing at the time. He quietly glanced over the paper, and, immediately taking up his pen, wrote after his name, "I can contribute nothing to the end in view."

Although Mr. Lincoln was my senior by eighteen years, in one important particular I certainly was in a marvelous degree his acknowledged superior. One of the first things I learned after getting fairly under way as a lawyer was to charge well for legal services,--a branch of the practice that Mr. Lincoln never could learn. In fact, the lawyers of the circuit often complained that his fees were not at all commensurate with the service rendered. He at length left that branch of the business wholly to me; and to my tender mercy clients were turned over, to be slaughtered according to my popular and more advanced ideas of the dignity of our profession. This soon led to serious and shocking embarrassment.

Early in our practice a gentleman named Scott placed in my hands a case of some importance. He had a demented sister who possessed property to the amount of $10,000, mostly in cash. A "conservator," as he was called, had been appointed to take charge of the estate, and we were employed to resist a motion to remove the conservator. A designing adventurer had become acquainted with the unfortunate girl, and knowing that she had money, sought to marry her; hence the motion. Scott, the brother and conservator, before we entered upon the case, insisted that I should fix the amount of the fee. I told him that it would be $250, adding, however, that he had better wait; it might not give us much trouble, and in that event a less amount would do. He agreed at once to pay $250, as he expected a hard contest over the motion.

The case was tried inside of twenty minutes; our success was complete. Scott was satisfied, and cheerfully paid over the money to me inside the bar, Mr. Lincoln looking on. Scott then went out, and Mr. Lincoln asked, "What did you charge that man?" I told him $250. Said he: "Lamon, that is all wrong. The service was not worth that sum. Give him back at least half of it."

I protested that the fee was fixed in advance; that Scott was perfectly satisfied, and had so expressed himself. "That may be," retorted Mr. Lincoln, with a look of distress and of undisguised displeasure, "but I am not satisfied. This is positively wrong. Go, call him back and return half the money at least, or I will not receive one cent of it for my share."

I did go, and Scott was astonished when I handed back half the fee.

This conversation had attracted the attention of the lawyers and the court. Judge David Davis, then on our circuit bench, called Mr. Lincoln to him. The judge never could whisper, but in this instance he probably did his best.

At all events, in attempting to whisper to Mr. Lincoln he trumpeted his rebuke in about these words, and in rasping tones that could be heard all over the court room: "Lincoln, I have been watching you and Lamon. You are impoverishing this bar by your picayune charges of fees, and the lawyers have reason to complain of you. You are now almost as poor as Lazarus, and if you don't make people pay you more for your services you will die as poor as Job's turkey!"

Judge O. L. Davis, the leading lawyer in that part of the State, promptly applauded this malediction from the bench; but Mr. Lincoln was immovable. "That money," said he, "comes out of the pocket of a poor, demented girl, and I would rather starve than swindle her in this manner."

That evening the lawyers got together and tried Mr. Lincoln before a moot tribunal called "The Ogmathorial Court." He was found guilty and fined for his awful crime against the pockets of his brethren of the bar. The fine he paid with great good humor, and then kept the crowd of lawyers in uproarious laughter until after midnight. He persisted in his revolt, however, declaring that with his consent his firm should never during its life, or after its dissolution, deserve the reputation enjoyed by those shining lights of the profession, "Catch 'em and Cheat 'em."

In these early days Mr. Lincoln was once employed in a case against a railroad company in Illinois. The case was concluded in his favor, except as to the pronouncement of judgment. Before this was done, he rose and stated that his opponents had not proved all that was justly due to them in offset, and proceeded to state briefly that justice required that an allowance should be made against his client for a certain amount. The court at once acquiesced in his statement, and immediately proceeded to pronounce judgment in accordance therewith. He was ever ready to sink his selfish love of victory as well as his partiality for his client's favor and interest for the sake of exact justice.

In many of the courts on the circuit Mr. Lincoln would be engaged on one side or the other of every case on the docket, and yet, owing to his low charges and the large amount of professional work which he did for nothing, at the time he left Springfield for Washington to take the oath of office as President of the United States he was not worth more than seven thousand dollars,--his property consisting of the house in which he had lived, and eighty acres of land on the opposite side of the river from Omaha, Neb. This land he had entered with his bounty land-warrant obtained for services in the Black Hawk War.[1]

[1] Page 20, line 21, after the word "war."

Mr. Lincoln did not think money for its own sake a fit object of any man's ambition.

Mr. Lincoln was always simple in his habits and tastes. He was economical in everything, and his wants were few. He was a good liver; and his family, though not extravagant, were much given to entertainments, and saw and enjoyed many ways of spending money not observable by him. After all his inexpensive habits, and a long life of successful law practice, he was reduced to the necessity of borrowing money to defray expenses for the first months of his residence at the White House. This money he repaid after receiving his salary as President for the first quarter.

A few months after meeting Mr. Lincoln, I attended an entertainment given at his residence in Springfield. After introducing me to Mrs. Lincoln, he left us in conversation. I remarked to her that her husband was a great favorite in the eastern part of the State, where I had been stopping. "Yes," she replied, "he is a great favorite everywhere. He is to be President of the United States some day; if I had not thought so I never would have married him, for you can see he is not pretty. But look at him! Doesn't he look as if he would make a magnificent President?"

"Magnificent" somewhat staggered me; but there was, without appearing ungallant, but one reply to make to this pointed question. I made it, but did so under a mental protest, for I am free to admit that he did not look promising for that office; on the contrary, to me he looked about as unpromising a candidate as I could well imagine the American people were ever likely to put forward. At that time I felt convinced that Mrs. Lincoln was running Abraham beyond his proper distance in that race. I did not thoroughly know the man then; afterward I never saw the time when I was not willing to apologize for my misguided secret protest. Mrs. Lincoln, from that day to the day of his inauguration, never wavered in her faith that her hopes in this respect would be realized.

In 1858, when Mr. Lincoln and Judge Douglas were candidates for the United States Senate, and were making their celebrated campaign in Illinois, General McClellan was Superintendent of the Illinois Central Railroad, and favored the election of Judge Douglas. At all points on the road where meetings between the two great politicians were held, either a special train or a special car was furnished to Judge Douglas; but Mr. Lincoln, when he failed to get transportation on the regular trains in time to meet his appointments, was reduced to the necessity of going as freight. There being orders from headquarters to permit no passenger to travel on freight trains, Mr. Lincoln's persuasive powers were often brought into requisition. The favor was granted or refused according to the politics of the conductor.

On one occasion, in going to meet an appointment in the southern part of the State,--that section of Illinois called Egypt,--Mr. Lincoln and I, with other friends, were traveling in the "caboose" of a freight train, when we were switched off the main track to allow a special train to pass in which Mr. Lincoln's more aristocratic rival was being conveyed. The passing train was decorated with banners and flags, and carried a band of music which was playing "Hail to the Chief." As the train whistled past, Mr. Lincoln broke out in a fit of laughter and said, "Boys, the gentleman in that car evidently smelt no royalty in our carriage."

On arriving at the point where these two political gladiators were to test their strength, there was the same contrast between their respective receptions. The judge was met at the station by the distinguished Democratic citizens of the place, who constituted almost the whole population, and was marched to the camping ground to the sound of music, shouts from the populace, and under floating banners borne by his enthusiastic admirers. Mr. Lincoln was escorted by a few Republican politicians; no enthusiasm was displayed, no music greeted his ears, nor, in fact, any other sound except the warble of the bull-frogs in a neighboring swamp. The signs and prospects for Mr. Lincoln's election by the support of the people looked gloomy indeed.

Judge Douglas spoke first, and so great was the enthusiasm excited by his speech that Mr. Lincoln's friends became apprehensive of trouble. When spoken to on the subject he said: "I am not going to be terrified by an excited populace, and hindered from speaking my honest sentiments upon this infernal subject of human slavery." He rose, took off his hat, and stood before that audience for a considerable space of time in a seemingly reflective mood, looking over the vast throng of people as if making a preliminary survey of their tendencies. He then bowed, and commenced by saying: "My fellow-citizens, I learn that my friend Judge Douglas said in a public speech that I, while in Congress, had voted against the appropriation for supplies to the Mexican soldiers during the late war. This, fellow-citizens, is a perversion of the facts. It is true that I was opposed to the policy of the Administration in declaring war against Mexico[2]; but when war was declared, I never failed to vote for the support of any proposition looking to the comfort of our poor fellows who were maintaining the dignity of our flag in a war that I thought unnecessary and unjust."[F] He gradually became more and more excited; his voice thrilled and his whole frame shook. I was at the time sitting on the stand beside Hon. O. B. Ficklin, who had served in Congress with Mr. Lincoln in 1847. Mr. Lincoln reached back and took Ficklin by the coat-collar, back of his neck, and in no gentle manner lifted him from his seat as if he had been a kitten, and said: "Fellow-citizens, here is Ficklin, who was at that time in Congress with me, and he knows it is a lie." He shook Ficklin until his teeth chattered. Fearing that he would shake Ficklin's head off, I grasped Mr. Lincoln's hand and broke his grip. Mr. Ficklin sat down, and Lincoln continued his address.

[2] Page 24, line 2, after the word "Mexico."

In a speech delivered in the House July 27, 1848, on General Politics, Mr. Lincoln said: "The declaration that we (the Whigs) have always opposed the Mexican War is true or false accordingly as one may understand the term 'opposing the war.' If to say 'the war was unnecessarily and unconstitutionally commenced by the President' be opposing the war, then the Whigs have very generally opposed it. Whenever they have spoken at all, they have said this; and they said it on what appeared good reasons to them: the marching an army into the midst of a peaceful Mexican settlement, frightening the inhabitants away, leaving their growing crops and other property to destruction to you may appear a perfectly amiable, peaceful, unprovoking procedure, but it does not appear so to us. So to call such an act to us appears no other than a naked, impudent absurdity, and we speak of it accordingly. But if, when the war had begun and had become the cause of the country, the giving of our money and our blood, in common with yours, was support of the war, then it is not true that we have always opposed the war."

On another occasion Mr. Lincoln said that the claim that the Mexican War was not aggressive reminded him of the farmer who asserted, "I ain't greedy 'bout land, I only just wants what jines mine."

[F] For some time before this speech Mr. Lincoln had been receiving letters from friends inquiring as to the truth or falsity of Mr. Douglas's charge. Knowing that he had opposed the war with Mexico, while in Congress, they were in doubt whether or not the charge was true, and believed that if true it would be dangerous to his prospects. To one of these anxious friends he writes under date of June 24, 1858: "Give yourself no concern about my voting against the supplies, unless you are without faith that a lie can be successfully contradicted. There is not a word of truth in the charge, and I am just considering a little as to the best shape to put a contradiction in. Show this to whom you please, but do not publish it in the papers."

After the speaking was over, Mr. Ficklin, who had been opposed to Lincoln in politics, but was on terms of warm personal friendship with him, turned to him and said: "Lincoln, you nearly shook all the Democracy out of me to-day."

Mr. Lincoln replied: "That reminds me of what Paul said to Agrippa, which in language and substance I will formulate as follows: I would to God that such Democracy as you folks here in Egypt have were not only almost, but altogether shaken out of, not only you, but all that heard me this day, and that you would all join in assisting in shaking off the shackles of the bondmen by all legitimate means, so that this country may be made free as the good Lord intended it."

Ficklin continued: "Lincoln, I remember of reading somewhere in the same book from which you get your Agrippa story, that Paul, whom you seem to desire to personate, admonished all servants (slaves) to be obedient to them that are their masters according to the flesh, in fear and trembling. It would seem that neither our Saviour nor Paul saw the iniquity of slavery as you and your party do. But you must not think that where you fail by argument to convince an old friend like myself and win him over to your heterodox abolition opinions, you are justified in resorting to violence such as you practiced on me to-day. Why, I never had such a shaking up in the whole course of my life. Recollect that that good old book that you quote from somewhere says in effect this, 'Woe be unto him who goeth to Egypt for help, for he shall fall. The holpen shall fall, and they shall all fall together.' The next thing we know, Lincoln, you and your party will be advocating a war to kill all of us pro-slavery people off."

"No," said Lincoln, "I will never advocate such an extremity; but it will be well for you folks if you don't force such a necessity on the country."

Lincoln then apologized for his rudeness in jostling the muscular Democracy of his friend, and they separated, each going his own way, little thinking then that what they had just said in badinage would be so soon realized in such terrible consequences to the country.

The following letter shows Lincoln's view of the political situation at that time:--

SPRINGFIELD, June 11, 1858.

W. H. LAMON, Esq.:

MY DEAR SIR,--Yours of the 9th written at Joliet is just received. Two or three days ago I learned that McLean had appointed delegates in favor of Lovejoy, and thenceforward I have considered his renomination a fixed fact. My opinion--if my opinion is of any consequence in this case, in which it is no business of mine to interfere--remains unchanged, that running an independent candidate against Lovejoy will not do; that it will result in nothing but disaster all round. In the first place, whoever so runs will be beaten and will be spotted for life; in the second place, while the race is in progress, he will be under the strongest temptation to trade with the Democrats, and to favor the election of certain of their friends to the

Legislature; thirdly, I shall be held responsible for it, and Republican members of the Legislature, who are partial to Lovejoy, will for that purpose oppose us; and, lastly, it will in the end lose us the District altogether. There is no safe way but a convention; and if in that convention, upon a common platform which all are willing to stand upon, one who has been known as an Abolitionist, but who is now occupying none but common ground, can get the majority of the votes to which all look for an election, there is no safe way but to submit.

As to the inclination of some Republicans to favor Douglas, that is one of the chances I have to run, and which I intend to run with patience.

I write in the court room. Court has opened, and I must close.

Yours as ever,

(Signed) A. LINCOLN.

During this senatorial campaign in 1858, Hon. James G. Blaine predicted in a letter, which was extensively published, that Douglas would beat Lincoln for the United States Senate, but that Lincoln would beat Douglas for President in 1860. Mr. Lincoln cut out the paragraph of the letter containing this prediction, and placed it in his pocket-book, where I have no doubt it was found after his death, for only a very short time before that event I saw it in his possession.[3]

[3] Page 27, line 19, after the word "possession."

Mr. Lincoln felt deeply the responsibility of his great trust; and he felt still more keenly the supposed impossibility of administering the government for the sole benefit of an organization which had no existence in one-half of the Union. He was therefore willing, not only to appoint Democrats to office, but to appoint them to the very highest offices within his gift. At this time he thought very highly of Mr. Stephens of Georgia, and would gladly have taken him into his cabinet but for the fear that Georgia might secede, and take Mr. Stephens along with her. He commissioned Thurlow Weed to place a seat in the Cabinet at the disposal of Mr. Gilmore of North Carolina; but Mr. Gilmore, finding that his state was likely to secede, was reluctantly compelled to decline it. I had thought that Mr. Lincoln had authorized his friend Mr. Speed to offer the Treasury Department to Mr. Guthrie of Kentucky. Mr. Speed writes of this incident in a letter to me dated June 24, 1872.

In one instance I find a palpable mistake. It is in regard to a tender to Mr. Guthrie through me of a position in his Cabinet. The history of that transaction was about this: I met Mr. Lincoln by appointment in Chicago after his election but before he had gone to Washington. He seemed very anxious to avoid bloodshed and said that he would do almost anything saving the sacrifice of personal honor and the dignity of the position to which he had been elevated to avoid war.

He asked about Mr. Guthrie and spoke of him as a suitable man for Secretary of War. He asked very particularly as to his strength with the people and if I knew him well enough to say what would be his course in the event of war. I frankly gave my opinion as to what I thought would be his course--which is not necessary here to repeat. He requested me to see Mr. Guthrie. But by all means to be guarded and not to give any man the advantage of the tender of a Cabinet appointment to be declined by an insulting letter. I did see Mr. Guthrie and never tendered him any office for I was not authorized to do so. This is a very different thing from being authorized to tender an appointment.

Yours truly J. F. SPEED.

When Mr. Lincoln was asked during conferences incident to making up his cabinet if it was just or wise to concede so many seats to the Democratic element of the Republican party he replied that as a Whig he thought he could afford to be liberal to a section of the Republican party without whose votes he could not have been elected.

After Mr. Lincoln's election he was sorely beset by rival claimants for the spoils of office in his own State, and distracted by jealousies among his own party adherents. The State was divided so far as the Republican party was concerned into three cliques or factions. The Chicago faction was headed by Norman B. Judd and Ebenezer Peck, the Bloomington faction by Judge David Davis, Leonard Swett, and others, and that of Springfield by J. K. Dubois, O. M. Hatch, William Butler, and others; and however anxious Mr. Lincoln might be to honor his State by a Cabinet appointment, he was powerless to do so without incurring the hostility of the factions from which he could not make a selection. Harmony was, however, in a large measure preserved among the Republican politicians by sending Judd as Minister to Prussia, and by anticipating a place on the Supreme Bench for Judge Davis. Swett wanted nothing, and middle Illinois was satisfied. Springfield controlled the lion's share of State patronage, and satisfaction was given all round as far as circumstances would allow.

Between the time of Mr. Lincoln's election and the 11th of February, 1861, he spent his time in a room in the State House which was assigned to him as an office. Young Mr. Nicolay, a very clever and competent clerk, was lent to him by the Secretary of State to do his writing. During this time he was overrun with visitors from all quarters of the country,--some to assist in forming his Cabinet, some to direct how patronage should be distributed, others to beg for or demand personal advancement. So painstaking was he, that every one of the many thousand letters which poured in upon him was read and promptly answered. The burden of the new and overwhelming labor came near prostrating him with serious illness.

Some days before his departure for Washington, he wrote to me at Bloomington that he desired to see me at once. I went to Springfield, and Mr. Lincoln said to me: "Hill, on the 11th I go to Washington, and I want you to go along with me. Our friends have already asked me to send you as Consul to Paris. You know I would cheerfully give you anything for which our friends may ask or which you may desire, but it looks as if we might have war. In that case I want you with me. In fact, I must have you. So get yourself ready and come along. It will be handy to have you around. If there is to be a fight, I want you to help me to do my share of it, as you have done in times past. You must go, and go to stay."

CHAPTER II.

JOURNEY FROM SPRINGFIELD TO WASHINGTON.

On the 11th of February, 1861, the arrangements for Mr. Lincoln's departure from Springfield were completed. It was intended to occupy the time remaining between that date and the 4th of March with a grand tour from State to State and city to city. Mr. Wood, "recommended by Senator Seward," was the chief manager. He provided special trains, to be preceded by pilot engines all the way through.

It was a gloomy day: heavy clouds floated overhead, and a cold rain was falling. Long before eight o'clock, a great mass of people had collected at the station of the Great Western Railway to witness the event of the day. At precisely five minutes before eight, Mr. Lincoln, preceded by Mr. Wood, emerged from a private room in the station, and passed slowly to the car, the people falling back respectfully on either side, and as many as possible shaking his hand. Having reached the train he ascended the rear platform, and, facing the throng which had closed around him, drew himself up to his full height, removed his hat, and stood for several seconds in profound silence. His eye roved sadly over that sea of upturned faces; and he thought he read in them again the sympathy and friendship which he had often tried, and which he never needed more than he did then. There was an unusual quiver on his lip, and a still more unusual tear on his furrowed cheek. His solemn manner, his long silence, were as full of melancholy eloquence as any words he could have uttered. Of what was he thinking? Of the mighty changes which had lifted him from the lowest to the highest estate in the nation; of the weary road which had brought him to this lofty summit; of his poverty-stricken boyhood; of his poor mother lying beneath the tangled underbrush in a distant forest? Whatever the particular character of his thoughts, it is evident that they were retrospective and painful. To those who were anxiously waiting to catch words upon which the fate of the nation might hang, it seemed long until he had mastered his feelings sufficiently to speak. At length he began in a husky tone of voice, and slowly and impressively delivered his farewell to his neighbors. Imitating his example, every man in the crowd stood with his head uncovered in the fast-falling rain.

"Friends, no one who has never been placed in a like position can understand my feelings at this hour, nor the oppressive sadness I feel at this parting. For more than a quarter of a century I have lived among you, and during all that time I have received nothing but kindness at your hands. Here I have lived from my youth, until now I am an old man. Here the most sacred ties of earth were assumed; here all my children were born; and here one of them lies buried. To you, dear friends, I owe all that I have, all that I am. 'All the strange, checkered past seems to crowd now upon my mind.' To-day I leave you. I go to assume a task more difficult than that which devolved upon Washington. Unless the great God, who assisted him, shall be with me and aid me, I must fail; but if the same omniscient mind and almighty arm that directed and protected him shall guide and support me, I shall not fail,--I shall succeed. Let us all pray that the God of our fathers may not forsake us now. To Him I commend you all. Permit me to ask that, with equal security and faith, you will invoke His wisdom and guidance for me. With these few words I must leave you,--for how long I know not. Friends, one and all, I must now bid you an affectionate farewell."

Few more impressive utterances were ever made by any one than found expression in this simple speech. This farewell meant more to him than to his hearers. To them it meant, "Good-by for the present,"--a commendation of his dearest friends to the watchful care of God until his return. To him it foreboded eternity ere their reunion,--his last solemn benediction until the resurrection. He never believed he would return to the hallowed scenes of his adopted State, to his friends and his home. He had felt for many years that he would suffer a violent death, and at different times expressed his apprehensions before and after his election as President.

The first night after our departure from Springfield was spent in Indianapolis. Governor Yates, the Hon. O. H. Browning, Jesse K. Dubois, O. M. Hatch, Josiah Allen, of Indiana, and others, after taking leave of Mr. Lincoln to return to their respective homes, took me into a room, locked the door, and proceeded in the most solemn and impressive manner to instruct me as to my duties as the special guardian of Mr. Lincoln's person during the rest of his journey to Washington. The lesson was concluded by Uncle Jesse, as Mr. Dubois was commonly called, who said: "Now, Lamon, we have regarded you as the Tom Hyer of Illinois, with Morrissey attachment. We intrust the sacred life of Mr. Lincoln to your keeping; and if you don't protect it, never return to Illinois, for we will murder you on sight."

With this amiable threat, delivered in a jocular tone, but with a feeling of deep, ill-disguised alarm for the safety of the President-elect, in which they all shared, the door was unlocked and they took their leave. If I had been remiss in my duty toward Mr. Lincoln during that memorable journey, I have no doubt those sturdy men would have made good some part of their threat.

The journey from Springfield to Philadelphia was not characterized by any scene unusual or more eventful than what was ordinary on such occasions, notwithstanding that so much has been written about thrilling dangers, all of which were imagined but not encountered. Mr. Lincoln's speeches were the all-absorbing events of the hour. The people everywhere were eager to hear a forecast of his policy, and he was as determined to keep silence on that subject until it was made manifest in his Inaugural Address. After having been en route a day or two, he told me that he had done much hard work in his life, but to make speeches day after day, with the object of speaking and saying nothing, was the hardest work he ever had done. "I wish," said he, "that this thing were through with, and I could find peace and quiet somewhere."

On arriving at Albany, N. Y., Mr. Thurlow Weed asked me where Mr. Lincoln was going to be domiciled in Washington until he was inaugurated. I told him Messrs. Trumbull and Washburne had provided quarters for him; that they had rented a house on Thirteenth or Fourteenth Street, N. W., for his reception, and that Mr. Lincoln had submitted the matter to me, asking me to confer with Capt. John Pope, one of our party who was an old friend of his, and to make just such arrangements as I thought best for his quarters in Washington. Mr. Weed said, "It will never do to allow him to go to a private house to be under the influence of State control. He is now public property, and ought to be where he can be reached by the people until he is inaugurated." We then agreed that Willard's Hotel would be the best place, and the following letter was written to Mr. Willard to arrange for the reception of the Presidential party:--

ALBANY, Feb. 19, 1861.

DEAR WILLARD,--Mr. Lincoln will be your guest.

In arranging his apartments, please reserve nearest him apartments for two of his friends, Judge Davis and Mr. Lamon.

Truly yours,

(Signed) THURLOW WEED.

Mrs. Lincoln and one son accompany him.

[Illustration: Hand written letter above]

This arrangement was reported to Mr. Lincoln, who said: "I fear it will give mortal offense to our friends, but I think the arrangement a good one. I can readily see that many other well meant plans will 'gang aglee,' but I am sorry. The truth is, I suppose I am now public property; and a public inn is the place where people can have access to me."

Mr. Lincoln had prepared his Inaugural Address with great care, and up to the time of his arrival in Washington he had not shown it to any one. No one had been consulted as to what he should say on that occasion. During the journey the Address was made an object of special care, and was guarded with more than ordinary vigilance. It was carefully stored away in a satchel, which for the most of the time received his personal supervision. At Harrisburg, however, the precious bag was lost sight of. This was a matter which for prudential reasons could not be much talked about, and concerning which no great amount of anxiety could be shown. Mr. Lincoln had about concluded that his Address was lost. It at length dawned upon him that on arriving at Harrisburg he had intrusted the satchel to his son Bob, then a boy in his teens. He at once hunted up the boy and asked him what he had done with the bag. Robert confessed that in the excitement of the reception he thought that he had given it to a waiter of the hotel or to some one, he couldn't tell whom. Lincoln was in despair. Only ten days remained until the inauguration, and no Address; not even a trace of the notes was preserved from which it had been prepared.

I had never seen Mr. Lincoln so much annoyed, so much perplexed, and for the time so angry. He seldom manifested a spirit of anger toward his children,--this was the nearest approach to it I had ever witnessed. He and I started in search of the satchel. We went first to the hotel office, where we were informed that if an employ?of the hotel had taken charge of it, it would be found in the baggage-room. On going there, we found a great pile of all kinds of baggage in promiscuous confusion. Mr. Lincoln's keen eye soon discovered a satchel which he thought his own; taking it in his hand eagerly he tried his key; it fitted the lock,--the bag opened, and to our astonishment it contained nothing but a soiled shirt, several paper collars, a pack of cards, and a bottle of whiskey nearly full. In spite of his perplexity, the ludicrous mistake overcame Mr. Lincoln's gravity, and we both laughed heartily, much to the amusement of the bystanders. Shortly afterward we found among the mass the bag containing the precious document.

I shall never forget Mr. Lincoln's expression and what he said when he first informed me of his supposed loss, and enlisted my services in search of it. He held his head down for a moment, and then whispered: "Lamon, I guess I have lost my certificate of moral character, written by myself. Bob has lost my gripsack containing my Inaugural Address. I want you to help me to find it. I feel a good deal as the old member of the Methodist Church did when he lost his wife at the camp-meeting, and went up to an old elder of the church and asked him if he could tell him whereabouts in hell his wife was. In fact, I am in a worse fix than my Methodist friend; for if it were nothing but a wife that was missing, mine would be sure to pop up serenely somewhere. That Address may be a loss to more than one husband in this country, but I shall be the greatest sufferer."

On our dark journey from Harrisburg to Philadelphia the lamps of the car were not lighted, because of the secret journey we were making. The loss of the Address and the search for it was the subject of a great deal of amusement. Mr. Lincoln said many funny things in connection with the incident. One of them was that he knew a fellow once who had saved up fifteen hundred dollars, and had placed it in a private banking establishment. The bank soon failed, and he afterward received ten per cent of his investment. He then took his one hundred and fifty dollars and deposited it in a savings bank, where he was sure it would be safe. In a short time this bank also failed, and he received at the final settlement ten per cent on the amount deposited. When the fifteen dollars was paid over to him, he held it in his hand and looked at it thoughtfully; then he said, "Now, darn you, I have got you reduced to a portable shape, so I'll put you in my pocket." Suiting the action to the word, Mr. Lincoln took his Address from the bag and carefully placed it in the inside pocket of his vest, but held on to the satchel with as much interest as if it still contained his "certificate of moral character."

While Mr. Lincoln, in the midst of his suite of attendants, was being borne in triumph through the streets of Philadelphia, and a countless multitude of people were shouting themselves hoarse, and jostling and crushing each other round his carriage, Mr. Felton, the president of the Philadelphia, Wilmington, and Baltimore Railway, was engaged with a private detective discussing the details of an alleged conspiracy to murder him at Baltimore. At various places along the route Mr. Judd, who was supposed to exercise unbounded influence over the new President, had received vague hints of the impending danger.

Mr. Lincoln reached Philadelphia on the afternoon of the 21st. The detective had arrived in the morning, and improved the interval to impress and enlist Mr. Felton. In the evening he got Mr. Judd and Mr. Felton into his room at the St. Louis Hotel, and told them all he had learned. Mr. Judd was very much startled, and was sure that it would be extremely imprudent for Mr. Lincoln to pass through Baltimore in open daylight, according to the published programme. But he thought the detective ought to see the President himself; and, as it was wearing toward nine o'clock, there was no time to lose. It was agreed that the part taken by the detective and Mr. Felton should be kept secret from every one but the President. Mr. Sanford, president of the American Telegraph Company, had also been co-operating in the business, and the same stipulation was made with regard to him.

Mr. Judd went to his own room at the Continental, and the detective followed. The crowd in the hotel was very dense, and it took some time to get a message to Mr. Lincoln. But it finally reached him, and he responded in person. Mr. Judd introduced the detective; and the latter told his story again. Mr. Judd and the detective wanted Mr. Lincoln to leave for Washington that night. This he flatly refused to do. He had engagements with the people, he said, to raise a flag over Independence Hall in the morning, and to exhibit himself at Harrisburg in the afternoon,--and these engagements he would not break in any event. But he would raise the flag, go to Harrisburg, get away quietly in the evening, and permit himself to be carried to Washington in the way they thought best. Even this, however, he conceded with great reluctance. He condescended to cross-examine the detective on some parts of his narrative; but at no time did he seem in the least degree alarmed. He was earnestly requested not to communicate the change of plan to any member of his party except Mr. Judd, nor permit even a suspicion of it to cross the mind of another.

In the mean time, Mr. Seward had also discovered the conspiracy, and despatched his son to Philadelphia to warn the President-elect of the terrible snare into whose meshes he was about to run. Mr. Lincoln turned him over to Judd, and Judd told him they already knew about it. He went away with just enough information to enable his father to anticipate the exact moment of Mr. Lincoln's surreptitious arrival in Washington.

Early on the morning of the 22d, Mr. Lincoln raised the flag over

Independence Hall, and departed for Harrisburg. On the way, Mr. Judd gave him a full and precise detail of the arrangements that had been made the previous night. After the conference with the detective, Mr. Sanford, Colonel Scott, Mr. Felton, and the railroad and telegraph officials had been sent for, and came to Mr. Judd's room. They occupied nearly the whole of the night in perfecting the plan. It was finally agreed that about six o'clock the next evening Mr. Lincoln should slip away from the Jones Hotel at Harrisburg, in company with a single member of his party. A special car and engine was to be provided for him on the track outside the depot; all other trains on the road were to be "side-tracked" until this one had passed. Mr. Sanford was to forward skilled "telegraph-climbers," and see that all the wires leading out of Harrisburg were cut at six o'clock, and kept down until it was known that Mr. Lincoln had reached Washington in safety. The detective was to meet Mr. Lincoln at the West Philadelphia Station with a carriage, and conduct him by a circuitous route to the Philadelphia, Wilmington, and Baltimore Station. Berths for four were to be pre-engaged in the sleeping-car attached to the regular midnight train for Baltimore. This train Mr. Felton was to cause to be detained until the conductor should receive a package, containing important "government despatches," addressed to "E. J. Allen, Willard's Hotel, Washington." This package was to be made up of old newspapers, carefully wrapped and sealed, and delivered to the detective to be used as soon as Mr. Lincoln was lodged in the car.

Mr. Lincoln acquiesced in this plan. Then Mr. Judd, forgetting the secrecy which the spy had so impressively enjoined, told Mr. Lincoln that the step he was about to take was one of such transcendent importance that he thought "it should be communicated to the other gentlemen of the party." Therefore, when they had arrived at Harrisburg, and the public ceremonies and speech-making were over, Mr. Lincoln retired to a private parlor in the Jones House; and Mr. Judd summoned to meet him there Judge Davis, Colonel Sumner, Major Hunter, Captain Pope, and myself. Judd began the conference by stating the alleged fact of the Baltimore conspiracy, how it was detected, and how it was proposed to thwart it by a midnight expedition to Washington by way of Philadelphia. It was a great surprise to all of us.

Colonel Sumner was the first to break the silence. "That proceeding," said he, "will be a damned piece of cowardice."

Mr. Judd considered this a "pointed hit," but replied that "that view of the case had already been presented to Mr. Lincoln." Then there was a general interchange of opinions, which Sumner interrupted by saying,--

"I'll get a squad of cavalry, sir, and cut our way to Washington, sir!"

"Probably before that day comes," said Mr. Judd, "the inauguration day will have passed. It is important that Mr. Lincoln should be in Washington on that day."

Thus far Judge Davis had expressed no opinion, but had put various questions to test the truthfulness of the story. He now turned to Mr. Lincoln, and said, "You personally heard the detective's story. You have heard this discussion. What is your judgment in the matter?"

"I have thought over this matter considerably since I went over the ground with the detective last night. The appearance of Mr. Frederick Seward with warning from another source confirms my belief in the detective's statement. Unless there are some other reasons besides fear of ridicule, I am disposed to carry out Judd's plan."

There was no longer any dissent as to the plan itself; but one question still remained to be disposed of. Who should accompany the President on his perilous ride? Mr. Judd again took the lead, declaring that he and Mr. Lincoln had previously determined that but one man ought to go, and that I had been selected as the proper person. To this Sumner violently demurred.

"I have undertaken," he exclaimed, "to see Mr. Lincoln to Washington!"

Mr. Lincoln was dining when a close carriage was brought to the side door of the hotel. He was called, hurried to his room, changed his coat and hat, and passed rapidly through the hall and out of the door. As he was stepping into the carriage, it became manifest that Sumner was determined to get in also. "Hurry with him!" whispered Judd to me; and at the same time, placing his hand on Sumner's shoulder, he said aloud, "One moment, Colonel!" Sumner turned round, and in that moment the carriage drove rapidly away. "A madder man," says Mr. Judd, "you never saw."

We got on board the car without discovery or mishap. Besides ourselves, there was no one in or about the car except Mr. Lewis, general superintendent of the Pennsylvania Central Railroad, and Mr. Franciscus, superintendent of the division over which we were about to pass. The arrangements for the special train were made ostensibly to take these two gentlemen to Philadelphia.

At ten o'clock we reached West Philadelphia, and were met by the detective and one Mr. Kenney, an under-official of the Philadelphia, Wilmington, and Baltimore Railroad, from whose hands the "important parcel" was to be delivered to the conductor of the 10.50 P.M. train. Mr. Lincoln, the detective, and myself seated ourselves in a carriage which stood in waiting; and Mr. Kenney sat upon the box with the driver. It was nearly an hour before the Baltimore train was to start; and Mr. Kenney found it necessary to consume the time by driving northward in search of some imaginary person.

As the moment for the departure of the Baltimore train drew near, the carriage paused in the dark shadows of the depot building. It was not considered prudent to approach the entrance.

We were directed to the sleeping-car. Mr. Kenney ran forward and delivered the "important package," and in three minutes the train was in motion. The tickets for the whole party had been procured by George R. Dunn, an express agent, who had selected berths in the rear of the car, and had insisted that the rear door of the car should be opened on the plea that one of the party was an invalid, who would arrive late, and did not desire to be carried through the narrow passage-way of the crowded car. Mr. Lincoln got into his berth immediately, the curtains were carefully closed, and the rest of the party waited until the conductor came round, when the detective handed him the "sick man's" ticket. During the night Mr. Lincoln indulged in a joke or two, in an undertone; but with that exception the two sections occupied by us were perfectly silent. The detective said he had men stationed at various places along the road to let him know if all was right; and he rose and went to the platform occasionally to observe their signals, returning each time with a favorable report.

At thirty minutes past three the train reached Baltimore. One of the spy's assistants came on board and informed him in a whisper that "all was right." Mr. Lincoln lay still in his berth; and in a few moments the car was being slowly drawn through the quiet streets of the city toward what was called the Washington depot. There again was another pause, but no sound more alarming than the noise of shifting cars and engines. The passengers, tucked away on their narrow shelves, dozed on as peacefully as if Mr. Lincoln had never been born, until they were awakened by the loud strokes of a huge club against a night-watchman's box, which stood within the depot and close to the track. It was an Irishman, trying to arouse a sleepy ticket-agent comfortably ensconced within. For twenty minutes the Irishman pounded the box with ever-increasing vigor, and at each blow shouted at the top of his voice, "Captain! it's four o'clock! it's four o'clock!" The Irishman seemed to think that time had ceased to run at four o'clock, and making no allowance for the period consumed by his futile exercises, repeated to the last his original statement that it was four o'clock. The passengers were intensely amused; and their jokes and laughter at the Irishman's expense were not lost upon the occupants of the two sections in the rear.

In due time the train sped out of the suburbs of Baltimore, and the apprehensions of the President and his friends diminished with each welcome revolution of the wheels. At six o'clock the dome of the Capitol came in sight, and a moment later we rolled into that long, unsightly building, the Washington depot. We passed out of the car unobserved, and pushed along with the living stream of men and women toward the outer door. One man alone in the great crowd seemed to watch Mr. Lincoln with special attention. Standing a little to one side, he looked very sharply at him, and, as he passed, seized hold of his hand, and said in a loud tone of voice, "Abe, you can't play that on me!" We were instantly alarmed, and would have struck the stranger had not Mr. Lincoln hastily said, "Don't strike him! It is Washburne. Don't you know him?" Mr. Seward had given to Mr. Washburne a hint of the information received through his son; and Mr. Washburne knew its value as well as another.

The detective admonished Washburne to keep quiet for the present, and we passed on together. Taking a hack, we drove toward Willard's Hotel. Mr. Lincoln, Mr. Washburne, and the detective got out in the street, and approached the ladies' entrance, while I drove on to the main entrance, and sent the proprietor to meet his distinguished guest at the side door. A few minutes later Mr. Seward arrived, and was introduced to the company by Mr. Washburne. He spoke in very strong terms of the great danger which Mr. Lincoln had so narrowly escaped, and most heartily applauded the wisdom of the "secret passage."

It now soon became apparent that Mr. Lincoln wished to be left alone. He said he was "rather tired;" and, upon this intimation, the party separated. The detective went to the telegraph-office and loaded the wires with despatches in cipher, containing the pleasing intelligence that "Plums" had brought "Nuts" through in safety.

Mr. Lincoln soon learned to regret the midnight ride to which he had yielded under protest. He was convinced that he had committed a grave mistake in listening to the solicitations of a professional spy and of friends too easily alarmed, and frequently upbraided me for having aided him to degrade himself at the very moment in all his life when his behavior should have exhibited the utmost dignity and composure. Neither he nor the country generally then understood the true facts concerning the dangers to his life. It is now an acknowledged fact that there never was a moment from the day he crossed the Maryland line, up to the time of his assassination, that he was not in danger of death by violence, and that his life was spared until the night of the 14th of April, 1865, only through the ceaseless and watchful care of the guards thrown around him.

CHAPTER III.

INAUGURATION.

If before leaving Springfield Mr. Lincoln had become weary of the pressure upon him for office, he found no respite on his arrival at the focus of political intrigue and corruption. The time intervening between his arrival at Washington and his Inauguration was, for the most part, employed in giving consideration to his Inaugural Address, the formation of his Cabinet, and the conventional duties required by his elevated position.

The question of the new Administration's policy absorbed nearly every other consideration. To get a Cabinet that would work harmoniously in carrying out the policy determined on by Mr. Lincoln was very difficult. He was pretty well determined on the construction of his Cabinet before he reached Washington; but in the minds of the public, beyond the generally accepted fact that Mr. Seward was to be the Premier of the new Administration, all was speculation and conjecture. All grades of opinion were advanced for his consideration: conciliation was strongly urged; a vigorous war policy; a policy of quiescent neutrality recommending delay of demonstrative action for or against war,--and all, or nearly all these suggestions were prompted by the most unselfish and patriotic motives. He was compelled to give a patient ear to these representations, and to hold his decisions till the last moment, in order that he might decide with a full view of the requirements of public policy and party fealty.[4]

[4] Page 49, line 5, after the word "fealty."

When Mr. Lincoln was being importuned to appoint to his Cabinet another man from Maryland rather than Mr. Blair, he said laughingly: "Maryland must, I think, be a good State to move from," and then told a story of a witness who on being asked his age replied, "Sixty." Being satisfied that he was much older, the judge repeated the question, and on receiving the same answer, admonished the witness, saying that the Court knew him to be much older than sixty. "Oh," said the witness, "you're thinking about that fifteen years that I lived down on eastern shore of Maryland; that was so much lost time and don't count."

As late as the second of March a large and respectable delegation of persons visited Mr. Lincoln to bring matters to a conclusion. Their object was to prevent at all hazards the appointment of Mr. Chase in the Cabinet. They were received civilly and treated courteously. The President listened to them with great patience. They were unanimous in their opposition to Mr. Chase. Mr. Seward's appointment, they urged, was absolutely and indispensably required to secure for the Administration either the support of the North or a respectful hearing at the South. They portrayed the danger of putting into the Cabinet a man like Mr. Chase, who was so notoriously identified with and supported by men who did not desire the perpetuation of the Union. They strongly insisted that Mr. Chase would be an unsafe counsellor, and that he and his supporters favored a Northern republic, extending from the Ohio River to Canada, rather than the Union which our fathers had founded. They urged another argument, which to them seemed of vital importance and conclusive,--that it would not be possible for Mr. Seward to sit in the Cabinet with Mr. Chase as a member. To think of it was revolting to him, and neither he nor his State could or would tolerate it.

These arguments, so earnestly put forth, distressed Mr. Lincoln greatly. At length, after a long pause, he replied that it was very difficult to reconcile conflicting claims and interests; that his greatest desire was to form an Administration that would command the confidence and respect of the country, and of the party which had placed him in power. He spoke of his high regard for Mr. Seward, of his eminent services, his great genius, and the respect in which he was held by the country. He said Mr. Chase had also great claims that no one could gainsay. His claims were, perhaps, not so great as Mr. Seward's; but this he would not then discuss: the party and the country wanted the hearty and harmonious co-operation of all good men without regard to sections.

Then there was an ominous pause. Mr. Lincoln went to a drawer and took out a paper, saying, "I had written out my choice and selection of members for the Cabinet after most careful and deliberate consideration; and now you are here to tell me I must break the slate and begin the thing all over again." He admitted that he had sometimes apprehended that it might be as they had suggested,--that he might be forced to reconsider what he regarded as his judicious conclusions; and in view of this possibility he had constructed an alternative list of members. He did not like the alternative list so well as the original. He had hoped to have Mr. Seward as Secretary of State and Mr. Chase his Secretary of Treasury. He expressed his regrets that he could not be gratified in this desire, and added that he could not reasonably expect to have things just as he wanted them. Silence prevailed for some time, and he then added: "This being the case, gentlemen, how would it do for us to agree upon a change like this? To appoint Mr. Chase Secretary of the Treasury, and offer the State Department to Mr. William L. Dayton, of New Jersey?"

The delegation was shocked, disappointed, outraged. Mr. Lincoln, continuing in the same phlegmatic manner, again referred to his high appreciation of the abilities of Mr. Seward. He said Mr. Dayton was an old Whig, like Mr. Seward and himself, and that he was from New Jersey, and was "next door to New York." Mr. Seward, he added, could go as Minister to England, where his genius would find wonderful scope in keeping Europe straight about our home troubles. The delegation was nonplussed. They, however, saw and accepted the inevitable. For the first time they realized that indomitable will of the President-elect which afterward became so notable throughout the trying times of his Administration. They saw that "the mountain would not come to Mahomet, with the conditions imposed, and so Mahomet had to go to the mountain." The difficulty was accommodated by Mr. Seward coming into the Cabinet with Mr. Chase, and the Administrative organization was effected to Mr. Lincoln's satisfaction.

Mr. Seward was a Republican with centralizing tendencies, and had been a prominent and powerful member of the old Whig party, which had gone into decay. Mr. Chase was a State's Rights Federal Republican, not having been strictly attached to either the Whig or the Democratic organization; he had for years been a conspicuous leader of the Antislavery party, which had risen on the ruins of the Whig party, while Mr. Seward had cautiously abstained from any connection with the Antislavery party per se. Mr. Lincoln adopted, whether consciously or unconsciously, the policy of Washington in bringing men of opposite principles into his Cabinet, as far as he could do so, hoping that they would harmonize in administrative measures; and in doing this in the case of Mr. Seward and Mr. Chase he entirely reversed the original arrangement,--by giving Mr. Seward, a Republican centralist, the post of Jefferson, a State's Rights Federal Republican; and to Mr. Chase, a Federal Republican, the post assigned to Hamilton, a centralist.

There was a prevailing opinion among a great many politicians that Mr. Seward had an overpowering influence with Mr. Lincoln; and the belief was general that he, in whose ability and moderation the conservative people at the North seemed to have the most confidence, would be the real head of the Administration. This supposition was a great mistake. It underrated the man who had been elected to wield the helm of government in the troubled waters of the brewing storm. Mr. Lincoln was as self-reliant a man as ever breathed the atmosphere of patriotism. Up to the 2d of March, Mr. Seward had no intimation of the purport of the Inaugural Address. The conclusion was inevitable that if he was to be at the head of the Administration, he would not have been left so long in the dark as to the first act of Mr. Lincoln's official life. When the last faint hope was destroyed that Mr. Seward was virtually to be President, the outlook of the country seemed to these politicians discouraging.

The 4th of March at last arrived. Mr. Lincoln's feelings, as the hour approached which was to invest him with greater responsibilities than had fallen upon any of his predecessors, may readily be imagined. If he saw in his elevation another step toward the fulfilment of that destiny which he at times believed awaited him, the thought served but to tinge with a peculiar, almost poetic, sadness the manner in which he addressed himself to the solemn duties of the hour.

There were apprehensions of danger to Mr. Lincoln's person, and extensive preparations were made for his protection, under the direction of Lieutenant-General Scott. The carriage in which the President-elect rode to the Capitol was closely guarded by marshals and cavalry, selected with care from the most loyal and efficient companies of the veteran troops and marines. Mr. Lincoln appeared as usual, composed and thoughtful, apparently unmoved and indifferent to the excitement around him. On arriving at the platform, he was introduced to the vast audience awaiting his appearance by Senator Baker, of Oregon. Stepping forward, in a manner deliberate and impressive, the President-elect delivered in a clear, penetrating voice his Inaugural Address, closing this remarkable production with the words, which so forcibly exemplified his character and so clearly indicated his goodness of heart: "I am loath to close. We are not enemies, but friends. We must not be enemies. Though passion may have strained, it must not break, our bonds of affection. The mystic chords of memory, stretching from every battle-field and patriot grave to every living heart and hearthstone all over this broad land, will yet swell the chorus of the Union when again touched, as surely they will be, by the better angels of our nature."

The immense audience present was deeply impressed, and with awe viewed the momentous character of the occasion they were given to contemplate. The Address produced comparatively little applause and no manifestations of disapprobation. All were moved with a profound anxiety concerning their own respective States and the future of their country; and the sentiments they had just heard uttered from the Chief Executive foreshadowed the storm awaiting the nation.

After the oath of office was administered to him by the venerable Chief-Justice of the United States, Judge Roger B. Taney, Mr. Lincoln was escorted to the Presidential Mansion in the same order that was observed in going to the Capitol, amid the firing of cannon and the sound of music. Mr. Buchanan accompanied him, and in taking his leave expressed his wish and hope, in earnest and befitting language, that Mr. Lincoln's Administration of the government would be a happy and prosperous one.

The Inauguration over, every one seemed to have a sense of relief: there had been no accident, no demonstration which could be construed as portending disturbance.

The New York delegation, on the night of the Inauguration, paid their respects to the President. He said to them that he was rejoiced to see the good feeling manifested by them, and hoped that our friends of the South would be satisfied, when they read his Inaugural Address, that he had made it as nearly right as it was possible for him to make it in accordance with the Constitution, which he thought was as good for the people who lived south of the Mason and Dixon line as for those who lived north of it.

CHAPTER IV.

GLOOMY FOREBODINGS OF COMING CONFLICT.

After the first shout of triumph and the first glow of exultation consequent on his Inauguration, Mr. Lincoln soon began to realize with dismay what was before him. Geographical lines were at last distinctly drawn. He was regarded as a sectional representative, elected President with most overwhelming majorities north of Mason and Dixon's line, and not a single electoral vote south of it. He saw a great people, comprising many millions and inhabiting a vast region of our common country, exasperated by calumny, stung by defeat, and alarmed by the threats of furious fanatics whom demagogues held up to them as the real and only leaders of the triumphant party. His election had brought the nation face to face with the perils that had been feared by every rank and party since the dawn of Independence,--with the very contingency, the crisis in which all venerable authority had declared from the beginning that the Union would surely perish, and the fragments, after exhausting each other by commercial restrictions and disastrous wars, would find ignominious safety in as many paltry despotisms as there were fragments.

On the 3d of March, 1861, the Thirty-sixth Congress had reached the prescribed period of its existence, and had died a constitutional death. Its last session of three months had been spent in full view of an awful public calamity, which it had made no effort to avert or to mitigate. It saw the nation compassed round with a frightful danger, but it proposed no plan either of conciliation or defence. It adjourned forever, and left the law precisely as it found it.

In his message to Congress, President Buchanan had said: "Congress alone has power to decide whether the present laws can or cannot be amended so as to carry out more effectually the objects of the Constitution." With Congress rested the whole responsibility of peace or war, and with them the message left it. But Congress behaved like a body of men who thought that the calamities of the nation were no special business of theirs. The members from the extreme South were watching for the proper moment to retire; those from the middle slave States were a minority which could only stand and wait upon the movements of others; while the great and all-powerful Northern party was what the French minister called "a mere aggregation of individual ambitions." They had always denied the possibility of a dissolution of the Union in any conjuncture of circumstances; and their habit of disregarding the evidence was too strong to be suddenly changed. In the philosophy of their politics it had not been dreamed of as a possible thing. Even when they saw it assume the shape of a fixed and terrible fact, they could not comprehend its meaning. They looked at the frightful phenomenon as a crowd of barbarians might look at an eclipse of the sun: they saw the light of heaven extinguished and the earth covered with strange and unaccountable darkness, but they could neither understand its cause nor foresee its end,--they knew neither whence it came nor what it portended. The nation was going to pieces, and Congress left it to its fate. The vessel, freighted with all the hopes and all the wealth of thirty millions of free people was drifting to her doom, and they who alone had power to control her course refused to lay a finger on the helm.

Only a few days before the convening of this Congress the following letter was written by Hon. Joseph Holt, Postmaster-General, afterward Secretary of War, under Buchanan:--

WASHINGTON, NOV. 30, 1860.

MY DEAR SIR,--I am in receipt of yours of the 27th inst., and thank you for your kindly allusion to myself, in connection with the fearful agitation which now threatens the dismemberment of our government. I think the President's message will meet your approbation, but I little hope that it will accomplish anything in moderating the madness that rules the hour. The indications are that the movement has passed beyond the reach of human control. God alone can disarm the cloud of its lightnings. South Carolina will be out of the Union, and in the armed assertion of a distinct nationality probably before Christmas. This is certain, unless the course of events is arrested by prompt and decided action on the part of the people and Legislatures of the Northern States; the other slave States will follow South Carolina in a few weeks or months. The border States, now so devoted to the Union, will linger a little while; but they will soon unite their fortunes with those of their Southern sisters. Conservative men have now no ground to stand upon, no weapon to battle with. All has been swept from them by the guilty agitations and infamous legislation of the North. I do not anticipate, with any confidence, that the North will act up to the solemn responsibilities of the crisis, by retracing those fatal steps which have conducted us to the very brink of perdition, politically, morally, and financially.

There is a feeling growing in the free States which says, "Let the South go!" and this feeling threatens rapidly to increase. It is, in part, the fruit of complete estrangement, and in part a weariness of this perpetual conflict between North and South, which has now lasted, with increasing bitterness, for the last thirty years. The country wants repose, and is willing to purchase it at any sacrifice. Alas for the delusion of the belief that repose will follow the overthrow of the government!

I doubt not, from the temper of the public mind, that the Southern States will be allowed to withdraw peacefully; but when the work of dismemberment begins, we shall break up the fragments from month to month, with the nonchalance with which we break the bread upon our breakfast-table. If all the grave and vital questions which will at once arise among these fragments of the ruptured Republic can be adjusted without resort to arms, then we have made vast progress since the history of our race was written. But the tragic events of the hour will show that we have made no progress at all. We shall soon grow up a race of chieftains, who will rival the political bandits of South America and Mexico, and who will carve out to us our miserable heritage with their bloody swords. The masses of the people dream not of these things. They suppose the Republic can be destroyed to-day, and that peace will smile over its ruins to-morrow. They know nothing of civil war: this Marah in the pilgrimage of nations has happily been for them a sealed fountain; they know not, as others do, of its bitterness, and that civil war is a scourge that darkens every fireside, and wrings every heart with anguish. They are to be commiserated, for they know not what to do. Whence is all this? It has come because the pulpit and press and the cowering, unscrupulous politicians of the North have taught the people that they are responsible for the domestic institutions of the South, and that they have been faithful to God only by being unfaithful to the compact which they have made to their fellow-men. Hence those Liberty Bills which degrade the statute-books of some ten of the free States, and are confessedly a shameless violation of the federal Constitution in a point vital to her honor. We have presented, from year to year, the humiliating spectacle of free and sovereign States, by a solemn act of legislation, legalizing the theft of their neighbors' property. I say theft, since it is not the less so because the subject of the despicable crime chances to be a slave, instead of a horse or bale of goods.

From this same teaching has come the perpetual agitation of the slavery question, which has reached the minds of the slave population of the South, and has rendered every home in that distracted land insecure. This is the feature of the irrepressible conflict with which the Northern people are not familiar. In almost every part of the South miscreant fanatics have been found, and poisonings and conflagrations have marked their footsteps. Mothers there lie down at night trembling beside their children, and wives cling to their husbands as they leave their homes in the morning. I have a brother residing in Mississippi, who is a lawyer by profession, and a cotton planter, but has never had any connection with politics. Knowing the calm and conservative tone of his character, I wrote him a few weeks since, and implored him to exert his influence in allaying the frenzy of the popular mind around him. He has replied to me at much length, and after depicting the machinations of the wretches to whom I have alluded, and the consternation which reigns in the homes of the South, he says it is the unalterable determination of the Southern people to overthrow the government as the only refuge which is left to them from these insupportable wrongs; and he adds: "On the success of this movement depends my every interest,--the safety of my roof from the firebrand, and of my wife and children from the poison and the dagger."

I give you his language because it truthfully expresses the Southern mind which at this moment glows as a furnace in its hatred to the North because of these infernal agitations. Think you that any people can endure this condition of things? When the Northern preacher infuses into his audience the spirit of assassins and incendiaries in his crusade against slavery, does he think, as he lies down quietly at night, of the Southern homes he has robbed of sleep, and the helpless women and children he has exposed to all the nameless horrors of servile insurrections?

I am still for the Union, because I have yet a faint, hesitating hope that the North will do justice to the South, and save the Republic, before the wreck is complete. But action, to be available, must be prompt. If the free States will sweep the Liberty Bills from their codes, propose a convention of the States, and offer guaranties which will afford the same repose and safety to

Southern homes and property enjoyed by those of the North, the impending tragedy may be averted, but not otherwise. I feel a positive personal humiliation as a member of the human family in the events now preparing. If the Republic is to be offered as a sacrifice upon the altar of American servitude, then the question of man's capacity for self-government is forever settled. The derision of the world will henceforth justly treat the pretension as a farce; and the blessed hope which for five thousand years our race, amid storms and battles, has been hugging to its bosom, will be demonstrated to be a phantom and a dream.

Pardon these hurried and disjointed words. They have been pressed out of my heart by the sorrows that are weighing upon it.

Sincerely your friend, J. HOLT.

Within forty-eight hours after the election of Mr. Lincoln, the Legislature of South Carolina called a State Convention. It met on the 17th of December, and three days later the inevitable ordinance of secession was formally adopted, and the little commonwealth began to act under the erroneous impression that she was a sovereign and independent nation. She benignantly accepted the postal service of the "late United States of America," and even permitted the gold and silver coins of the federal government to circulate within her sacred limits. But intelligence from the rest of the country was published in her newspapers under the head of "foreign news;" her governor appointed a "cabinet," commissioned "ambassadors," and practised so many fantastic imitations of greatness and power, that, but for the serious purpose and the bloody event, his proceedings would have been very amusing. It was a curious little comedy between the acts of a hideous tragedy.

In the practice which provoked the fury of his Northern countrymen, the slaveholder could see nothing but what was right in the sight of God, and just as between man and man. Slavery, he said, was as old almost as time. From the hour of deliverance to the day of dispersion, it had been practised by the peculiar people of God, with the awful sanction of a theocratic State. When the Saviour came with his fan in his hand, he not only spared it from all rebuke, but recognized and regulated it as an institution in which he found no evil. The Church had bowed to the authority and emulated the example of the Master. With her aid and countenance, slavery had flourished in every age and country since the Christian era; in new lands she planted it, in the old she upheld and encouraged it. Even the modest of the sectaries had bought and sold, without a shade of doubt or a twinge of conscience, the bondmen who fell to their lot, until the stock was exhausted or the trade became unprofitable. To this rule the Puritans and Quakers were no exceptions. Indeed, it was but a few years since slavery in Massachusetts had been suffered to die of its own accord, and the profits of the slave-trade were still to be seen in the stately mansions and pleasant gardens of her maritime towns.

The Southern man could see no reason of State, of law, or of religion which required him to yield his most ancient rights and his most valuable property to the new-born zeal of adversaries whom he more than suspected of being actuated by mere malignity under the guise of philanthropy. All that he knew or had ever known of the policy of the State, of religion, or of law was on the side of slavery. It was his inheritance in the land descended from his remotest ancestry; recorded in the deeds and written in the wills of his nearest kindred; interwoven more or less intimately with every tradition and every precious memory; the basis of public economy and of private prosperity, fostered by the maternal care of Great Britain, and, unlike any other domestic institution, solemnly protected by separate and distinct provisions in the fundamental law of the federal Union. It was, therefore, as much a part of his religion to cherish and defend it as it was part of the religion of an Abolitionist to denounce and assail it. To him, at least, it was still pure and of good report; he held it as sacred as marriage, as sacred as the relation of parent and child. Forcible abolition was in his eyes as lawless and cruel as arbitrary divorce, or the violent abduction of his offspring; it bereft his fireside, broke up his family, set his own household in arms against him, and deluded to their ruin those whom the Lord had given into his hand for a wise and beneficent purpose. He saw in the extinction of slavery the extinction of society and the subversion of the State; his imagination could compass no crime more daring in the conception, or more terrible in the execution. He saw in it the violation of every law, human and divine, from the Ten Commandments to the last Act of Assembly,--the inauguration of every disaster and of every enormity which men in their sober senses equally fear and detest; it was the knife to his throat, the torch to his roof, a peril unutterable to his wife and daughter, and certain penury, or worse, to such of his posterity as might survive to other times. We smile at his delusion, and laugh at his fears; but we forget that they were shared by eight millions of intelligent people, and had been entertained by the entire generation of patriots and statesmen who made the Union,--by Jefferson who opposed slavery and "trembled" for the judgment, as by the New-England ship-owner and the Georgia planter, who struck hands to continue the African slave-trade till 1808.

Mr. Lincoln himself, with that charity for honest but mistaken opinions which more than once induced him to pause long and reflect seriously before committing his Administration to the extremities of party rage, declared in an elaborate speech, that, had his lot been cast in the South, he would no doubt have been a zealous defender of the "peculiar institution,"--and confessed, that, were he then possessed of unlimited power, he would not know how to liberate the slaves without fatally disturbing the peace and prosperity of the country. He had once said in a speech; "The Southern people are just what we would be in their situation. If slavery did not now exist among them, they would not introduce it: if it did now exist among us, we should not instantly give it up. This I believe of the masses North and South. Doubtless, there are individuals on both sides who would not hold slaves under any circumstances; and others would gladly introduce slavery anew if it were out of existence. We know that some Southern men do free their slaves, go North, and become tip-top Abolitionists; while some Northern men go South, and become cruel slave-masters."

Judge Jeremiah S. Black, in a paper written in response to a memorial address on William H. Seward, said: "The Southern people sprang from a race accustomed for two thousand years to dominate over all other races with which it came in contact. They supposed themselves greatly superior to negroes, most of them sincerely believing that if they and the African must live together, the best and safest relations that could be established between them was that of master and servant.... Some of them believed slavery a dangerous evil, but did not see how to get rid of it. They felt as Jefferson did, that they had the wolf by the ears: they could neither hold on with comfort nor let go with safety, and it made them extremely indignant to be goaded in the rear. In all that country from the Potomac to the Gulf there was probably not one man who felt convinced that this difficult subject could be determined for them by strangers and enemies; seeing that we in the North had held fast to every pound of human flesh we owned, and either worked it to death or sold it for a price, our provision for the freedom of unborn negroes did not tend much to their edification. They had no confidence in that 'ripening' influence of humanity which turned up the white of its eyes at a negro compelled to hoe corn and pick cotton, and yet gloated over the prospect of insurrection and massacre."

Further, emancipation was a question of figures as well as feeling. The loss of four millions of slaves, at an average value of six hundred dollars each, constituted in the aggregate a sacrifice too vast to be contemplated for a moment. Yet this was but a single item. The cotton crop of 1860 was worth the round sum of a hundred and ninety-eight million dollars, while that of 1859 was worth two hundred and forty-seven million dollars, and the demand still in excess of the supply. It formed the bulk of our exchanges with Europe; paid our foreign indebtedness; maintained a great marine; built towns, cities, and railways; enriched factors, brokers, and bankers; filled the federal treasury to overflowing, and made the foremost nations of the world commercially our tributaries and politically our dependants. A short crop embarrassed and distressed all western Europe; a total failure, a war, or non-intercourse, would reduce whole communities to famine, and probably precipitate them into revolution. It was an opinion generally received, and scarcely questioned anywhere, that cotton-planting could be carried on only by African labor, and that African labor was possible only under compulsion. Here, then, was another item of loss, which, being prospective, could neither be measured by statistics nor computed in figures. Add to this the sudden conversion of millions of producers into mere consumers, the depreciation of real estate, the depreciation of stocks and securities as of banks and railways, dependent for their value upon the inland commerce in the products of slave-labor, with the waste, disorder, and bloodshed inevitably attending a revolution like this, and you have a sum-total literally appalling. Could any people on earth tamely submit to spoliation so thorough and so fatal? The very Bengalese would muster the last man, and stake the last jewel, to avert it.

In the last days of March, 1861, I was sent by President Lincoln on a confidential mission to Charleston, South Carolina. It was in its nature one of great delicacy and importance; and the state of the public mind in the South at that juncture made it one not altogether free from danger to life and limb, as I was rather roughly reminded before the adventure was concluded. Throughout the entire land was heard the tumult of mad contention; the representative men, the politicians and the press of the two sections were hurling at one another deadly threats and fierce defiance; sober and thoughtful men heard with sickening alarm the deep and not distant mutterings of the coming storm; and all minds were agitated by gloomy forebodings, distressing doubts, and exasperating uncertainty as to what the next move in the strange drama would be. Following the lead of South

Carolina, the secession element of other Southern States had cut them loose, one by one, from their federal moorings, and "The Confederate States of America" was the result. It was at the virtual Capital of the State which had been the pioneer in all this haughty and stupendous work of rebellion that I was about to trust my precious life and limbs as a stranger within her gates and an enemy to her cause.

Up to this time, Mr. Lincoln had been slow to realize or to acknowledge, even to himself, the awful gravity of the situation, and the danger that the gathering clouds portended. Certain it is that Mr. Seward wildly underrated the courage and determination of the Southern people, and both men indulged the hope that pacific means might yet be employed to arrest the tide of passion and render a resort to force unnecessary. Mr. Seward was inclined, as the world knows, to credit the Southern leaders with a lavish supply of noisy bravado, quite overlooking the dogged pertinacity and courage which Mr. Lincoln well knew would characterize those men, as well as the Southern masses, in case of armed conflict between the sections. Mr. Lincoln had Southern blood in his veins, and he knew well the character of that people. He believed it possible to effect some accommodation by dealing directly with the most chivalrous among their leaders; at all events he thought it his duty to try, and my embassy to Charleston was one of his experiments in that direction.

It was believed in the South that Mr. Seward had given assurances, before and after Lincoln's inauguration, that no attempt would be made to reinforce the Southern forts, or to resupply Fort Sumter, under a Republican Administration. This made matters embarrassing, as Mr. Lincoln's Administration had, on the contrary, adopted the policy of maintaining the federal authority at all points, and of tolerating no interference in the enforcement of that authority from any source whatever.

When my mission to Charleston was suggested by Mr. Lincoln, Mr. Seward promptly opposed it. "Mr. President," said he, "I greatly fear that you are sending Lamon to his grave. I fear they may kill him in Charleston. Those people are greatly excited, and are very desperate. We can't spare Lamon, and we shall feel very badly if anything serious should happen to him."

"Mr. Secretary," replied Mr. Lincoln, "I have known Lamon to be in many a close place, and he has never been in one that he didn't get out of. By Jing! I'll risk him. Go, Lamon, and God bless you! Bring back a Palmetto, if you can't bring us good news."

Armed with certain credentials--from the President, Mr. Seward, General Scott, Postmaster-General Blair, and others--I set out on my doubtful and ticklish adventure.

While I was preparing my baggage at Willard's Hotel, General (then Mr. Stephen A.) Hurlbut, of Illinois, entered my room, and seeing how I was engaged inquired as to the object. He being an old and reliable friend, I told him without hesitation; and he immediately asked if he might not be allowed to accompany me. He desired, he said, to pay a last visit to Charleston, the place of his birth, and to a sister living there, before the dread outbreak which he knew was coming. I saw no objection. He hurried to his rooms to make his own preparations, whence, an hour later, I took him and his wife to the boat.

On arriving at Charleston about eight o'clock Saturday night, the Hurlbuts went to the house of a kinsman, and I went to the Charleston Hotel. It so happened that several young Virginians arrived on the same train, and stopped at the same hotel. They all registered from Virginia, and made the fact known with some show of enthusiasm that they had come to join the Confederate army. I registered simply "Ward H. Lamon," followed by a long dash of the pen.

That evening, and all the next day (Sunday), little attention was paid to me, and no one knew me. I visited the venerable and distinguished lawyer, Mr. James L. Petigru, and had a conference with him,--having been enjoined to do so by Mr. Lincoln, who personally knew that Mr. Petigru was a Union man. At the close of the interview Mr. Petigru said to me that he seldom stirred from his house; that he had no sympathy with the rash movements of his people, and that few sympathized with him; that the whole people were infuriated and crazed, and that no act of headlong violence by them would surprise him. In saying farewell, with warm expressions of good-will, he said that he hoped he should not be considered inhospitable if he requested me not to repeat my visit, as every one who came near him was watched, and intercourse with him could only result in annoyance and danger to the visitor as well as to himself, and would fail to promote any good to the Union cause. It was now too late, he said; peaceable secession or war was inevitable.

Governor Pickens and his admirable and beautiful wife were boarding at the Charleston Hotel. Early Monday morning I sent my card to the governor requesting an interview, and stating that I was from the President of the United States. The answer came that he would see me as soon as he was through with his breakfast. I then strolled downstairs into the main lobby and corridors, where, early as the hour was, I soon discovered that something wonderful was "in the wind," and, moreover, that that wonderful something was embodied in my own person. I was not, like Hamlet, "the glass of fashion and the mould of form," yet I was somehow "the observed of all observers." I was conscious that I did not look like "the expectancy and rose of the fair state;" that my "personal pulchritude," as a witty statesman has it, was not overwhelming to the beholder; and yet I found myself at that moment immensely, not to say alarmingly, attractive.

The news had spread far and wide that a great Goliath from the North, a "Yankee Lincoln-hireling," had come suddenly into their proud city, uninvited, unheralded. Thousands of persons had gathered to see the strange ambassador. The corridors, the main office and lobby, were thronged, and the adjacent streets were crowded as well with excited spectators, mainly of the lower order,--that class of dowdy patriots who in times of public commotion always find the paradise of the coward, the bruiser, and the blackguard. There was a wagging of heads, a chorus of curses and epithets not at all complimentary, and all eyes were fixed upon the daring stranger, who seemed to be regarded not as the bearer of the olive-branch of peace, but as a demon come to denounce the curse of war, pestilence, and famine. This was my initiation into the great "Unpleasantness," and the situation was certainly painful and embarrassing; but there was plainly nothing to do but to assume a bold front.

I pressed my way through the mass of excited humanity to the clerk's counter, examined the register, then turned, and with difficulty elbowed my way through the dense crowd to the door of the breakfast-room. There I was touched upon the shoulder by an elderly man, who asked in a tone of peremptory authority,--

"Are you Mark Lamon?"

"No, sir; I am Ward H. Lamon, at your service."

"Are you the man who registered here as Lamon, from Virginia?"

"I registered as Ward H. Lamon, without designating my place of residence. What is your business with me, sir?"

"Oh, well," continued the man of authority, "have you any objection to state what business you have here in Charleston?"

"Yes, I have." Then after a pause, during which I surveyed my questioner with as much coolness as the state of my nerves would allow, I added, "My business is with your governor, who is to see me as soon as he has finished his breakfast. If he chooses to impart to you my business in this city, you will know it; otherwise, not."

"Beg pardon; if you have business with our governor, it's all right; we'll see."

Shortly after breakfast I was waited upon by one of the governor's staff, a most courtly and agreeable gentleman, in full military uniform, who informed me that the governor was ready to receive me.

My interview with Governor Pickens was, to me, a memorable one. After saying to him what President Lincoln had directed me to say, a general discussion took place touching the critical state of public affairs. With a most engaging courtesy, and an open frankness for which that brave man was justly celebrated, he told me plainly that he was compelled to be both radical and violent; that he regretted the necessity of violent measures, but that he could see no way out of existing difficulties but to fight out. "Nothing," said he, "can prevent war except the acquiescence of the President of the United States in secession, and his unalterable resolve not to attempt any reinforcement of the Southern forts. To think of longer remaining in the Union is simply preposterous. We have five thousand well-armed soldiers around this city; all the States are arming with great rapidity; and this means war with all its consequences. Let your President attempt to reinforce Sumter, and the tocsin of war will be sounded from every hill-top and valley in the South."

This settled the matter so far as accommodation was concerned. There was no doubt in my mind that Pickens voiced the sentiment of Rebellion.

My next duty was to confer with Major Anderson at the beleaguered fort.

On my intimating a desire to see that officer, Governor Pickens promptly placed in my hands the following:--

STATE OF SOUTH CAROLINA, EXECUTIVE DEPARTMENT, 25 March, 1861.

Mr. Lamon, from the President of the United States, requests to see Major Anderson at Fort Sumter, on business entirely pacific; and my aid, Colonel Duryea, will go with him and return, merely to see that every propriety is observed toward Mr. Lamon.

F. W. PICKENS, Governor.

A flag-of-truce steamer was furnished by the governor, under charge of Colonel Duryea, a genial and accomplished gentleman to whom I am indebted for most considerate courtesy, and I proceeded to Fort Sumter. I found Anderson in a quandary, and deeply despondent. He fully realized the critical position he and his men occupied, and he apprehended the worst possible consequences if measures were not promptly taken by the government to strengthen him. His subordinates generally, on the contrary, seemed to regard the whole affair as a sort of picnic, and evinced a readiness to meet any fate. They seemed to be "spoiling for a fight," and were eager for anything that might relieve the monotony of their position. War seemed as inevitable to them as to Governor Pickens.

After a full and free conference with Major Anderson, I returned to the Charleston Hotel. The excited crowds were still in the streets, and the hotel was overflowing with anxious people. The populace seemed maddened by their failure to learn anything of the purpose or results of my visit. The aspect of things was threatening to my personal safety, and Governor Pickens had already taken steps to allay the excitement.

A rope had been procured by the rabble and thrown into one corner of the reading-room; and as I entered the room I was accosted by a seedy patriot, somewhat past the middle age. He was dressed in a fork-tailed coat with brass buttons, which looked as if it might have done service at Thomas Jefferson's first reception. He wore a high bell-crowned hat, with an odor and rust of antiquity which seemed to proclaim it a relic from the wardrobe of Sir Walter Raleigh. His swarthy throat was decorated with a red bandana cravat and a shirt-collar of amazing amplitude, and of such fantastic pattern that it might have served as a "fly" to a Sibley tent. This individual was in a rage. Kicking the rope into the middle of the room, and squaring himself before me, he said,--

"Do you think that is strong enough to hang a damned ---- Lincoln abolition hireling?"

To this highly significant interrogatory I replied, aiming my words more at the crowd than at the beggarly ruffian who had addressed me, "Sir, I am a Virginian by birth, and a gentleman, I hope, by education and instinct. I was sent here by the President of the United States to see your governor -"

The seedy spokesman interrupted with, "Damn your President!"

I continued: "You, sir, are surrounded by your friends--by a mob; and you are brutal and cowardly enough to insult an unoffending stranger in the great city that is noted for its hospitality and chivalry; and let me tell you that your conduct is cowardly in the extreme. Among gentlemen, the brutal epithets you employ are neither given nor received."

This saucy speech awoke a flame of fury in the mob, and there is no telling what might have happened but for the lucky entrance into the room at that moment of Hon. Lawrence Keitt, who approached me and laying his hand familiarly on my shoulder, said,--

"Why, Lamon, old fellow, where did you come from? I am glad to see you."

The man with the brass buttons showed great astonishment. "Keitt," said he, "do you speak to that Lincoln hireling?"

"Stop!" thundered Keitt; "you insult Lamon, and you insult me! He is a gentleman, and my friend. Come, Lamon, let us take a drink."

The noble and generous Keitt knew me well, and it may be supposed that his "smiling" invitation was music in one sinner's ears at least. Further insults to the stranger from the loafer element of Charleston were not indulged in. The extremes of Southern character--the top and the bottom of the social scale in the slaveholding States--were exemplified in the scene just described, by Keitt and the blustering bully with the shirt-collar. The first, cultivated, manly, noble, hospitable, brave, and generous; the other, mean, unmanly, unkempt, untaught, and reeking with the fumes of the blackguard and the brute.[5]

[5] Page 78, line 7, after the word "brute."

That neither section had the monopoly of all the virtues reminds us of the conversation between General Butler and a gentleman from Georgia in 1861, when the latter said, "I do not believe there is an honest man in Massachusetts." After a moment's reflection he added: "I beg to assure you, Mr. Butler, I mean nothing personal." The General responded: "I believe there are a great many honest men in Georgia; but in saying so, sir, I too mean nothing personal."

My instructions from Mr. Lincoln required me to see and confer with the postmaster of Charleston. By this time the temper of the riotous portion of the populace, inflamed by suspicion and disappointed rage, made my further appearance on the streets a hazardous adventure. Again Governor Pickens, who despised the cowardice as he deplored the excesses of the mob, interposed his authority. To his thoughtful courtesy I was indebted for the following pass, which enabled me to visit the postmaster without molestation:--

HEADQUARTERS, 25 March, 1861.

The bearer, Mr. Lamon, has business with Mr. Huger, Postmaster of Charleston, and must not be interrupted by any one, as his business in Charleston is entirely pacific in all matters.

F. W. PICKENS, Governor.

At eight o'clock that Monday night I took the train for my return to Washington. At a station in the outskirts of the city my friends, General Hurlbut and wife, came aboard. Hurlbut knew the conductor, who gave him seats that were as private as possible. Very soon the conductor slipped a note into my hands that was significant as well as amusing. It was from General Hurlbut, and was in the following words:--

Don't you recognize us until this train gets out of South Carolina. There is danger ahead, and a damned sight of it.

STEVE.

This injunction was scrupulously observed. I learned afterward that about all of Hurlbut's time in Charleston had been employed in eluding the search of the vigilants, who, it was feared, would have given him a rough welcome to Charleston if they had known in time of his presence there.

Without further adventure we reached Washington in safety, only a few days before the tocsin of war was sounded by the firing on Fort Sumter. On my return, the President learned for the first time that Hurlbut had been in South Carolina. He laughed heartily over my unvarnished recital of Hurlbut's experience in the hot-bed of secession, though he listened with profound and saddened attention to my account of the condition of things in the fort on the one hand, and in the State and city on the other.

I brought back with me a Palmetto branch, but I brought no promise of peace. I had measured the depth of madness that was hurrying the Southern masses into open rebellion; I had ascertained the real temper and determination of their leaders by personal contact with them; and this made my mission one that was not altogether without profit to the great man at whose bidding I made the doubtful journey.

CHAPTER V.

HIS SIMPLICITY.

Political definitions have undergone some curious changes in this country since the beginning of the present century. In the year 1801, Thomas Jefferson was the first "republican" President of the United States, as the term was then defined. Sixty years later, Abraham Lincoln was hailed as our first Republican President. The Sage of Monticello was, indeed, the first to introduce at the Executive Mansion a genuine republican code of social and official etiquette. It was a wide departure from the ceremonial and showy observances for which Hamilton, his great rival, had so long contended, and which were peculiarly distasteful to the hardy freemen of the new Republic.

Mr. Lincoln profoundly admired the Virginian. Nothing in the career or the policy of Jefferson was nearer his heart than the homely and healthful republicanism implied in the term "Jeffersonian simplicity." While Mr.

Lincoln occupied the White House, his intercourse with his fellow-citizens was fashioned after the Jeffersonian idea. He believed that there should be the utmost freedom of intercourse between the people and their President. Jefferson had the truly republican idea that he was the servant of the people, not their master. That was Lincoln's idea also. Jefferson welcomed to the White House the humble mechanic and the haughty aristocrat with the same unaffected cordiality. Mr. Lincoln did the same. "There is no smell of royalty about this establishment," was a jocular expression which I have heard Mr. Lincoln use many times; and it was thoroughly characteristic of the man.

"Lincolnian simplicity" was, in fact, an improvement on the code of his illustrious predecessor. The doors of the White House were always open. Mr. Lincoln was always ready to greet visitors, no matter what their rank or calling,--to hear their complaints, their petitions, or their suggestions touching the conduct of public affairs. The ease with which he could be approached vastly increased his labor. It also led to many scenes at the White House that were strangely amusing and sometimes dramatic.

Early in the year 1865, certain influential citizens of Missouri, then in Washington, held a meeting to consider the disturbed state of the border counties, and to formulate a plan for securing Executive interference in behalf of their oppressed fellow-citizens. They "where-ased" and "resolved" at great length, and finally appointed a committee charged with the duty of visiting Mr. Lincoln, of stating their grievances, and of demanding the removal of General Fisk and the appointment of Gen. John B. McPherson in his place. The committee consisted of an ex-governor and several able and earnest gentlemen deeply impressed with the importance of their mission.

They entered the White House with some trepidation. It was at a critical period of the war, and they supposed it would be difficult to get the ear of the President. Grant was on the march to Richmond, and Sherman's army was returning from the sea. The committee knew that Mr. Lincoln would be engaged in considering the momentous events then developing, and they were therefore greatly surprised to find the doors thrown open to them. They were cordially invited to enter Mr. Lincoln's office.

The ex-governor took the floor in behalf of the oppressed Missourians. He first presented the case of a certain lieutenant, who was described as a very lonely Missourian, an orphan, his family and relatives having joined the Confederate army. Through evil reports and the machinations of enemies this orphan had got into trouble. Among other things the orator described the orphan's arrest, his trial and conviction on the charge of embezzling the money of the government; and he made a moving appeal to the President for a reopening of the case and the restoration of the abused man to his rank and pay in the army. The papers in the case were handed to Mr. Lincoln, and he was asked to examine them for himself.

The bulky package looked formidable. Mr. Lincoln took it up and began reading aloud: "Whereas, conduct unbecoming an officer and a gentleman"--"Whereas, without resentment the said lieutenant received a letter from a man named ----, stating that the President must be a negro;" and "Whereas, the said lieutenant corruptly received while an officer on duty, from a man in ----, the sum of forty dollars--"

"Stop there!" exclaimed the lieutenant, who was at that moment behind the ex-governor's chair. "Why, Mr. Lincoln--beg pardon--Mr. President, it wa'n't but thirty dollars."

"Yes," said the governor, "that charge, Mr. President, is clearly wrong. It was only thirty dollars, as we can prove."

"Governor," said Mr. Lincoln, who was by this time thoroughly amused, but grave as a judge, "that reminds me of a man in Indiana, who was in a battle of words with a neighbor. One charged that the other's daughter had three illegitimate children. 'Now,' said the man whose family was so outrageously scandalized, 'that's a lie, and I can prove it, for she only has two.' This case is no better. Whether the amount was thirty dollars or thirty thousand dollars, the culpability is the same." Then, after reading a little further, he said: "I believe I will leave this case where it was left by the officers who tried it."

The ex-governor next presented a very novel case. With the most solemn deliberation he began: "Mr. President, I want to call your attention to the case of Betsy Ann Dougherty,--a good woman. She lived in ---- County, and did my washing for a long time. Her husband went off and joined the rebel army, and I wish you would give her a protection paper." The solemnity of this appeal struck Mr. Lincoln as uncommonly ridiculous.

The two men looked at each other,--the governor desperately in earnest, and the President masking his humor behind the gravest exterior. At last Mr. Lincoln asked with inimitable gravity, "Was Betsy Ann a good washerwoman?"

"Oh, yes, sir; she was indeed."

"Was your Betsy Ann an obliging woman?"

"Yes, she was certainly very kind," responded the governor, soberly.

"Could she do other things than wash?" continued Mr. Lincoln, with the same portentous gravity.

"Oh, yes; she was very kind--very."

"Where is Betsy Ann?"

"She is now in New York, and wants to come back to Missouri; but she is afraid of banishment."

"Is anybody meddling with her?"

"No; but she is afraid to come back unless you will give her a protection paper."

Thereupon Mr. Lincoln wrote on a visiting card the following:--

Let Betsy Ann Dougherty alone as long as she behaves herself.

A. LINCOLN.

He handed this card to her advocate, saying, "Give this to Betsy Ann."

"But, Mr. President, couldn't you write a few words to the officers that would insure her protection?"

"No," said Mr. Lincoln, "officers have no time now to read letters. Tell Betsy Ann to put a string in this card and hang it round her neck. When the officers see this, they will keep their hands off your Betsy Ann."

A critical observer of this ludicrous scene could not fail to see that Mr. Lincoln was seeking needed relaxation from overburdening cares, relief from the severe mental strain he was daily undergoing. By giving attention to mirth-provoking trifles along with matters of serious concern, he found needed diversion. We can never know how much the country profited by the humor-loving nature of this wonderful man.

After patiently hearing all the Missouri committee had to say, and giving them the best assurances circumstances would allow, he dismissed them from his presence, enjoyed a hearty laugh, and then relapsed into his accustomed melancholy, contemplative mood, as if looking for something else,--looking for the end. He sat for a time at his desk thinking, then turning to me he said: "This case of our old friend, the governor, and his Betsy Ann, is a fair sample of the trifles I am constantly asked to give my attention to. I wish I had no more serious questions to deal with. If there were more Betsy Anns and fewer fellows like her husband, we should be better off. She seems to have laundered the governor to his full satisfaction, but I am sorry she didn't keep her husband washed cleaner."

Mr. Lincoln was by nature singularly merciful. The ease with which he could be reached by persons who might profit by his clemency gave rise to many notable scenes in the White House during the war.

Mr. Wheeler tells of a young man who had been convicted by a military court of sleeping at his post,--a grave offence, for which he had been sentenced to death. He was but nineteen years of age, and the only son of a widowed mother. He had suffered greatly with homesickness, and overpowered at night with cold and watching, was overcome by sleep. He had always been an honest, faithful, temperate soldier. His comrades telegraphed his mother of his fate. She at once went to Orlando Kellogg, whose kind heart promptly responded to her request, and he left for Washington by the first train. He arrived in that city at midnight. The boy was to be executed on the afternoon of the next day. With the aid of his friend, Mr. Wheeler, he passed the military guard about the White House and reached the doorkeeper, who, when he knew Mr. Kellogg's errand, took him to Mr. Lincoln's sleeping-room. Arousing Mr. Lincoln, Mr. Kellogg made known the emergency in a few words. Without stopping to dress, the President went to another room and awakened a messenger. Then sitting down, still in undress, he wrote a telegram to the officer commanding at Yorktown to suspend the execution of the boy until further orders. The telegram was sent at once to the War Department, with directions to the messenger to remain until an answer was received. Getting uneasy at the seeming delay, Mr. Lincoln dressed, went to the Department, and remained until the receipt of his telegram was acknowledged. Then turning to Kellogg, with trembling voice he said, "Now you just telegraph that mother that her boy is safe, and I will go home and go to bed. I guess we shall all sleep better for this night's work."

A somewhat similar proof of Mr. Lincoln's mercy is the story told of a very young man living in one of the southern counties of Kentucky, who had been enticed into the rebel army. After remaining with it in Tennessee a few months he became disgusted or weary, and managed to make his way back to his home. Soon after his arrival, some of the military stationed in the town heard of his return and arrested him as a rebel spy, and, after a military trial, he was condemned to be hanged. His family was overwhelmed with distress and horror. Mr. Lincoln was seen by one of his friends from Kentucky, who explained his errand and asked for mercy. "Oh, yes, I understand; some one has been crying, and worked upon your feelings, and you have come here to work on mine."

His friend then went more into detail, and assured him of his belief in the truth of the story. After some deliberation, Mr. Lincoln, evidently scarcely more than half convinced, but still preferring to err on the side of mercy, replied: "If a man had more than one life, I think a little hanging would not hurt this one; but after he is once dead we cannot bring him back, no matter how sorry we may be; so the boy shall be pardoned." And a reprieve was given on the spot.

The following incident will illustrate another phase of Mr. Lincoln's character. A man who was then in jail at Newburyport, Mass., as a convicted slave-trader, and who had been fined one thousand dollars and sentenced to imprisonment for five years, petitioned for a pardon. The petition was accompanied by a letter to the Hon. John B. Alley, a member of Congress from Lynn, Mass. Mr. Alley presented the papers to the President, with a letter from the prisoner acknowledging his guilt and the justice of his sentence. He had served out the term of sentence of imprisonment, but was still held on account of the fine not being paid. Mr. Lincoln was much moved by the pathetic appeal. He then, after pausing some time, said to Mr. Alley: "My friend, this appeal is very touching to my feelings, and no one knows my weakness better than you. It is, if possible, to be too easily moved by appeals for mercy; and I must say that if this man had been guilty of the foulest murder that the arm of man could perpetrate, I might forgive him on such an appeal. But the man who could go to Africa and rob her of her children, and then sell them into interminable bondage, with no other motive than that which is furnished by dollars and cents, is so much worse than the most depraved murderer that he can never receive pardon at my hand. No, sir; he may stay in jail forever before he shall have liberty by any act of mine."

After the war had been fairly inaugurated, and several battles had been fought, a lady from Alexandria visited Mr. Lincoln, and importuned him to give an order for the release of a certain church in that place which had been seized and used as a hospital. He asked and was told the name of the church, and that there were but three or four wounded persons occupying it, and that the inhabitants wanted it to worship in. Mr. Lincoln asked her if she had applied to the post surgeon at Alexandria to give it up. She answered that she had, and that she could do nothing with him. "Well, madam," said he, "that is an end of it then. We put him there to attend to just such business, and it is reasonable to suppose that he knows better what should be done under the circumstances than I do."

More for the purpose of testing the sentiments of this visitor than for any other reason, Mr. Lincoln said: "You say you live in Alexandria. How much would you be willing to subscribe towards building a hospital there?"

She replied: "You may be aware, Mr. Lincoln, that our property has been very much embarrassed by the war, and I could not afford to give much for such a purpose."

"Yes," said Mr. Lincoln, "and this war is not over yet; and I expect we shall have another fight soon, and that church may be very useful as a hospital in which to nurse our poor wounded soldiers. It is my candid opinion that God wants that church for our wounded fellows. So, madam, you will excuse me. I can do nothing for you."

Afterward, in speaking of this incident, Mr. Lincoln said that the lady as a representative of her class in Alexandria reminded him of the story of the young man who had an aged father and mother owning considerable property. The young man being an only son, and believing that the old people had lived out their usefulness, assassinated them both. He was accused, tried, and convicted of the murder. When the judge came to pass sentence upon him, and called upon him to give any reason he might have why the sentence of death should not be passed upon him, he with great promptness replied that he hoped the court would be lenient upon him because he was a poor orphan!

Two ladies from Tennessee called at the White House one day, and begged Mr. Lincoln to release their husbands, who were rebel prisoners at Johnson's Island. One of the fair petitioners urged as a reason for the liberation of her husband that he was a very religious man; and she rang the changes on this pious plea ad nauseam. "Madam," said Mr. Lincoln, "you say your husband is a religious man. Perhaps I am not a good judge of such matters, but in my opinion the religion that makes men rebel and fight against their government is not the genuine article; nor is the religion the right sort which reconciles them to the idea of eating their bread in the sweat of other men's faces. It is not the kind to get to heaven on." After another interview, however, the order of release was made,--Mr. Lincoln remarking, with impressive solemnity, that he would expect the ladies to subdue the rebellious spirit of their husbands, and to that end he thought it would be well to reform their religion. "True patriotism," said he, "is better than the wrong kind of piety."

This is in keeping with a significant remark made by him to a clergyman, in the early days of the war. "Let us have faith, Mr. President," said the minister, "that the Lord is on our side in this great struggle." Mr. Lincoln quietly answered: "I am not at all concerned about that, for I know that the Lord is always on the side of the right; but it is my constant anxiety and prayer that I and this nation may be on the Lord's side."

Clergymen were always welcomed by Mr. Lincoln at the White House with the respectful courtesy due to their sacred calling. During the progress of the war, and especially in its earlier stages, he was visited almost daily by reverend gentlemen, sometimes as single visitors, but more frequently in delegations. He was a patient listener to the words of congratulation, counsel, admonition, exhortation, and sometimes reproof, which fell from the lips of his pious callers, and generally these interviews were entertaining and agreeable on both sides. It sometimes happened, however, that these visits were painfully embarrassing to the President. One delegation, for example, would urge with importunate zeal a strict observance of the Sabbath day by the army; others would insist upon a speedy proclamation of emancipation; while some recounted the manifold errors of commanding generals, complained of the tardy action of the government in critical emergencies, and proposed sweeping changes of policy in the conduct of the war.

There was scarcely a day when there were not several delegations of this kind to visit him, and a great deal of the President's valuable time was employed in this unimportant manner. One day he was asked by one of these self-constituted mentors, how many men the rebels had in the field? Mr. Lincoln promptly but seriously answered, "Twelve hundred thousand, according to the best authority." His listeners looked aghast. "Good heavens!" they exclaimed in astonishment. "Yes, sir; twelve hundred thousand, no doubt of it. You see, all of our generals when they get whipped say the enemy outnumbers them from three or five to one, and I must believe them. We have four hundred thousand men in the field, and three times four make twelve,--don't you see it? It is as plain to be seen as the nose on a man's face; and at the rate things are now going, with the great amount of speculation and the small crop of fighting, it will take a long time to overcome twelve hundred thousand rebels in arms. If they can get subsistence they have everything else, except a just cause. Yet it is said that 'thrice is he armed that hath his quarrel just.' I am willing, however, to risk our advantage of thrice in justice against their thrice in numbers."

On but one occasion that I can now recall was Mr. Lincoln's habitual good humor visibly overtaxed by these well-meaning but impatient advisers. A committee of clergymen from the West called one day; and the spokesman, fired with uncontrollable zeal, poured forth a lecture which was fault-finding in tone from beginning to end. It was delivered with much energy, and the shortcomings of the Administration were rehearsed with painful directness. The reverend orator made some keen thrusts, which evoked hearty applause from other gentlemen of the committee.

Mr. Lincoln's reply was a notable one. With unusual animation, he said: "Gentlemen, suppose all the property you possess were in gold, and you had placed it in the hands of Blondin to carry across the Niagara River on a rope. With slow, cautious, steady step he walks the rope, bearing your all. Would you shake the cable, and keep shouting to him, 'Blondin! stand up a little straighter! Blondin! stoop a little more; go a little faster; lean more to the south! Now lean a little more to the north!'--would that be your behavior in such an emergency? No; you would hold your breath, every one of you, as well as your tongues. You would keep your hands off until he was safe on the other side. This government, gentlemen, is carrying an immense weight; untold treasures are in its hands. The persons managing the ship of state in this storm are doing the best they can. Don't worry them with needless warnings and complaints. Keep silence, be patient, and we will get you safe across. Good day, gentlemen. I have other duties pressing upon me that must be attended to."

This incident made Mr. Lincoln a little shy of preachers for a time. "But the latch-string is out," said he, "and they have the right to come here and preach to me if they will go about it with some gentleness and moderation." He firmly believed that--

"To speak his thoughts is every freeman's right, In peace and war, in council and in fight."

And from this republican idea he would suffer not the slightest departure while he was President.

Soon after the affair just described, a man of remarkable appearance presented himself at the White House and requested an audience with Mr. Lincoln. He was a large, fleshy man, of a stern but homely countenance, and of a solemn and dignified carriage. He was dressed in a neatly-fitting swallow-tailed coat, ruffled shirt of faultless fabric, white cravat, and orange-colored gloves. An immense fob chain, to which was attached a huge topaz seal, swung from his watch-pocket, and he carried a large gold-headed cane. His whole appearance was that of a man of great intellect, of stern qualities, of strong piety, and of dignified uncomeliness. He looked in every way like a minister of the gospel, whose vigorous mind was bent on godly themes, and whose present purpose was to discourse to Mr. Lincoln on matters of grave import.

"I am in for it now," thought the President. "This pious man means business. He is no common preacher. Evidently his gloomy mind is big with a scheme of no ordinary kind."

The ceremony of introduction was unusually formal, and the few words of conversation that followed were constrained. The good man spoke with great deliberation, as if feeling his way cautiously; but the evident restraint which his manner imposed upon Mr. Lincoln seemed not to please him. The sequel was amazing.

Quitting his chair, the portly visitor extended his hand to Mr. Lincoln, saying as the latter rose and confronted him: "Well, Mr. President, I have no business with you, none whatever. I was at the Chicago convention as a friend of Mr. Seward. I have watched you narrowly ever since your inauguration, and I called merely to pay my respects. What I want to say is this: I think you are doing everything for the good of the country that is in the power of man to do. You are on the right track. As one of your constituents I now say to you, do in future as you damn please, and I will support you!" This was spoken with tremendous effect.

"Why," said Mr. Lincoln in great astonishment, "I took you to be a preacher. I thought you had come here to tell me how to take Richmond," and he again grasped the hand of his strange visitor. Accurate and penetrating as Mr. Lincoln's judgment was concerning men, for once he had been wholly mistaken. The scene was comical in the extreme. The two men stood gazing at each other. A smile broke from the lips of the solemn wag and rippled over the wide expanse of his homely face like sunlight overspreading a continent, and Mr. Lincoln was convulsed with laughter.

"Sit down, my friend," said the President; "sit down. I am delighted to see you. Lunch with us to-day. Yes, you must stay and lunch with us, my friend, for I have not seen enough of you yet."

The stranger did lunch with Mr. Lincoln that day. He was a man of rare and racy humor,--and the good cheer, the fun, the wit, the anecdotes and sparkling conversation that enlivened the scene was the work of two of the most original characters ever seen in the White House.

Shortly after the election of Mr. Lincoln, I talked with him earnestly about the habits, manners, customs, and style of the people with whom he had now to associate, and the difference between his present surroundings and those of his Illinois life, and wherein his plain, practical, common-sense actions differed from the polite, graceful, and elegant bearing of the cultivated diplomat and cultured gentlemen of polite society. Thanks to his confidence in my friendship and his affectionate forbearance with me, he would listen to me with the most attentive interest, always evincing the strongest desire to correct anything in which he failed to be and appear like the people with whom he acted; for it was one of the cardinal traits of his character to be like, of, and for the people, whether in exalted or humble life.

A New Hampshire lady having presented to him a soft felt hat of her own manufacture, he was at a loss what to do on his arrival in Washington, as the felt hat seemed unbecoming for a President-elect. He therefore said to me: "Hill, this hat of mine won't do. It is a felt one, and I have been uncomfortable in it ever since we left Harrisburg. Give me that plug of yours, until you can go out in the city and buy one either for yourself or for me. I think your hat is about the style. I may have to do some trotting around soon, and if I can't feel natural with a different hat, I may at least look respectable in it."

I went to a store near by and purchased a hat, and by the ironing process soon had it shaped to my satisfaction; and I must say that when Mr. Lincoln put it on, he looked more presentable and more like a President than I had ever seen him. He had very defective taste in the choice of hats, the item of dress that does more than any other for the improvement of one's personal appearance.

After the hat reform, I think Mr. Lincoln still suffered much annoyance from the tyranny of fashion in the matter of gloves. His hat for years served the double purpose of an ornamental head-gear and a kind of office or receptacle for his private papers and memoranda. But the necessity to wear gloves he regarded as an affliction, a violation of the statute against "cruelty to animals." Many amusing stories could be told of Mr. Lincoln and his gloves. At about the time of his third reception he had on a tight-fitting pair of white kids, which he had with difficulty got on. He saw approaching in the distance an old Illinois friend named Simpson, whom he welcomed with a genuine Sangamon County shake, which resulted in bursting his white-kid glove with an audible sound. Then raising his brawny hand up before him, looking at it with an indescribable expression, he said,--while the whole procession was checked, witnessing this scene,--"Well, my old friend, this is a general bustification. You and I were never intended to wear these things. If they were stronger they might do well enough to keep out the cold, but they are a failure to shake hands with between old friends like us. Stand aside, Captain, and I'll see you shortly." The procession then advanced. Simpson stood aside, and after the unwelcome pageantry was terminated, he rejoined his old Illinois friend in familiar intercourse.

Mr. Lincoln was always delighted to see his Western friends, and always gave them a cordial welcome; and when the proprieties justified it, he met them on the old familiar footing, entertaining them with anecdotes in unrestrained, free-and-easy conversation. He never spoke of himself as President,--always referred to his office as "this place;" would often say to an old friend, "Call me Lincoln: 'Mr. President' is entirely too formal for us." Shortly after the first inauguration, an old and respected friend accompanied by his wife visited Washington, and as a matter of course paid their respects to the President and his family, having been on intimate social terms with them for many years. It was proposed that at a certain time Mr. and Mrs. Lincoln should call at the hotel where they were stopping and take them out for a ride in the Presidential carriage,--a gorgeous and grandly caparisoned coach, the like of which the visitors had seldom seen before that time. As close as the intimacy was, the two men had never seen each other with gloves on in their lives, except as a protection from the cold. Both gentlemen, realizing the propriety of their use in the changed condition of things, discussed the matter with their respective wives, who decided that gloves were the proper things. Mr. Lincoln reluctantly yielded to this decree, and placed his in his pocket, to be used or not according to circumstances. On arriving at the hotel he found his friend, who doubtless had yielded to his wife's persuasion, gloved in the most approved style. The friend, taking in the situation, was hardly seated in the carriage when he began to take off the clinging kids; and at the same time Mr. Lincoln began to draw his on,--seeing which they both burst into a hearty laugh, when Mr. Lincoln exclaimed, "Oh, why should the spirit of mortals be proud?" Then he added, "I suppose it is polite to wear these things, but it is positively uncomfortable for me to do so. Let us put them in our pockets; that is the best place for them, and we shall be able to act more like folks in our bare hands." After this the ride was as enjoyable as any one they had ever taken in early days in a lumber wagon over the prairies of Illinois.

An instance showing that the deserving low-born commanded Mr. Lincoln's respect and consideration as well as the high-born and distinguished, may be found in what he said on one occasion to an Austrian count during the rebellion. The Austrian minister to this government introduced to the President a count, subject of the Austrian government, who was desirous of obtaining a position in the American army. Being introduced by the accredited minister of Austria, he required no further recommendation to secure the appointment; but fearing that his importance might not be fully appreciated by the republican President, the count was particular in impressing the fact upon him that he bore that title, and that his family was ancient and highly respectable. Mr. Lincoln listened with attention, until this unnecessary commendation was mentioned; then, with a merry twinkle in his eye, he tapped the aristocratic sprig of hereditary nobility on the shoulder in the most fatherly way, as if the gentleman had made a confession of some unfortunate circumstance connected with his lineage, for which he was in no way responsible, saying, "Never mind, you shall be treated with just as much consideration for all that. I will see to it that your bearing a title sha'n't hurt you."

CHAPTER VI.

HIS TENDERNESS.

Mr. Lincoln was one of the bravest men that ever lived, and one of the gentlest. The instances in his earlier career in which he put his life in peril to prevent injury to another are very numerous. I have often thought that his interposition in behalf of the friendless Indian who wandered into camp during the Black Hawk war and was about to be murdered by the troops, was an act of chivalry unsurpassed in the whole story of knighthood. So in the rough days of Gentryville and New Salem, he was always on the side of the weak and the undefended; always daring against the bully; always brave and tender; always invoking peace and good-will, except where they could be had only by dishonor. He could not endure to witness the needless suffering even of a brute. When riding once with a company of young ladies and gentlemen, dressed up in his best, he sprang from his horse and released a pig which was fast in a fence and squealing in pain, because, as he said in his homely way, the misery of the poor pig was more than he could bear.

Hon. I. N. Arnold tells of an incident in the early days of Mr. Lincoln's practice at the Springfield bar. He was coming home from a neighboring county seat, with a party of lawyers, riding two by two along a country lane. Lincoln and a comrade brought up the rear, and when the others stopped to water their horses his comrade came up alone. "Where is Lincoln?" was the inquiry. "Oh," replied the friend, "when I saw him last he had caught two young birds which the wind had blown out of their nest, and was hunting up the nest to put them back into it."

How instinctively Mr. Lincoln turned from the deliberate, though lawful and necessary, shedding of blood during the war is well known. His Secretaries of War, his Judge-Advocate General, and generals in the field, were often put to their wits' end to maintain the discipline of the army against this constant softness of the President's good heart.

Upward of twenty deserters were sentenced at one time to be shot. The warrants for their execution were sent to Mr. Lincoln for his approval; but he refused to sign them. The commanding general to whose corps the condemned men belonged was indignant. He hurried to Washington. Mr. Lincoln had listened to moving petitions for mercy from humane persons who, like himself, were shocked at the idea of the cold-blooded execution of more than a score of misguided men. His resolution was fixed, but his rule was to see every man who had business with him. The irate commander, therefore, was admitted into Mr. Lincoln's private office. With soldierly bluntness he told the President that mercy to the few was cruelty to the many; that Executive clemency in such a case would be a blow at military discipline; and that unless the condemned men were made examples of, the army itself would be in danger. "General," said Mr. Lincoln, "there are too many weeping widows in the United States now. For God's sake don't ask me to add to the number; for, I tell you plainly, I won't do it!" He believed that kind words were better for the poor fellows than cold lead; and the sequel showed that he was right.

Death warrants: execution of unfortunate soldiers,--how he dreaded and detested them, and longed to restore every unfortunate man under sentence to life and honor in his country's service! I had personally an almost unlimited experience with him in this class of cases, and could fill volumes with anecdotes exhibiting this trait in the most touching light, though the names of the persons concerned--disgraced soldiers, prisoners of war, civilian spies--would hardly be recognized by the readers of this generation.

But it was the havoc of the war, the sacrifice of patriotic lives, the flow of human blood, the mangling of precious limbs in the great Union host that shocked him most,--indeed, on some occasions shocked him almost beyond his capacity to control either his judgment or his feelings. This was especially the case when the noble victims were of his own acquaintance, or of the narrower circle of his familiar friends; and then he seemed for the moment possessed of a sense of personal responsibility for their individual fate, which was at once most unreasonable and most pitiful. Of this latter class were many of the most gallant men of Illinois and Indiana, who fell dead or cruelly wounded in the early battles of the Southwest.

The "Black boys" were notable among the multitude of eager youths who rushed to the field at the first call to arms. Their mother, the widow of a learned Presbyterian minister, had married Dr. Fithian, of Danville, Ill.; and the relations between Dr. Fithian and his stepsons were of the tenderest paternal nature. His pride in them and his devotion to them was the theme of the country side. Mr. Lincoln knew them well. In his frequent visits to Danville on the circuit he seldom failed to be the guest of their mother and the excellent Dr. Fithian. They were studious and industrious boys, earning with their own hands at least a part of the money required for their education. When Sumter was fired upon they were at Wabash College, Crawfordsville, Ind., and immediately enlisted as privates in the Crawfordsville Guards. Their career in the field needs no recital here. Mr. Lincoln watched it with intense interest. At the battle of Pea Ridge, having reached high rank,--each promotion for some special act of gallantry,--they both fell desperately wounded within five minutes of each other, and only thirty yards apart. Dr. Fithian hastened to them with a father's solicitude, and nursed them back to life, through fearful vicissitudes. They had scarcely returned to the army when the elder, John Charles Black, again fell, terribly mangled, at Prairie Grove. He was hopelessly shattered; yet he remained in the service and at the front until the last gun was fired, and is now among the badly wounded survivors of the war. I shall never forget the scene, when I took to Mr. Lincoln a letter written by Dr. Fithian to me, describing the condition of the "Black boys," and expressing his fears that they could not live. Mr. Lincoln read it, and broke into tears: "Here, now," he cried, "are these dear, brave boys killed in this cursed war! My God, my God! It is too bad! They worked hard to earn money enough to educate themselves, and this is the end! I loved them as if they were my own." I took his directions about my reply to Dr. Fithian, and left him in one of the saddest moods in which I ever saw him, burdened with an unreasonable sense of personal responsibility for the lives of these gallant men.

Lieut.-Colonel William McCullough, of whom a very eminent gentleman said on a most solemn occasion, "He was the most thoroughly courageous man I have ever known," fell leading a hopeless charge in Mississippi. He had entered the service at the age of fifty, with one arm and one eye. He had been clerk of McLean County Circuit Court, Ill., for twenty years, and Mr. Lincoln knew him thoroughly. His death affected the President profoundly, and he wrote to the Colonel's daughter, now Mrs. Frank D. Orme, the following peculiar letter of condolence:--

EXECUTIVE MANSION, WASHINGTON, Dec. 23, 1862.

DEAR FANNY,--It is with deep regret that I learn of the death of your kind and brave father, and especially that it is affecting your young heart beyond what is common in such cases. In this sad world of ours sorrow comes to all, and to the young it comes with bitterer agony because it takes them unawares. The older have learned ever to expect it. I am anxious to afford some alleviation of your present distress. Perfect relief is not possible, except with time. You cannot now realize that you will ever feel better. Is not this so? And yet it is a mistake. You are sure to be happy again. To know this, which is certainly true, will make you some less miserable now. I have had experience enough to know what I say, and you need only to believe it to feel better at once. The memory of your dear father, instead of an agony, will yet be a sad, sweet feeling in your heart, of a purer and holier sort than you have known before.

Please present my kind regards to your afflicted mother.

Your sincere friend, A. LINCOLN.

MISS FANNY MCCULLOUGH, Bloomington, Ill.

Gen. W. H. L. Wallace, who fell at Shiloh, was a friend whom Lincoln held in the tenderest regard. He knew his character as a man and his inestimable value as a soldier quite as well as they are now known to the country. Those who have read General Grant's "Memoirs" will understand from that great general's estimate of him what was the loss of the federal service in the untimely death of Wallace. Mr. Lincoln felt it bitterly and deeply. But his was a public and a private grief united, and his lamentations were touching to those who heard them, as I did. The following account of General Wallace's death is taken from an eloquent memorial address, by the Hon. Leonard Swett in the United States Circuit Court, upon our common friend the late Col. T. Lyle Dickey, who was the father-in-law of Wallace:--

"Mrs. Gen. W. H. L. Wallace, who was Judge Dickey's eldest daughter, as the battle of Shiloh approached, became impressed with the sense of impending danger to her husband, then with Grant's army. This impression haunted her until she could stand it no longer; and in one of the most severe storms of the season, at twelve o'clock at night, she started alone for the army where her husband was. At Cairo she was told that no women could be permitted to go up the Tennessee River. But affection has a persistency which will not be denied. Mrs. Wallace finding a party bearing a flag to the Eleventh Infantry from the ladies of Ottawa, to be used instead of their old one, which had been riddled and was battle-worn, got herself substituted to carry that flag: and thus with one expedient and another she finally reached Shiloh, six hundred miles from home and three hundred through a hostile country, and through the more hostile guards of our own forces.

"She arrived on Sunday, the 6th of April, 1862, when the great storm-centre of that battle was at its height, and in time to receive her husband as he was borne from the field terribly mangled by a shot in the head, which he had received while endeavoring to stay the retreat of our army as it was falling back to the banks of the river on that memorable Sunday, the first day of that bloody battle. She arrived in time to recognize him, and be recognized by him; and a few days afterward, saying, 'We shall meet again in heaven,' he died in the arms of that devoted wife, surrounded by Judge Dickey and his sons and the brothers of General Wallace."

These are but a few cases of death and mutilation in the military service cited to show how completely Mr. Lincoln shared the sufferings of our soldiers. It was with a weight of singular personal responsibility that some of these misfortunes and sorrows seemed to crowd upon his sympathetic heart.

Soon after his election in 1864, when any other man would have been carried away on the tide of triumph and would have had little thought for the sorrows of a stranger, he found time to write the following letter:--

EXECUTIVE MANSION, Nov. 21, 1864.

DEAR MADAM,--I have been shown, in the files of the War Department, a statement of the Adjutant-General of Massachusetts, that you are the mother of five sons who have died gloriously on the field of battle. I feel how weak and fruitless must be any words of mine which should attempt to beguile you from the grief of a loss so overwhelming. But I cannot refrain from tendering to you the consolation that may be found in the thanks of the republic they died to save. I pray that our Heavenly Father may assuage the anguish of your bereavement, and leave you only the cherished memory of the loved and lost and the solemn pride that must be yours to have laid so costly a sacrifice upon the altar of freedom.

Yours very sincerely and respectfully, ABRAHAM LINCOLN.

TO MRS. BIXBY BOSTON, MASS.

Once when Mr. Lincoln had released a prisoner at the request of his mother she, in expressing her gratitude, said, "Good-bye, Mr. Lincoln. I shall probably never see you again till we meet in heaven." She had the President's hand in hers, and he was deeply moved. He instantly took her hand in both of his and, following her to the door, said, "I am afraid with all my troubles I shall never get to the resting place you speak of, but if I do I am sure I shall find you. Your wish that you will meet me there has fully paid for all I have done for you."

Perhaps none of Mr. Lincoln's ambitions were more fully realized than the wish expressed to Joshua F. Speed: Die when I may, I want it said of me by those who know me best that I always plucked a thistle and planted a flower where I thought a flower would grow.

CHAPTER VII.

DREAMS AND PRESENTIMENTS.

That "every man has within him his own Patmos," Victor Hugo was not far wrong in declaring. "Revery," says the great French thinker, "fixes its gaze upon the shadow until there issues from it light. Some power that is very high has ordained it thus." Mr. Lincoln had his Patmos, his "kinship with the shades;" and this is, perhaps, the strangest feature of his character. That his intellect was mighty and of exquisite mould, that it was of a severely logical cast, and that his reasoning powers were employed in the main on matters eminently practical, all men know who know anything about the real Lincoln. The father of modern philosophy tells us that "the master of superstition is the people; and in all superstitions wise men follow fools." Lord Bacon, however, was not unwilling to believe that storms might be dispersed by the ringing of bells,--a superstition that is not yet wholly dead, even in countries most distinguished by modern enlightenment. Those whom the great Englishman designated "masters of superstition,--fools," were the common people whose collective wisdom Mr. Lincoln esteemed above the highest gifts of cultured men. That the Patmos of the plain people, as Mr. Lincoln called them, was his in a large measure he freely acknowledged; and this peculiarity of his nature is shown in his strange dreams and presentiments, which sometimes elated and sometimes disturbed him in a very astonishing degree.

From early youth he seemed conscious of a high mission. Long before his admission to the bar, or his entrance into politics, he believed that he was destined to rise to a great height; that from a lofty station to which he should be called he would be able to confer lasting benefits on his fellow-men. He believed also that from a lofty station he should fall. It was a vision of grandeur and of gloom which was confirmed in his mind by the dreams of his childhood, of his youthful days, and of his maturer years. The plain people with whom his life was spent, and with whom he was in cordial sympathy, believed also in the marvellous as revealed in presentiments and dreams; and so Mr. Lincoln drifted on through years of toil and exceptional hardship, struggling with a noble spirit for honest promotion,--meditative, aspiring, certain of his star, but appalled at times by its malignant aspect. Many times prior to his election to the Presidency he was both elated and alarmed by what seemed to him a rent in the veil which hides from mortal view what the future holds. He saw, or thought he saw, a vision of glory and of blood, himself the central figure in a scene which his fancy transformed from giddy enchantment to the most appalling tragedy.

On the day of his renomination at Baltimore, Mr. Lincoln was engaged at the War Department in constant telegraphic communication with General Grant, who was then in front of Richmond. Throughout the day he seemed wholly unconscious that anything was going on at Baltimore in which his interests were in any way concerned. At luncheon time he went to the White House, swallowed a hasty lunch, and without entering his private office hurried back to the War Office. On his arrival at the War Department the first dispatch that was shown him announced the nomination of Andrew Johnson for Vice-President.

"This is strange," said he, reflectively; "I thought it was usual to nominate the candidate for President first."

His informant was astonished. "Mr. President," said he, "have you not heard of your own renomination? It was telegraphed to you at the White House two hours ago."

Mr. Lincoln had not seen the dispatch, had made no inquiry about it, had not even thought about it. On reflection, he attached great importance to this singular occurrence. It reminded him, he said, of an ominous incident of mysterious character which occurred just after his election in 1860. It was the double image of himself in a looking-glass, which he saw while lying on a lounge in his own chamber at Springfield. There was Abraham Lincoln's face reflecting the full glow of health and hopeful life; and in the same mirror, at the same moment of time, was the face of Abraham Lincoln showing a ghostly paleness. On trying the experiment at other times, as confirmatory tests, the illusion reappeared, and then vanished as before.

Mr. Lincoln more than once told me that he could not explain this phenomenon; that he had tried to reproduce the double reflection at the

Executive Mansion, but without success; that it had worried him not a little; and that the mystery had its meaning, which was clear enough to him. To his mind the illusion was a sign,--the life-like image betokening a safe passage through his first term as President; the ghostly one, that death would overtake him before the close of the second. Wholly unmindful of the events happening at Baltimore, which would have engrossed the thoughts of any other statesman in his place that day,--forgetful, in fact, of all earthly things except the tremendous events of the war,--this circumstance, on reflection, he wove into a volume of prophecy, a sure presage of his re-election. His mind then instantly travelled back to the autumn of 1860; and the vanished wraith--the ghostly face in the mirror, mocking its healthy and hopeful fellow--told him plainly that although certain of re-election to the exalted office he then held, he would surely hear the fatal summons from the silent shore during his second term. With that firm conviction, which no philosophy could shake, Mr. Lincoln moved on through a maze of mighty events, calmly awaiting the inevitable hour of his fall by a murderous hand.

How, it may be asked, could he make life tolerable, burdened as he was with that portentous horror which though visionary, and of trifling import in our eyes, was by his interpretation a premonition of impending doom? I answer in a word: His sense of duty to his country; his belief that "the inevitable" is right; and his innate and irrepressible humor.

But the most startling incident in the life of Mr. Lincoln was a dream he had only a few days before his assassination. To him it was a thing of deadly import, and certainly no vision was ever fashioned more exactly like a dread reality. Coupled with other dreams, with the mirror-scene and with other incidents, there was something about it so amazingly real, so true to the actual tragedy which occurred soon after, that more than mortal strength and wisdom would have been required to let it pass without a shudder or a pang. After worrying over it for some days, Mr. Lincoln seemed no longer able to keep the secret. I give it as nearly in his own words as I can, from notes which I made immediately after its recital. There were only two or three persons present. The President was in a melancholy, meditative mood, and had been silent for some time. Mrs. Lincoln, who was present, rallied him on his solemn visage and want of spirit. This seemed to arouse him, and without seeming to notice her sally he said, in slow and measured tones:--

"It seems strange how much there is in the Bible about dreams. There are, I think, some sixteen chapters in the Old Testament and four or five in the New in which dreams are mentioned; and there are many other passages scattered throughout the book which refer to visions. If we believe the Bible, we must accept the fact that in the old days God and His angels came to men in their sleep and made themselves known in dreams. Nowadays dreams are regarded as very foolish, and are seldom told, except by old women and by young men and maidens in love."

Mrs. Lincoln here remarked: "Why, you look dreadfully solemn; do you believe in dreams?"

"I can't say that I do," returned Mr. Lincoln; "but I had one the other night which has haunted me ever since. After it occurred, the first time I opened the Bible, strange as it may appear, it was at the twenty-eighth chapter of Genesis, which relates the wonderful dream Jacob had. I turned to other passages, and seemed to encounter a dream or a vision wherever I looked. I kept on turning the leaves of the old book, and everywhere my eye fell upon passages recording matters strangely in keeping with my own thoughts,--supernatural visitations, dreams, visions, etc."

He now looked so serious and disturbed that Mrs. Lincoln exclaimed: "You frighten me! What is the matter?"

"I am afraid," said Mr. Lincoln, observing the effect his words had upon his wife, "that I have done wrong to mention the subject at all; but somehow the thing has got possession of me, and, like Banquo's ghost, it will not down."

This only inflamed Mrs. Lincoln's curiosity the more, and while bravely disclaiming any belief in dreams, she strongly urged him to tell the dream which seemed to have such a hold upon him, being seconded in this by another listener. Mr. Lincoln hesitated, but at length commenced very deliberately, his brow overcast with a shade of melancholy.

"About ten days ago," said he, "I retired very late. I had been up waiting for important dispatches from the front. I could not have been long in bed when I fell into a slumber, for I was weary. I soon began to dream. There seemed to be a death-like stillness about me. Then I heard subdued sobs, as if a number of people were weeping. I thought I left my bed and wandered downstairs. There the silence was broken by the same pitiful sobbing, but the mourners were invisible. I went from room to room; no living person was in sight, but the same mournful sounds of distress met me as I passed along. It was light in all the rooms; every object was familiar to me; but where were all the people who were grieving as if their hearts would break? I was puzzled and alarmed. What could be the meaning of all this? Determined to find the cause of a state of things so mysterious and so shocking, I kept on until I arrived at the East Room, which I entered. There I met with a sickening surprise. Before me was a catafalque, on which rested a corpse wrapped in funeral vestments. Around it were stationed soldiers who were acting as guards; and there was a throng of people, some gazing mournfully upon the corpse, whose face was covered, others weeping pitifully. 'Who is dead in the White House?' I demanded of one of the soldiers. 'The President,' was his answer; 'he was killed by an assassin!' Then came a loud burst of grief from the crowd, which awoke me from my dream. I slept no more that night; and although it was only a dream, I have been strangely annoyed by it ever since."

"That is horrid!" said Mrs. Lincoln. "I wish you had not told it. I am glad I don't believe in dreams, or I should be in terror from this time forth."

"Well," responded Mr. Lincoln, thoughtfully, "it is only a dream, Mary. Let us say no more about it, and try to forget it."

This dream was so horrible, so real, and so in keeping with other dreams and threatening presentiments of his, that Mr. Lincoln was profoundly disturbed by it. During its recital he was grave, gloomy, and at times visibly pale, but perfectly calm. He spoke slowly, with measured accents and deep feeling. In conversations with me he referred to it afterward, closing one with this quotation from "Hamlet": "To sleep; perchance to dream! ay, there's the rub!" with a strong accent on the last three words.

Once the President alluded to this terrible dream with some show of playful humor. "Hill," said he, "your apprehension of harm to me from some hidden enemy is downright foolishness. For a long time you have been trying to keep somebody--the Lord knows who--from killing me. Don't you see how it will turn out? In this dream it was not me, but some other fellow, that was killed. It seems that this ghostly assassin tried his hand on some one else. And this reminds me of an old farmer in Illinois whose family were made sick by eating greens. Some poisonous herb had got into the mess, and members of the family were in danger of dying. There was a half-witted boy in the family called Jake; and always afterward when they had greens the old man would say, 'Now, afore we risk these greens, let's try 'em on Jake. If he stands 'em, we're all right.' Just so with me. As long as this imaginary assassin continues to exercise himself on others I can stand it." He then became serious and said: "Well, let it go. I think the Lord in His own good time and way will work this out all right. God knows what is best."

These words he spoke with a sigh, and rather in a tone of soliloquy, as if hardly noting my presence.

Mr. Lincoln had another remarkable dream, which was repeated so frequently during his occupancy of the White House that he came to regard it as a welcome visitor. It was of a pleasing and promising character, having nothing in it of the horrible. It was always an omen of a Union victory, and came with unerring certainty just before every military or naval engagement where our arms were crowned with success. In this dream he saw a ship sailing away rapidly, badly damaged, and our victorious vessels in close pursuit. He saw, also, the close of a battle on land, the enemy routed, and our forces in possession of vantage ground of incalculable importance. Mr. Lincoln stated it as a fact that he had this dream just before the battles of Antietam, Gettysburg, and other signal engagements throughout the war.

The last time Mr. Lincoln had this dream was the night before his assassination. On the morning of that lamentable day there was a Cabinet meeting at which General Grant was present. During an interval of general discussion, the President asked General Grant if he had any news from General Sherman, who was then confronting Johnston. The reply was in the negative, but the general added that he was in hourly expectation of a dispatch announcing Johnston's surrender. Mr. Lincoln then with great impressiveness said: "We shall hear very soon, and the news will be important." General Grant asked him why he thought so. "Because," said Mr. Lincoln, "I had a dream last night; and ever since this war began I have had the same dream just before every event of great national importance. It portends some important event that will happen very soon."

After this Mr. Lincoln became unusually cheerful. In the afternoon he ordered a carriage for a drive. Mrs. Lincoln asked him if he wished any one to accompany them. "No, Mary," said he, "I prefer that we ride by ourselves to-day."

Mrs. Lincoln said afterwards that she never saw him look happier than he did during that drive. In reply to a remark of hers to that effect, Mr. Lincoln said: "And well may I feel so, Mary; for I consider that this day the war has come to a close. Now, we must try to be more cheerful in the future; for between this terrible war and the loss of our darling son we have suffered much misery. Let us both try to be happy."

On the night of the fatal 14th of April, 1865, when the President was assassinated, Mrs. Lincoln's first exclamation was, "His dream was prophetic."

History will record no censure against Mr. Lincoln for believing, like the first Napoleon, that he was a man of destiny; for such he surely was, if the term is at all admissible in a philosophic sense. And our estimate of his greatness must be heightened by conceding the fact that he was a believer in certain phases of the supernatural. Assured as he undoubtedly was by omens which to his mind were conclusive that he would rise to greatness and power, he was as firmly convinced by the same tokens that he would be suddenly cut off at the height of his career and the fulness of his fame. He always believed that he would fall by the hand of an assassin; and yet with that appalling doom clouding his life,--a doom fixed and irreversible, as he was firmly convinced,--his courage never for a moment forsook him, even in the most trying emergencies. Can greatness, courage, constancy in the pursuit of exalted aims, be tried by a severer test? He believed with Tennyson that--

"Because right is right, to follow right Were wisdom in the scorn of consequence."

Concerning presentiments and dreams Mr. Lincoln had a philosophy of his own, which, strange as it may appear, was in perfect harmony with his character in all other respects. He was no dabbler in divination,--astrology, horoscopy, prophecy, ghostly lore, or witcheries of any sort. With Goethe, he held that "Nature cannot but do right eternally." Dreams and presentiments, in his judgment, are not of supernatural origin; that is, they proceed in natural order, their essence being preternatural, but not above Nature. The moving power of dreams and visions of an extraordinary character he ascribed, as did the Patriarchs of old, to the Almighty Intelligence that governs the universe, their processes conforming strictly to natural laws. "Nature," said he, "is the workmanship of the Almighty; and we form but links in the general chain of intellectual and material life."

Mr. Lincoln had this further idea. Dreams being natural occurrences, in the strictest sense, he held that their best interpreters are the common people; and this accounts in large measure for the profound respect he always had for the collective wisdom of plain people,--"the children of Nature," he called them,--touching matters belonging to the domain of psychical mysteries. There was some basis of truth, he believed, for whatever obtained general credence among these "children of Nature;" and as he esteemed himself one of their number, having passed the greater part of his life among them, we can easily account for the strength of his convictions on matters about which they and he were in cordial agreement.

The natural bent of Mr. Lincoln's mind, aided by early associations, inclined him to read books which tended to strengthen his early convictions on occult subjects. Byron's "Dream" was a favorite poem, and I have often heard him repeat the following lines:--

"Sleep hath its own world, A boundary between the things misnamed Death and existence: Sleep hath its own world And a wide realm of wild reality. And dreams in their development have breath, And tears and tortures, and the touch of joy; They leave a weight upon our waking thoughts, They take a weight from off our waking toils, They do divide our being."

He seemed strangely fascinated by the wonderful in history,--such as the fall of Geta by the hand of Caracalla, as foretold by Severus; the ghosts of Caracalla's father and murdered brother threatening and upbraiding him; and kindred passages. It is useless further to pursue this account of Mr. Lincoln's peculiar views concerning these interesting mysteries. Enough has been said to show that the more intense the light which is poured upon what may be regarded as Mr. Lincoln's weakest points, the greater and grander will his character appear.

CHAPTER VIII.

THE HUMOROUS SIDE OF HIS CHARACTER.

No one knew better than Mr. Lincoln that genuine humor is "a plaster that heals many a wound;" and certainly no man ever had a larger stock of that healing balm or knew better how to use it. His old friend I. N. Arnold once remarked that Lincoln's laugh had been his "life-preserver." Wit, with that illustrious man, was a jewel whose mirth-moving flashes he could no more repress than the diamond can extinguish its own brilliancy. In no sense was he vain of his superb ability as a wit and story-teller.

Noah Brooks says in an article written for Harper's Monthly, three months after Mr. Lincoln's death, that the President once said, that, as near as he could reckon, about one sixth only of the stories credited to him were old acquaintances,--all the others were the productions of other and better story-tellers than himself. "I remember," said he, "a good story when I hear it; but I never invented anything original. I am only a retail-dealer." No man was readier than he to acknowledge the force of Shakespeare's famous lines,

"A jest's prosperity lies in the ear Of him that hears it; never in the tongue Of him that makes it."

Mr. Lincoln's stories were generally told with a well-defined purpose,--to cheer the drooping spirits of a friend; to lighten the weight of his own melancholy,--"a pinch, as it were, of mental snuff,"--to clinch an argument, to expose a fallacy, or to disarm an antagonist; but most frequently he employed them simply as "labor-saving contrivances." He believed, with the great Ulysses of old, that there is naught "so tedious as a twice-told tale;" and during my long and intimate acquaintance with Mr. Lincoln I seldom heard him relate a story the second time. The most trifling circumstances, or even a word, was enough to remind him of a story, the aptness of which no one could fail to see. He cared little about high-flown words, fine phrases, or merely ornamental diction; and yet, for one wholly without scholastic training, he was master of a style which was remarkable for purity, terseness, vigor, and force. As Antenor said of the Grecian king, "he spoke no more than just the thing he thought;" and that thought he clothed in the simplest garb, often sacrificing the elegant and poetic for the homely and prosaic in the structure of his sentences.

In one of his messages to Congress Mr. Lincoln used the term "sugar-coated." When the document was placed in the hands of the public printer, Hon. John D. Defrees, that officer was terribly shocked and offended. Mr. Defrees was an accomplished scholar, a man of fastidious taste, and a devoted friend of the President, with whom he was on terms of great intimacy. It would never do to leave the forbidden term in the message; it must be expunged,--otherwise it would forever remain a ruinous blot on the fair fame of the President. In great distress and mortification the good Defrees hurried away to the White House, where he told Mr. Lincoln plainly that "sugar-coated" was not in good taste.

"You ought to remember, Mr. President," said he, "that a message to the Congress of the United States is quite a different thing from a speech before a mass meeting in Illinois; that such messages become a part of the history of the country, and should therefore be written with scrupulous care and propriety. Such an expression in a State paper is undignified, and if I were you I would alter the structure of the whole sentence."

Mr. Lincoln laughed, and then said with a comical show of gravity: "John, that term expresses precisely my idea, and I am not going to change it. 'Sugar-coated' must stand! The time will never come in this country when the people will not understand exactly what 'sugar-coated' means."

Mr. Defrees was obliged to yield, and the message was printed without amendment.

One day at a critical stage of the war, Mr. Lincoln sat in his office in deep meditation. Being suddenly aroused, he said to a gentleman whose presence he had not until that moment observed: "Do you know that I think General ---- is a philosopher? He has proved himself a really great man. He has grappled with and mastered that ancient and wise admonition, 'Know thyself;' he has formed an intimate acquaintance with himself, knows as well for what he is fitted and unfitted as any man living. Without doubt he is a remarkable man. This war has not produced another like him."

"Why is it, Mr. President," asked his friend, "that you are now so highly pleased with General ----? Has your mind not undergone a change?"

"Because," replied Mr. Lincoln, with a merry twinkle of the eye, "greatly to my relief, and to the interests of the country, he has resigned. And now I hope some other dress-parade commanders will study the good old admonition, 'Know thyself,' and follow his example."

On the 3d of February, 1865, during the so-called Peace Conference at Hampton Roads between Mr. Lincoln and Mr. Seward on the one side and the Messrs. Stephens, Campbell, and Hunter on the other, Mr. Hunter remarked that the recognition of the Confederate government by President Lincoln was indispensable as the first step towards peace; and he made an ingenious argument in support of his proposition, citing as a precedent for the guidance of constitutional rulers in dealing with insurgents the case of

Charles I. and his rebel Parliament. This reference to King Charles as a model for imitation by a President of the United States was a little unfortunate, but Mr. Lincoln was more amused than offended by it. Turning to Mr. Hunter he said: "On the question of history I must refer you to Mr. Seward, who is posted in such matters. I don't pretend to be; but I have a tolerably distinct recollection, in the case you refer to, that Charles lost his head, and I have no head to spare."

Mr. Hunter, during the same conference, in speaking of emancipation, remarked that the slaves had always been accustomed to work on compulsion, under an overseer; and he apprehended they would, if suddenly set free, precipitate themselves and the whole social fabric of the South into irretrievable ruin. In that case neither the whites nor the blacks would work. They would all starve together. To this Mr. Lincoln replied: "Mr. Hunter, you ought to know a great deal more about this matter than I do, for you have always lived under the slave system. But the way you state the case reminds me of an Illinois farmer who was not over-fond of work, but was an adept in shirking. To this end he conceived a brilliant scheme of hog culture. Having a good farm, he bought a large herd of swine. He planted an immense field in potatoes, with the view of turning the whole herd into it late in the fall, supposing they would be able to provide for themselves during the winter. One day his scheme was discussed between himself and a neighbor, who asked him how the thing would work when the ground was frozen one or two feet deep. He had not thought of that contingency, and seemed perplexed over it. At length he answered: 'Well, it will be a leetle hard on their snouts, I reckon; but them shoats will have to root, hog, or die.' And so," concluded Mr. Lincoln, "in the dire contingency you name, whites and black alike will have to look out for themselves; and I have an abiding faith that they will go about it in a fashion that will undeceive you in a very agreeable way."

During the same conference, in response to certain remarks by the

Confederate commissioners requiring explicit contradiction, Mr. Lincoln animadverted with some severity upon the conduct of the rebel leaders, and closed with the statement that they had plainly forfeited all right to immunity from punishment for the highest crime known to the law. Being positive and unequivocal in stating his views concerning individual treason, his words seemed to fall upon the commissioners with ominous import. There was a pause, during which Mr. Hunter regarded the speaker with a steady, searching look. At length, carefully measuring his own words, Mr. Hunter said: "Then, Mr. President, if we understand you correctly, you think that we of the Confederacy have committed treason; that we are traitors to your government; that we have forfeited our rights, and are proper subjects for the hangman. Is not that about what your words imply?"

"Yes," said Mr. Lincoln, "you have stated the proposition better than I did. That is about the size of it!"

There was another pause, and a painful one, after which Mr. Hunter, with a pleasant smile, replied: "Well, Mr. Lincoln, we have about concluded that we shall not be hanged as long as you are President--if we behave ourselves."

There is here as high a compliment as could have been paid to Mr. Lincoln,--a trust in his magnanimity and goodness of heart. From the gentleness of his character, such were the sentiments he inspired even among his enemies,--that he was incapable of inflicting pain, punishment, or injury if it could possibly be avoided; that he was always resolutely merciful and forbearing.

On his return to Washington after this conference, Mr. Lincoln recounted the pleasure he had had in meeting Alexander H. Stephens, who was an invalid all his life; and in commenting upon his attenuated appearance as he looked after emerging from layers of overcoats and comforters, Mr. Lincoln said, "Was there ever such a nubbin after so much shucking?"

At one time when very lively scenes were being enacted in West Virginia, a Union general allowed himself and his command to be drawn into a dangerous position, from which it was feared he would be unable to extricate himself without the loss of his whole command. In speaking of this fiasco, Mr. Lincoln said: "General ---- reminds me of a man out West who was engaged in what they call heading a barrel. He worked diligently for a time driving down the hoops; but when the job seemed completed, the head would fall in, and he would have to do the work all over again. Suddenly, after a deal of annoyance, a bright idea struck him. He put his boy, a chunk of a lad, into the barrel to hold up the head while he pounded down the hoops. This worked like a charm. The job was completed before he once thought about how he was to get the little fellow out again. Now," said Mr. Lincoln, "that is a fair sample of the way some people do business. They can succeed better in getting themselves and others corked up than in getting uncorked."

During the year 1861 it was difficult to preserve peace and good order in the city of Washington. Riots and disturbances were occurring daily, and some of them were of a serious and sometimes dangerous nature. The authorities were in constant apprehension, owing to the disloyal sentiment prevailing, that a riot might occur of such magnitude as to endanger the safety of the capital; and this necessitated the utmost vigilance on their part to preserve order.

On one occasion, when the fears of the loyal element of the city were excited to fever-heat, a free fight near the old National Theatre occurred about eleven o'clock one night. An officer in passing the place observed what was going on; and seeing the great number of persons engaged, he felt it to be his duty to command the peace. The imperative tone of his voice stopped the fighting for a moment; but the leader, a great bully, roughly pushed back the officer, and told him to go away, or he would whip him. The officer again advanced and said, "I arrest you," attempting to place his hand on the man's shoulder, when the bully struck a fearful blow at the officer's face. This was parried, and instantly followed by a blow from the fist of the officer, striking the fellow under the chin and knocking him senseless. Blood issued from his mouth, nose, and ears. It was believed that the man's neck was broken. A surgeon was called, who pronounced the case a critical one, and the wounded man was hurried away on a litter to the hospital. There the physicians said there was concussion of the brain, and that the man would die. All medical skill that the officer could procure was employed in the hope of saving the life of the man. His conscience smote him for having, as he believed, taken the life of a fellow-creature, and he was inconsolable.

Being on terms of intimacy with the President, about two o'clock that night the officer went to the White House, woke up Mr. Lincoln, and requested him to come into his office, where he told him his story. Mr. Lincoln listened with great interest until the narrative was completed, and then asked a few questions; after which he remarked: "I am sorry you had to kill the man; but these are times of war, and a great many men deserve killing. This one, according to your story, is one of them; so give yourself no uneasiness about the matter. I will stand by you."

"That is not why I came to you. I knew I did my duty, and had no fears of your disapproval of what I did," replied the officer; and then he added: "Why I came to you was, I felt great grief over the unfortunate affair, and I wanted to talk to you about it."

Mr. Lincoln then said, with a smile, placing his hand on the officer's shoulder: "You go home now and get some sleep; but let me give you this piece of advice,--hereafter, when you have occasion to strike a man, don't hit him with your fist; strike him with a club, a crowbar, or with something that won't kill him."

The officer then went home, but not to sleep. The occurrence had a great effect upon him, and was a real source of discomfort to his mind during the fourteen months the unfortunate invalid lived, and it left a sincere regret impressed upon him ever after; but the conciliatory and kindly view prompted by Mr. Lincoln's tender heart, and his fidelity to friendship on that occasion, is to this day cherished in the officer's memory with a feeling of consecration.

About the first time Mr. Lincoln contemplated leaving Washington, he was to attend some gathering of the people in Baltimore, Philadelphia, or New York. A committee waited upon him and urged his attendance on the occasion, saying that they were sure Mr. Garrett, the president of the only road then going east out of Washington, would take great pleasure in furnishing a special train of cars for him. "Well," said the President, "I have no doubt of that. I know Mr. Garrett well, and like him very much; but if I were to believe (which I don't) everything some people say of him about his 'secesh' principles, he might say to you as was said by the superintendent of a railroad to a son of one of my predecessors in office. Some two years after the death of President Harrison, the son of the incumbent of this office, contemplating an excursion for his father somewhere or other, went to order a special train of cars. At that time politics were very bitter between the Whigs and the Democrats, and the railroad superintendent happened to be an uncompromising Whig. The son made known his demand, which was bluntly refused by the railroad official, saying that his road was not running special trains for the accommodation of Presidents just then. 'What!' said the young man, 'did you not furnish a special train for the funeral of General Harrison?' 'Yes,' said the superintendent, very calmly; 'and if you will only bring your father here in that shape you shall have the best train on the road.' But, gentlemen," continued Mr. Lincoln, "I have no doubts of Mr. Garrett's loyalty for the government or his respect for me personally, and I will take pleasure in going."

General James B. Fry, the Provost-Marshal General during Mr. Lincoln's Administration, was designated by the Secretary of War as a special escort to accompany Mr. Lincoln to the field of Gettysburg upon the occasion of the anniversary of that battle. The general, on arriving at the White House and finding the President late in his preparations for the trip, remarked to him that it was late, and there was little time to lose in getting to the train. "Well," said Mr. Lincoln, "I feel about that as the convict did in Illinois, when he was going to the gallows. Passing along the road in custody of the sheriff, and seeing the people who were eager for the execution crowding and jostling one another past him, he at last called out, 'Boys! you needn't be in such a hurry to get ahead, for there won't be any fun till I get there.'"

General Fry also tells of a conversation between Mr. Lincoln and Mr. Stanton, in relation to the selection of brigadier-generals. Mr. Lincoln was heard to say: "Well, Mr. Secretary, I concur in pretty much all you say. The only point I make is, that there has got to be something done which will be unquestionably in the interest of the Dutch; and to that end I want Schimmelpfennig appointed." The secretary replied: "Mr. President, perhaps this Schimmel--what's-his-name--is not as highly recommended as some other German officer." "No matter about that," said Mr. Lincoln; "his name will make up for any difference there may be, and I'll take the risk of his coming out all right." Then, with a laugh, he repeated, dwelling upon each syllable of the name and accenting the last one, "Schim-mel-pfen-nig must be appointed."

Mr. Welles, in speaking of the complication into which Spain attempted to draw the government of the United States in regard to reclaiming her possessions in San Domingo, says that the pressure was great on both sides, and the question a grave and delicate one as to what position we should take and what course pursue. On the one side Spain, whose favor we wished to conciliate, and on the other the appeal of the negroes against Spanish oppression. Mr. Seward detailed the embarrassments attending the negotiations to Mr. Lincoln, whose countenance indicated that his mind was relieved before Mr. Seward had concluded. He remarked that the dilemma of the Secretary of State reminded him of an interview between two negroes in Tennessee; one was a preacher, who, with the crude and strange notions of his ignorant race, was endeavoring to admonish and enlighten his brother African of the importance of religion and the danger of the future. "'Dar are,' said Josh the preacher, 'two roads befo' you, Joe; be careful which ob dem you take. Narrow am de way dat leads straight to destruction; but broad am de way dat leads right to damnation.' Joe opened his eyes with affright, and under the inspired eloquence of the awful danger before him, exclaimed, 'Josh, take which road you please; I shall go troo de woods.' I am not willing," said the President, "to assume any new troubles or responsibilities at this time, and shall therefore avoid going to the one place with Spain or with the negro to the other, but shall take to the woods. We will maintain an honest and strict neutrality."

When Attorney-General Bates resigned, late in 1864, after the resignation of Postmaster-General Blair in that year, the Cabinet was left without a Southern member. A few days before the meeting of the Supreme Court, which then met in December, Mr. Lincoln sent for Titian F. Coffey, and said: "My Cabinet has shrunk up North, and I must find a Southern man. I suppose if the twelve Apostles were to be chosen nowadays, the shrieks of locality would have to be heeded."

Mr. Coffey acted as Attorney-General during the time intervening between the resignation of Mr. Bates and the appointment of Mr. Speed. He tells about a delegation that called on Mr. Lincoln to ask the appointment of a gentleman as commissioner to the Sandwich Islands. They presented their case as earnestly as possible; and besides their candidate's fitness for the place they urged that he was in bad health, and that a residence in that balmy climate would be of great benefit to him. The President closed the interview with this discouraging remark: "Gentlemen, I am sorry to say that there are eight other applicants for that place, and they are all sicker than your man."

In 1858 Mr. Lincoln was engaged at Bloomington, in a case of very great importance. The attorney on the other side was a young lawyer of fine abilities, who has since become a judge. He was a sensible and sensitive young man, and the loss of a case always gave him great pain,--to avoid which he invariably manifested an unusual zeal, and made great preparation for the trial of his cases. This case of which I speak lasted till late at night, when it was submitted to the jury. In anticipation of a favorable verdict, the young attorney spent a sleepless night in anxiety, and early next morning learned to his great chagrin that he had lost the case. Mr. Lincoln met him at the court house some time after the jury had come in, and asked him what had become of his case. With lugubrious countenance and in a melancholy tone the young man replied, "It's gone to hell." "Oh, well," said Mr. Lincoln, "then you will see it again."

Mr. Lincoln had shown great wisdom in appreciating the importance of holding such Democrats as Mr. Douglas close to the Administration, on the issue of a united country or a dissolution of the Union. He said: "They are just where we Whigs were in 1848, about the Mexican war. We had to take the Locofoco preamble when Taylor wanted help, or else vote against helping Taylor; and the Democrats must vote to hold the Union now, without bothering whether we or the Southern men got things where they are; and we must make it easy for them to do this, for we cannot live through the case without them." He further said: "Some of our friends are opposed to an accommodation because the South began the trouble and is entirely responsible for the consequences, be they what they may. This reminds me of a story told out in Illinois where I lived. There was a vicious bull in a pasture, and a neighbor passing through the field, the animal took after him. The man ran to a tree, and got there in time to save himself; and being able to run round the tree faster than the bull, he managed to seize him by the tail. His bullship seeing himself at a disadvantage, pawed the earth and scattered gravel for awhile, then broke into a full run, bellowing at every jump, while the man, holding on to the tail, asked the question, 'Darn you, who commenced this fuss?' Now, our plain duty is to settle the fuss we have before us, without reference to who commenced it."

Mr. Lincoln told another anecdote in connection with the probable adjustment of the difficulties. Said he: "Once on a time, a number of very pious gentlemen, all strict members of the church, were appointed to take in charge and superintend the erection of a bridge over a very dangerous and turbulent river. They found great difficulty in securing the services of an engineer competent for the work. Finally, Brother Jones said that Mr. Meyers had built several bridges, and he had no doubt he could build this one. Mr. Meyers was sent for. The committee asked, 'Can you build this bridge?' 'Yes,' was the answer, 'I can build a bridge to the infernal regions, if necessary.' The committee was shocked, and Brother Jones felt called upon to say something in defence of his friend, and commenced by saying: 'Gentlemen, I know my friend Meyers so well, and he is so honest a man and so good an architect, that if he states positively that he can build a bridge to hell, why, I believe he can do it; but I feel bound to say that I have my doubts about the abutment on the infernal side.' So," said Mr. Lincoln, "when the politicians told me that the Northern and Southern wings of the Democracy could be harmonized, why, I believed them of course; but I had always my doubts about the abutment on the other side."

Anthony J. Bleeker tells his experience in applying for a position under Mr. Lincoln. He was introduced by Mr. Preston King, and made his application verbally, handing the President his vouchers. The President requested him to read them, which he commenced to do. Before Mr. Bleeker had got half through with the documents, the President cried out, "Oh, stop! you are like the man who killed the dog." Not feeling particularly flattered by the comparison, Mr. Bleeker inquired, "In what respect?" Mr. Lincoln replied, "He had a vicious animal which he determined to dispatch, and accordingly knocked out his brains with a club. He continued striking the dog until a friend stayed his hand, exclaiming, 'You needn't strike him any more, the dog is dead; you killed him at the first blow.' 'Oh, yes,' said he, 'I know that; but I believe in punishment after death.' So, I see, you do." Mr. Bleeker acknowledged that it was possible to do too much sometimes, and he in his turn told an anecdote of a good priest who converted an Indian from heathenism to Christianity; the only difficulty he had with him was to get him to pray for his enemies. "The Indian had been taught by his father to overcome and destroy them. 'That,' said the priest, 'may be the Indian's creed, but it is not the doctrine of Christianity or the Bible. Saint Paul distinctly says, "If thine enemy hunger, feed him; if he thirst, give him drink."' The Indian shook his head at this and seemed dejected, but when the priest added, '"For in so doing thou shalt heap coals of fire on his head,"' the poor convert was overcome with emotion, fell on his knees, and with outstretched hands and uplifted eyes invoked all sorts of blessings on his adversary's head, supplicating for pleasant hunting-grounds, a large supply of squaws, lots of papooses, and all other Indian comforts, till the good priest interrupted him (as you did me), exclaiming, 'Stop, my son! You have discharged your Christian duty, and have done more than enough.' 'Oh, no, father,' says the Indian, 'let me pray! I want to burn him down to the stump!'" Mr. Bleeker got the position.

"Mr. Lincoln," wrote one who knew him very well,[G] "was a good judge of men, and quickly learned the peculiar traits of character in those he had to deal with. He pointed out a marked trait in one of the Northern governors who was earnest, able, and untiring in keeping up the war spirit of his State, but was at times overbearing and exacting in his intercourse with the general government. Upon one occasion he complained and protested more bitterly than usual, and warned those in authority that the execution of their orders in his State would be beset by difficulties and dangers. The tone of his dispatches gave rise to an apprehension that he might not co-operate fully in the enterprise in hand. The Secretary of War, therefore, laid the dispatches before the President for advice or instructions. They did not disturb Mr. Lincoln in the least. In fact, they rather amused him. After reading all the papers, he said in a cheerful and reassuring tone: 'Never mind, those dispatches don't mean anything. Just go right ahead. The governor is like the boy I saw once at the launching of a ship. When everything was ready, they picked out a boy and sent him under the ship to knock away the trigger and let her go. At the critical moment everything depended on the boy. He had to do the job well by a direct, vigorous blow, and then lie flat and keep still while the ship slid over him. The boy did everything right; but he yelled as if he were being murdered, from the time he got under the keel until he got out. I thought the skin was all scraped off his back; but he wasn't hurt at all. The master of the yard told me that this boy was always chosen for that job, that he did his work well, that he never had been hurt, but that he always squealed in that way. That's just the way with Governor ----. Make up your minds that he is not hurt, and that he is doing his work right, and pay no attention to his squealing. He only wants to make you understand how hard his task is, and that he is on hand performing it.'"

[G] General Fry, in the New York "Tribune."

Time proved that the President's estimation of the governor was correct.

Upon another occasion a Governor went to the office of the Adjutant-General bristling with complaints. The Adjutant, finding it impossible to satisfy his demands, accompanied him to the Secretary of War's office, whence, after a stormy interview with Secretary Stanton he went alone to see the President. The Adjutant-General expected important orders from the President or a summons to the White House for explanation. After some hours the Governor returned and said with a pleasant smile that he was going home by the next train and merely dropped in to say good-bye, making no allusion to the business upon which he came nor his interview with the President. As soon as the Adjutant-General could see Mr. Lincoln he told him he was very anxious to learn how he disposed of Governor ----, as he had started to see him in a towering rage, and said he supposed it was necessary to make large concessions to him as he seemed after leaving the President to be entirely satisfied. "O, no," replied Mr. Lincoln, "I did not concede anything. You know how that Illinois farmer managed the big log that lay in the middle of his field? To the inquiries of his neighbors one Sunday he announced that he had got rid of the big log. 'Got rid of it!' said they. 'How did you do it? It was too big to haul out, too knotty to split, and too wet and soggy to burn. What did you do?' 'Well, now, boys,' replied the farmer, 'if you won't divulge the secret, I'll tell you how I got rid of it. I plowed around it.' Now," said Lincoln, "don't tell anybody, but that is the way I got rid of Governor ----, I plowed around him, but it took me three mortal hours to do it, and I was afraid every minute he would see what I was at."

Mr. Lincoln enjoyed telling of the youth who emigrated to the West and wrote back East to his father who was something of a politician: "Dear Dad,--I have settled at ---- and like it first rate. Do come out here, for almighty mean men get office here."

Thurlow Weed tells of breakfasting with Lincoln and Judge Davis while in Springfield in December prior to Mr. Lincoln's first inauguration. Judge Davis remarked Mr. Weed's fondness for sausage and said, "You seem fond of our Chicago sausages." To which Mr. Weed responded that he was, and thought the article might be relied on where pork was cheaper than dogs. "That," said Mr. Lincoln, "reminds me of what occurred down in Joliet, where a popular grocer supplied all the villagers with sausages. One Saturday evening, when his grocery was filled with customers, for whom he and his boys were busily engaged in weighing sausages, a neighbor with whom he had had a violent quarrel that day came into the grocery, made his way up to the counter, holding two enormous dead cats by the tail, which he deliberately threw onto the counter saying, 'This makes seven to-day. I'll call round Monday and get my money for them.'"

Mr. Lincoln read men and women quickly, and was so keen a judge of their peculiarities that none escaped his observation.

Once a very attractive woman consumed a good deal of Mr. Lincoln's time. He finally dismissed her with a card directed to Secretary Stanton on which he had written: "This woman, dear Stanton, is a little smarter than she looks to be."

CHAPTER IX.

THE ANTIETAM EPISODE.--LINCOLN'S LOVE OF SONG.

In the autumn of 1862 I chanced to be associated with Mr. Lincoln in a transaction which, though innocent and commonplace in itself, was blown by rumor and surmise into a revolting and deplorable scandal. A conjectural lie, although mean, misshapen, and very small at its birth, grew at length into a tempest of defamation, whose last echoes were not heard until its noble victim had yielded his life to a form of assassination only a trifle more deadly.

Mr. Lincoln was painted as the prime mover in a scene of fiendish levity more atrocious than the world had ever witnessed since human nature was shamed and degraded by the capers of Nero and Commodus. I refer to what is known as the Antietam song-singing; and I propose to show that the popular construction put upon that incident was wholly destitute of truth.

Mr. Lincoln persistently declined to read the harsh comments of the newspaper press and the fierce mouthings of platform orators; and under his advice I as persistently refused to make any public statement concerning that ill-judged affair. He believed with Sir Walter Scott, that, if a cause of action is good, it needs no vindication from the actor's motives; if bad, it can derive none. When I suggested to him that the slander ought to be refuted,--that a word from him would silence his defamers,--Mr. Lincoln replied with great earnestness: "No, Hill; there has already been too much said about this falsehood. Let the thing alone. If I have not established character enough to give the lie to this charge, I can only say that I am mistaken in my own estimate of myself. In politics, every man must skin his own skunk. These fellows are welcome to the hide of this one. Its body has already given forth its unsavory odor."

The newspapers and the stump-speakers went on "stuffing the ears of men with false reports" until the fall of 1864, when I showed to Mr. Lincoln a letter, of which the following is a copy. It is a fair sample of hundreds of letters received by me about that time, the Antietam incident being then discussed with increased virulence and new accessions of false coloring.

PHILADELPHIA, Sept. 10, 1864.

WARD H. LAMON:

Dear Sir,--Enclosed is an extract from the New York "World" of Sept. 9, 1864:--

"ONE OF MR. LINCOLN'S JOKES.--The second verse of our campaign song published on this page was probably suggested by an incident which occurred on the battle-field of Antietam a few days after the fight. While the President was driving over the field in an ambulance, accompanied by Marshal Lamon, General McClellan, and another officer, heavy details of men were engaged in the task of burying the dead. The ambulance had just reached the neighborhood of the old stone bridge, where the dead were piled highest, when Mr. Lincoln, suddenly slapping Marshal Lamon on the knee, exclaimed: 'Come, Lamon, give us that song about Picayune Butler;

McClellan has never heard it.' 'Not now, if you please,' said General McClellan, with a shudder; 'I would prefer to hear it some other place and time.'"

This story has been repeated in the New York "World" almost daily for the last three months. Until now it would have been useless to demand its authority. By this article it limits the inquiry to three persons as its authority,--Marshal Lamon, another officer, and General McClellan. That it is a damaging story, if believed, cannot be disputed. That it is believed by some, or that they pretend to believe it, is evident by the accompanying verse from the doggerel, in which allusion is made to it:--

"Abe may crack his jolly jokes O'er bloody fields of stricken battle, While yet the ebbing life-tide smokes From men that die like butchered cattle; He, ere yet the guns grow cold, To pimps and pets may crack his stories," etc.

I wish to ask you, sir, in behalf of others as well as myself, whether any such occurrence took place; or if it did not take place, please to state who that "other officer" was, if there was any such, in the ambulance in which the President "was driving over the field [of Antietam] whilst details of men were engaged in the task of burying the dead." You will confer a great favor by an immediate reply.

Most respectfully your obedient servant, A. J. PERKINS.

Along with the above I submitted to Mr. Lincoln my own draft of what I conceived to be a suitable reply. The brutal directness and falsity of the "World's" charge, and the still more brutal and insulting character of the doggerel with which it was garnished, impelled me to season my reply to Mr. Perkins's letter with a large infusion of "vinegar and gall." After carefully reading both letters, Mr. Lincoln shook his head. "No, Lamon," said he, "I would not publish this reply; it is too belligerent in tone for so grave a matter.

There is a heap of 'cussedness' mixed up with your usual amiability, and you are at times too fond of a fight. If I were you, I would simply state the facts as they were. I would give the statement as you have here, without the pepper and salt. Let me try my hand at it." He then took up a pen and wrote the following. It was to be copied by me and forwarded to Mr. Perkins as my refutation of the slander.

"The President has known me intimately for nearly twenty years, and has often heard me sing little ditties. The battle of Antietam was fought on the 17th day of September, 1862. On the first day of October, just two weeks after the battle, the President, with some others including myself, started from Washington to visit the Army, reaching Harper's Ferry at noon of that day. In a short while General McClellan came from his headquarters near the battle-ground, joined the President, and with him reviewed the troops at Bolivar Heights that afternoon, and at night returned to his headquarters, leaving the President at Harper's Ferry. On the morning of the second the President, with General Sumner, reviewed the troops respectively at Loudon Heights and Maryland Heights, and at about noon started to General McClellan's headquarters, reaching there only in time to see very little before night. On the morning of the third all started on a review of the third corps and the cavalry, in the vicinity of the Antietam battle-ground. After getting through with General Burnside's corps, at the suggestion of General McClellan he and the President left their horses to be led, and went into an ambulance or ambulances to go to General Fitz John Porter's corps, which was two or three miles distant. I am not sure whether the President and General McClellan were in the same ambulance, or in different ones; but myself and some others were in the same with the President. On the way, and on no part of the battle-ground, and on what suggestions I do not remember, the President asked me to sing the little sad song that follows, which he had often heard me sing, and had always seemed to like very much. I sang it. After it was over, some one of the party (I do not think it was the President) asked me to sing something else; and I sang two or three little comic things, of which 'Picayune Butler' was one. Porter's corps was reached and reviewed; then the battle-ground was passed over, and the most noted parts examined; then, in succession, the cavalry and Franklin's corps were reviewed, and the President and party returned to General McClellan's headquarters at the end of a very hard, hot, and dusty day's work. Next day, the 4th, the President and General McClellan visited such of the wounded as still remained in the vicinity, including the now lamented General Richardson; then proceeded to and examined the South-Mountain battle-ground, at which point they parted,--General McClellan returning to his camp, and the President returning to Washington, seeing, on the way, General Hartsoff, who lay wounded at Frederick Town.

"This is the whole story of the singing and its surroundings. Neither General McClellan nor any one else made any objections to the singing; the place was not on the battle-field; the time was sixteen days after the battle; no dead body was seen during the whole time the President was absent from Washington, nor even a grave that had not been rained on since it was made."

This perfectly truthful statement was written by Mr. Lincoln about the 12th of September, 1864, less than two years after the occurrence of the events therein described. It was done slowly, and with great deliberation and care. The statement, however, was never made public. Mr. Lincoln said to me: "You know, Hill, that this is the truth and the whole truth about that affair; but I dislike to appear as an apologist for an act of my own which I know was right. Keep this paper, and we will see about it." The momentous and all-engrossing events of the war caused the Antietam episode to be forgotten by the President for a time; the statement was not given to the press, but has remained in my possession until this day.

Mark how simple the explanation is! Mr. Lincoln did not ask me to sing "Picayune Butler." No song was sung on the battle-field. The singing occurred on the way from Burnside's corps to Fitz John Porter's corps, some distance from the battle-ground, and sixteen days after the battle. Moreover, Mr. Lincoln had said to me, "Lamon, sing one of your little sad songs,"--and thereby hangs a tale which is well worth the telling, as it illustrates a striking phase of Mr. Lincoln's character which has never been fully revealed.

I knew well what Mr. Lincoln meant by "the little sad songs." The sentiment that prompted him to call for such a song had its history, and one of deep and touching interest to me. One "little sad song"--a simple ballad entitled "Twenty Years Ago"--was, above all others, his favorite. He had no special fondness for operatic music; he loved simple ballads and ditties, such as the common people sing, whether of the comic or pathetic kind; but no one in the list touched his great heart as did the song of "Twenty Years Ago." Many a time, in the old days of our familiar friendship on the Illinois circuit, and often at the White House when he and I were alone, have I seen him in tears while I was rendering, in my poor way, that homely melody. The late Judge David Davis, the Hon. Leonard Swett, and Judge Corydon Beckwith were equally partial to the same ballad. Often have I seen those great men overcome by the peculiar charm they seemed to find in the sentiment and melody of that simple song. The following verses seemed to affect Mr. Lincoln more deeply than any of the others:--

"I've wandered to the village, Tom; I've sat beneath the tree Upon the schoolhouse play-ground, that sheltered you and me: But none were left to greet me, Tom, and few were left to know Who played with us upon the green, some twenty years ago.

"Near by the spring, upon the elm you know I cut your name,-- Your sweetheart's just beneath it, Tom; and you did mine the same. Some heartless wretch has peeled the bark,--'twas dying sure but slow, Just as she died whose name you cut, some twenty years ago.

"My lids have long been dry, Tom, but tears came to my eyes; I thought of her I loved so well, those early broken ties: I visited the old churchyard, and took some flowers to strew Upon the graves of these we loved, some twenty years ago."

This is the song Mr. Lincoln called for, and the one I sang to him in the vicinity of Antietam. He was at the time weary and sad. As I well knew it would, the song only deepened his sadness. I then did what I had done many times before: I startled him from his melancholy by striking up a comic air, singing also a snatch from "Picayune Butler," which broke the spell of "the little sad song," and restored somewhat his accustomed easy humor. It was not the first time I had pushed hilarity--simulated though it was--to an extreme for his sake. I had often recalled him from a pit of melancholy into which he was prone to descend, by a jest, a comic song, or a provoking sally of a startling kind; and Mr. Lincoln always thanked me afterward for my well-timed rudeness "of kind intent."

This reminds me of one or two little rhythmic shots I often fired at him in his melancholy moods, and it was a kind of nonsense that he always keenly relished. One was a parody on "Life on the Ocean Wave."

Mr. Lincoln would always laugh immoderately when I sang this jingling nonsense to him. It reminded him of the rude and often witty ballads that had amused him in his boyhood days. He was fond of negro melodies, and "The Blue-Tailed Fly" was a favorite. He often called for that buzzing ballad when we were alone, and he wanted to throw off the weight of public and private cares.

A comic song in the theatre always restored Mr. Lincoln's cheerful good-humor. But while he had a great fondness for witty and mirth-provoking ballads, our grand old patriotic airs and songs of the tender and sentimental kind afforded him the deepest pleasure. "Ben Bolt" was one

111

of his favorite ballads; so was "The Sword of Bunker Hill;" and he was always deeply moved by "The Lament of the Irish Emigrant," especially the following touching lines:--

"I'm very lonely now, Mary, For the poor make no new friends; But, oh, they love the better still The few our Father sends! And you were all I had, Mary, My blessing and my pride; There's nothing left to care for now, Since my poor Mary died."

Many examples can be given illustrative of this phase of Mr. Lincoln's character,--the blending of the mirthful and the melancholy in his singular love of music and verse. When he was seventeen years old, his sister was married. The festivities of the occasion were made memorable by a song entitled "Adam and Eve's Wedding Song," which many believed was composed by Mr. Lincoln himself. The conceits embodied in the verses were old before Mr. Lincoln was born; but there is some intrinsic as well as extrinsic evidence to show that the doggerel itself was his.

ADAM AND EVE'S WEDDING SONG.

When Adam was created, he dwelt in Eden's shade, As Moses has recorded; and soon an Eve was made. Ten thousand times ten thousand Of creatures swarmed around Before a bride was formed, And yet no mate was found.

The Lord then was not willing The man should be alone, But caused a sleep upon him, And took from him a bone.

And closed the flesh in that place of; And then he took the same, And of it made a woman, And brought her to the man.

Then Adam he rejoiced To see his loving bride,-- A part of his own body, The product of his side.

This woman was not taken From Adam's feet, we see; So he must not abuse her, The meaning seems to be.

This woman was not taken From Adam's head, we know; To show she must not rule him, 'Tis evidently so.

This woman she was taken From under Adam's arm; So she must be protected From injuries and harm.

But the lines which Mr. Lincoln liked best of all, and which were repeated by him more often than any other, were--

"Oh, why should the spirit of mortal be proud?"

Mr. Carpenter in his "Six Months at the White House" gives them in full as follows:--

"Oh, why should the spirit of mortal be proud? Like a swift-flecting meteor, a fast-flying cloud, A flash of the lightning, a break of the wave, He passeth from life to his rest in the grave.

"The leaves of the oak and the willow shall fade, Be scattered around, and together be laid; And the young and the old, and the low and the high, Shall moulder to dust, and together shall lie.

"The infant a mother attended and loved; The mother that infant's affection who proved; The husband that mother and infant who blest,-- Each, all, are away to their dwellings of rest.

"The maid on whose cheek, on whose brow, in whose eye, Shone beauty and pleasure, her triumphs are by; And the memory of those who loved her and praised, Are alike from the minds of the living erased.

"The hand of the king that the sceptre hath borne, The brow of the priest that the mitre hath worn, The eye of the sage, and the heart of the brave, Are hidden and lost in the depths of the grave.

"The peasant whose lot was to sow and to reap, The herdsman who climbed with his goats up the steep, The beggar who wandered in search of his bread, Have faded away like the grass that we tread.

"The saint who enjoyed the communion of Heaven, The sinner who dared to remain unforgiven, The wise and the foolish, the guilty and just, Have quietly mingled their bones in the dust.

"So the multitude goes, like the flower or the weed, That withers away to let others succeed; So the multitude comes, even those we behold, To repeat every tale that has often been told.

"For we are the same our fathers have been; We see the same sights our fathers have seen; We drink the same stream, we view the same sun, And run the same course our fathers have run.

"The thoughts we are thinking our fathers would think; From the death we are shrinking our fathers would shrink; To the life we are clinging they also would cling, But it speeds from us all like a bird on the wing.

"They loved, but the story we cannot unfold; They scorned, but the heart of the haughty is cold; They grieved, but no wail from their slumber will come; They joyed, but the tongue of their gladness is dumb.

"They died,--ay, they died: we things that are now, That walk on the turf that lies over their brow, And make in their dwellings a transient abode,

Meet the things that they met on their pilgrimage road.

"Yea, hope and despondency, pleasure and pain, Are mingled together in sunshine and rain; And the smile and the tear, the song and the dirge, Still follow each other like surge upon surge.

"'Tis the wink of an eye, 'tis the draught of a breath, From the blossom of health to the paleness of death, From the gilded saloon to the bier and the shroud,-- Oh, why should the spirit of mortal be proud?"

These curiously sad lines were chosen by Mr. Lincoln when he was a very young man to commemorate a grief which lay with continual heaviness on his heart, but to which he could not otherwise allude,--the death of Ann Rutledge, in whose grave Mr. Lincoln said that his heart lay buried. He muttered these verses as he rambled through the woods; he was heard to murmur them as he slipped into the village at nightfall; they came unbidden to his lips in all places, and very often in his later life. In the year of his nomination, he repeated them to some friends. When he had finished them, he said "they sounded to him as much like true poetry as anything that he had ever heard." The poem is now his; it is imperishably associated with his memory and interwoven with the history of his greatest sorrow. Mr. Lincoln's adoption of it has saved it from oblivion, and translated it from the "poet's corner" of the country newspaper to a place in the story of his own life.

But enough has been given to show that Mr. Lincoln was as incapable of insulting the dead, in the manner credited to him in the Antietam episode, as he was of committing mean and unmanly outrages upon the living. If hypercritical and self-appointed judges are still disposed to award blame for anything that happened on that occasion, let their censure fall upon me, and not upon the memory of the illustrious dead, who was guiltless of wrong and without the shadow of blame for the part he bore in that misjudged affair.

My own part in the incident, in the light of the facts here given, needs no apology.

CHAPTER X.

HIS LOVE OF CHILDREN.

No sketch of Mr. Lincoln's character can be called complete which does not present him as he appeared at his own fireside, showing his love for his own children, his tenderness toward the little ones generally, and how in important emergencies he was influenced by them. A great writer has said that it were "better to be driven out from among men than to be disliked by children." So Mr. Lincoln firmly believed; and whenever it chanced that he gave offence to a child unwittingly he never rested until he had won back its favor and affection. He beheld in the face of a little child a record of innocence and love, of truth and trust; and in the society of children he was always happy.

Owing, perhaps, to his homely countenance and ungainly figure, strange children generally repelled his first advances; but I never saw him fail to win the affection of a child when its guileless friendship became a matter of interest to him. He could persuade any child from the arms of its mother, nurse, or play-fellow, there being a peculiar fascination in his voice and manner which the little one could not resist. As a student of child nature and a lover of its artless innocence, he had no patience with people who practise upon the credulity of children; and it was a rule of his life never to mislead a child, even in the most trifling matter, or if in his power to prevent it to be misled or deceived by others. On making the acquaintance of a child he at once became its friend, and never afterward forgot its face or the circumstances under which the acquaintance was formed; for his little friends always made some impression on his mind and feelings that was certain to be lasting.

A striking instance of this character deserves especial mention. Shortly after his first election to the Presidency he received a pleasant letter from a little girl living in a small town in the State of New York. The child told him that she had seen his picture, and it was her opinion, as she expressed it in her artless way, that he "would be a better looking man if he would let his beard grow." Mr. Lincoln passed that New York town on his way to Washington, and his first thought on reaching the place was about his little correspondent. In his brief speech to the people he made a pleasing reference to the child and her charming note. "This little lady," said he, "saw from the first that great improvement might be made in my personal appearance. You all see that I am not a very handsome man; and to be honest with you, neither I nor any of my friends ever boasted very much about my personal beauty." He then passed his hand over his face and continued: "But I intend to follow that little girl's advice, and if she is present I would like to speak to her." The child came forward timidly, and was warmly greeted by the President-elect. He took her in his arms and kissed her affectionately, expressing the hope that he might have the pleasure of seeing his little friend again sometime.

Shortly after this, Mr. Lincoln, for the first time in his life, allowed his beard to grow all over his face, with the exception of the upper lip; and this fashion he continued as long as he lived. In speaking of the incident which led him to wear a full beard, he afterward remarked, reflectively, "How small a thing will sometimes change the whole aspect of our lives!"

That Mr. Lincoln realized that an improvement was necessary in his personal appearance is evidenced by many amusing stories told by him. The one he especially enjoyed telling was, how once, when "riding the circuit," he was accosted in the cars by a stranger, who said, "Excuse me, sir, but I have an article in my possession which belongs to you." "How is that?" Mr. Lincoln asked, much astonished. The stranger took a knife from his pocket, saying, "This knife was placed in my hands some years ago with the injunction that I was to keep it until I found a man uglier than myself. I have carried it from that time to this. Allow me now to say, sir, that I think you are fairly entitled to the property."

Mr. Carpenter, the artist who painted the picture of "The Proclamation of Emancipation," tells in his book of an incident which occurred the day following the adjournment of the Baltimore Convention: "Various political organizations called to pay their respects to the President. While the Philadelphia delegation was being presented, the chairman of that body, in introducing one of the members, said: 'Mr. President, this is Mr. S. of the second district of our State,--a most active and earnest friend of yours and the cause. He has, among other things, been good enough to paint, and present to our league rooms, a most beautiful portrait of yourself.' Mr. Lincoln took the gentleman's hand in his, and shaking it cordially said, with a merry voice, 'I presume, sir, in painting your beautiful portrait, you took your idea of me from my principles and not from my person.'"

Before leaving the old town of Springfield, Mr. Lincoln was often seen, on sunny afternoons, striking out on foot to a neighboring wood, attended by his little sons. There he would romp with them as a companion, and enter with great delight into all their childish sports. This joyous companionship with his children suffered no abatement when he became a resident of the White House and took upon himself the perplexing cares of his great office. To find relief from those cares he would call his boys to some quiet part of the house, throw himself at full length upon the floor, and abandon himself to their fun and frolic as merrily as if he had been of their own age. The two children who were his play-fellows in these romping scenes the first year of his residence at the Executive Mansion were Willie and Thomas, the latter of whom he always called "Tad;" and these children were the youngest of his family.

In February, 1862, this fond father was visited by a sorrowful bereavement. The Executive Mansion was turned into a house of mourning. Death had chosen a shining mark, and the beloved Willie, the apple of his father's eye, the brightest and most promising of his children, was taken away. The dreadful stroke wellnigh broke the President's heart, and certainly an affliction more crushing never fell to the lot of man. In the lonely grave of the little one lay buried Mr. Lincoln's fondest hopes, and, strong as he was in the matter of self-control, he gave way to an overmastering grief, which became at length a serious menace to his health. Never was there witnessed in an American household a scene of distress more touching than that in which the President and Mrs. Lincoln mingled their tears over the coffin that inclosed the lifeless form of their beloved child. A deep and settled despondency took possession of Mr. Lincoln; and when it is remembered that this calamity--for such it surely was--befell him at a critical period of the war, just when the resources of his mighty intellect were most in demand, it will be understood how his affliction became a matter of the gravest concern to the whole country, and especially to those who stood in close personal and official relations with him.

The measures taken by his friends to break the force of his great grief, and to restore him to something like his old-time cheerfulness, seemed for a while unavailing. The nearest approach to success in this humane endeavor was made, I believe, by the Rev. Dr. Vinton, of Trinity Church, New York, who visited the White House not long after the death of Willie. The doctor's effort led to a very remarkable scene, one that shows how terrible is a great man's grief. Mr. Lincoln had a high respect for Dr. Vinton. He knew him to be an able man, and believed him to be conscientious and sincere. The good doctor, profoundly impressed with the importance of his mission, determined that in administering consolation to the stricken President it would be necessary to use great freedom of speech. Mr. Lincoln was over-burdened with the weight of his public cares, weak in body, and sick in mind; and his thoughts seemed to linger constantly about the grave of his lost darling. Ill health and depression made him apparently listless, and this the worthy doctor mistook for a sign of rebellion against the just decree of Providence. He began by exhorting the President to remember his duty to the common Father who "giveth and taketh away," and to whom we owe cheerful obedience and thanks for worldly afflictions as well as for temporal benefits. He chided Mr. Lincoln for giving way to excessive grief, declaring without reserve that the indulgence of such grief, though natural, was sinful; that greater fortitude was demanded; that his duties to the living were imperative; and that, as the chosen leader of the people in a national crisis, he was unfitting himself for the discharge of duties and responsibilities which could not be evaded. Mr. Lincoln listened patiently and respectfully for a time to this strong and pointed exhortation. He was evidently much affected by it, but as the doctor proceeded he became lost in his own reflections. From this revery he was aroused by words which had a magical effect.

"To mourn excessively for the departed as lost," continued Dr. Vinton, "is foreign to our religion. It belongs not to Christianity, but to heathenism. Your son is alive in Paradise."

When these last words were uttered, Mr. Lincoln, as if suddenly awakened from a dream, exclaimed, "Alive! alive! Surely you mock me!" These magic words had startled him, and his countenance showed that he was profoundly distressed.

Without heeding the President's emotion, the doctor continued, in a tone of deep solemnity, "Seek not your son among the dead, for he is not there. God is not the God of the dead, but of the living. Did not the ancient patriarch mourn for his son as dead? 'Joseph is not, and Simeon is not, and ye will take Benjamin also.' The fact that Benjamin was taken away made him the instrument, eventually, in saving the whole family." Applying this Scriptural test, the doctor told Mr. Lincoln that his little son had been called by the

All-Wise and Merciful Father to His upper kingdom; that, like Joseph, the departed boy might be the means of saving the President's household; and that it must be considered as a part of the Lord's plan for the ultimate happiness of the family.

Mr. Lincoln was deeply moved by this consolatory exhortation. The respected divine had touched a responsive chord. His strong words, spoken with such evident sincerity and in a manner so earnest and impressive, brought strength as well as comfort to the illustrious mourner; and there is no doubt that this remarkable interview had a good effect in helping to recall to Mr. Lincoln a more healthful state of feeling, and in restoring his accustomed self-control. Willie had inherited the amiable disposition and a large share of the talent of his father. He was a child of great promise, and his death was sincerely mourned by all who knew him.

Mr. Lincoln's fondness for his children knew no bounds. It wellnigh broke his heart to use his paternal authority in correcting their occasional displays of temper or insubordination; but when occasion required the sacrifice, he showed great firmness in teaching them the strictest obedience. I remember a very amusing instance of this sort of contest between his indulgent fondness and his sense of what was due to his guiding authority as a father.

At the time to which I refer, Tad seemed to his fond father the most lovable object on earth. That fondness had been intensified by the death of Willie just mentioned. In one of the vacant rooms of the White House Tad had fitted up, with the aid of the servants, a miniature theatre. The little fellow had rare skill and good taste in such matters, and after long and patient effort the work was completed. There were the stage, the orchestra, the parquet, the curtains, and all the paraphernalia pertaining to what he called "a real theatre," and Tad was in a delirium of childish joy. About this time, just after the review of Burnside's division of the army of the Potomac, a certain photographer came to the Executive Mansion to make some stereoscopic studies of the President's office for Mr. Carpenter, who had been much about the house. Mr. Carpenter and the photographer appeared at the same time. The artists told Mr. Lincoln that they must have a dark closet in which to develop their pictures. There was such a closet attached to the room which Tad had appropriated for his theatre, and it could not be reached without passing through the room.

With Mr. Lincoln's permission the artists took possession of the "theatre," and they had taken several pictures before Tad discovered the trespass upon his premises. When he took in the situation there was an uproar. Their occupancy of his "theatre," without his consent, was an offence that stirred his wrath into an instant blaze. The little fellow declared indignantly that he would not submit to any such impudence. He locked the door and carried off the key. The artists hunted him up, and coaxed, remonstrated, and begged, but all in vain. The young theatre manager, in a flame of passion, blamed Carpenter with the whole outrage. He declared that they should neither use his room nor go into it to get their instruments and chemicals. "No one," said he, "has any business in my room, unless invited by me, and I never invited you." Here was a pretty state of things. Tad was master of the situation.

Finally, Mr. Lincoln was appealed to. Tad was called, and Mr. Lincoln said to him, "Go, now, and unlock the door." The offended boy went off to his mother's room, muttering a positive refusal to obey his father's command. On hearing of the child's disobedience, Mr. Lincoln soon had the key, and "the theatre" was again invaded by the artists. Soon after this, Mr. Lincoln said to Carpenter, half apologetically: "Tad is a peculiar child. He was violently excited when I went to him for the key. I said to him, 'Tad, do you know that you are making your father very unhappy? You are causing a deal of trouble.' He burst into tears, and gave up the key. I had not the heart to say much to him in the way of reproof, for the little man certainly thought his rights had been shamefully disregarded." The distress which this unlucky affair brought upon his little pet caused Mr. Lincoln more concern than anything else connected with it.

During the first year of the war, owing to the great press of business, it was at times difficult to get at the President. Some four or five distinguished gentlemen from Kentucky, who had come to visit him as commissioners or agents from that State, had been endeavoring, for a number of days, without success, to see him. Mr. Lincoln having learned the object of their intended visit to him through some source or other, wanted to avoid the interview if possible, and had given them no opportunity for presenting themselves. One day after waiting in the lobby for several hours, they were about to give up the effort in despair, and in no amiable terms expressed their disappointment as they turned to the head of the stairs, saying something about "seeing old Abe." Tad caught at these words, and asked them if they wanted to see "old Abe," laughing at the same time. "Yes," they replied. "Wait a minute," said Tad, and he rushed into his father's office and said, "Papa, may I introduce some friends to you?" His father, always indulgent and ready to make him happy, kindly said, "Yes, my son, I will see your friends." Tad went to the Kentuckians again, and asked a very dignified looking gentleman of the party what his name was. He was told his name. He then said, "Come, gentlemen," and they followed him. Leading them up to Mr. Lincoln, Tad, with much dignity, said, "Papa, let me introduce to you Judge ----, of Kentucky;" and quickly added, "Now, Judge, you introduce the other gentlemen." The introductions were gone through with, and they turned out to be the gentlemen Mr. Lincoln had been avoiding for a week. Mr. Lincoln reached for the boy, took him on his lap, kissed him, and told him it was all right, and that he had introduced his friend like a little gentleman as he was. Tad was eleven years old at this time.

Mr. Lincoln was pleased with Tad's diplomacy, and often laughed at the incident as he told others of it. One day while caressing the boy, he asked him why he called those gentlemen "his friends." "Well," said Tad, "I had seen them so often, and they looked so good and sorry, and said they were from Kentucky, that I thought they must be our friends." "That is right, my son," said Mr. Lincoln; "I would have the whole human race your friends and mine, if it were possible."

CHAPTER XI.

THE TRUE HISTORY OF THE GETTYSBURG SPEECH.

Among the many historic scenes in which President Lincoln was an actor there is not one, perhaps, where a single incident gave rise to speculations so groundless and guesses so wide of the truth as his justly celebrated Gettysburg speech.[H] Since his death there has been an enormous expenditure, not to say a very great waste, of literary talent on that extraordinary address, as there has been on almost everything else he did, or was supposed to have done, from his boyhood until the moment of his assassination. That reporters, critics, chroniclers, eulogists, flatterers, and biographers have not only failed to give a true account of that famous speech, but that they have subjected Mr. Lincoln's memory to hurtful misrepresentation, it is the purpose of this chapter to show.

[H] Fourscore and seven years ago our fathers brought forth on this Continent a new nation, conceived in liberty, and dedicated to the proposition that all men are created equal.

Now we are engaged in a civil war, testing whether that nation, or any nation so conceived and so dedicated, can long endure. We are met on a great battle-field of that war. We have come to dedicate a portion of that field as a final resting-place for those who gave their lives that that nation might live. It is altogether fitting and proper that we should do this.

But in a larger sense we cannot dedicate, we cannot consecrate, we cannot hallow, this ground. The brave men, living and dead, who struggled here, have consecrated it far above our poor power to add or detract. The world will little note, nor long remember, what we say here; but it can never forget what they did here. It is for us the living, rather, to be dedicated here to the unfinished work which they who fought here have thus far so nobly advanced. It is rather for us to be here dedicated to the great task remaining before us; that from these honored dead we take increased devotion to that cause for which they gave the last full measure of devotion; that we here highly resolve that these dead shall not have died in vain; that this nation, under God, shall have a new birth of freedom; and that government of the people, by the people, for the people, shall not perish from the earth.

It was my good fortune to have known Mr. Lincoln long and well,--so long and so intimately that as the shadows lengthen and the years recede I am more and more impressed by the rugged grandeur and nobility of his character, his strength of intellect, and his singular purity of heart. Surely I am the last man on earth to say or do aught in derogation of his matchless worth, or to tarnish the fair fame of him who was, during eighteen of the most eventful years of my life, a constant, considerate, and never-failing friend.

The world has long since conceded that Abraham Lincoln was great in all the elements that go to make up human greatness. He had a stamp of originality entirely his own. With his unique individuality and his commanding intellect--at once strong, sagacious, and profoundly acute and critical--were associated a mental integrity and a moral purpose as firm as granite, a thorough knowledge of himself, and a modesty that scorned not only self-laudation but eulogy by others for fame or achievements not his own. An act accomplished by him, either in his character of a citizen or as a public servant, he regarded more as a duty discharged than as an achievement of which to be proud. He was charitable to a fault; and yet no man ever discriminated more narrowly in forming a judgment concerning the character, the acts, and the motives of other men, or had a keener appreciation of merit or demerit in others. With his characteristic honesty and simplicity we may well suppose, that, were he alive to-day, he would feel under little obligation to the swarm of fulsome eulogists who have made up a large part of the current chronicles of his life and public conduct by ascribing to him ornamental virtues which he never possessed, and motives, purposes, and achievements which he would promptly disown if he could now speak for himself.

Discriminating observers and students of history have not failed to note the fact that the ceremony of Mr. Lincoln's apotheosis was not only planned but executed by men who were unfriendly to him while he lived, and that the deification took place with showy magnificence some time after the great man's lips were sealed in death. Men who had exhausted the resources of their skill and ingenuity in venomous detraction of the living Lincoln, especially during the last years of his life, were the first, when the assassin's bullet had closed the career of the great-hearted statesman, to undertake the self-imposed task of guarding his memory,--not as a human being endowed with a mighty intellect and extraordinary virtues, but as a god. In fact, the tragic death of Mr. Lincoln brought a more fearful panic to his former traducers than to his friends. The latter's legacy was deep sorrow and mourning; the former were left to the humiliating necessity of a change of base to place themselves en rapport with the millions who mourned the loss of their greatest patriot and statesman.

If there was one form of flattery more offensive to the noble and manly pride of Mr. Lincoln than all others, it was that in which credit was given him for a meritorious deed done by some other man, or which ascribed to him some sentimental or saintly virtue that he knew he did not possess. In the same spirit he rejected all commendations or flattering compliments touching anything which he had written or spoken, when, in his own judgment, there was nothing especially remarkable in the speech or the composition referred to. Although superior, I readily concede, to any other man I have ever known, Mr. Lincoln was yet thoroughly human; and with his exact knowledge of his own character,--its weakness and its strength,--he once said to me, speaking of what historians and biographers might say of him, "Speak of me as I am; nothing extenuate, nor set down aught in malice." He had a clear perception of the value of that history which is truthful; and he believed that hosannas sung to the memory of the greatest of men, as if they were demi-gods, are hurtful to their fame.

A day or two before the dedication of the National Cemetery at Gettysburg, Mr. Lincoln told me that he would be expected to make a speech on the occasion; that he was extremely busy, and had no time for preparation; and that he greatly feared he would not be able to acquit himself with credit, much less to fill the measure of public expectation. From his hat (the usual receptacle for his private notes and memoranda) he drew a sheet of foolscap, one side of which was closely written with what he informed me was a memorandum of his intended address. This he read to me, first remarking that it was not at all satisfactory to him. It proved to be in substance, if not in exact words, what was afterwards printed as his famous Gettysburg speech.

After its delivery on the day of commemoration, he expressed deep regret that he had not prepared it with greater care. He said to me on the stand, immediately after concluding the speech: "Lamon, that speech won't scour! It is a flat failure, and the people are disappointed." (The word "scour" he often used in expressing his positive conviction that a thing lacked merit, or would not stand the test of close criticism or the wear of time.) He seemed deeply concerned about what the people might think of his address; more deeply, in fact, than I had ever seen him on any public occasion. His frank and regretful condemnation of his effort, and more especially his manner of expressing that regret, struck me as somewhat remarkable; and my own impression was deepened by the fact that the orator of the day, Mr. Everett, and Secretary Seward both coincided with Mr. Lincoln in his unfavorable view of its merits.

The occasion was solemn, impressive, and grandly historic. The people, it is true, stood apparently spell-bound; and the vast throng was hushed and awed into profound silence while Mr. Lincoln delivered his brief speech. But it seemed to him that this silence and attention to his words arose more from the solemnity of the ceremonies and the awful scenes which gave rise to them, than from anything he had said. He believed that the speech was a failure. He thought so at the time, and he never referred to it afterwards, in conversation with me, without some expression of unqualified regret that he had not made the speech better in every way.

On the platform from which Mr. Lincoln delivered his address, and only a moment after it was concluded, Mr. Seward turned to Mr. Everett and asked him what he thought of the President's speech. Mr. Everett replied, "It is not what I expected from him. I am disappointed." Then in his turn Mr. Everett asked, "What do you think of it, Mr. Seward?" The response was, "He has made a failure, and I am sorry for it. His speech is not equal to him." Mr. Seward then turned to me and asked, "Mr. Marshal, what do you think of it?" I answered, "I am sorry to say that it does not impress me as one of his great speeches."

In the face of these facts it has been repeatedly published that this speech was received by the audience with loud demonstrations of approval; that "amid the tears, sobs, and cheers it produced in the excited throng, the orator of the day, Mr. Everett, turned to Mr. Lincoln, grasped his hand and exclaimed, 'I congratulate you on your success!' adding in a transport of heated enthusiasm, 'Ah, Mr. President, how gladly would I give my hundred pages to be the author of your twenty lines!'" Nothing of the kind occurred. It is a slander on Mr. Everett, an injustice to Mr. Lincoln, and a falsification of history. Mr. Everett could not have used the words attributed to him, in the face of his own condemnation of the speech uttered a moment before, without subjecting himself to the charge of being a toady and a hypocrite;

and he was neither the one nor the other.

As a matter of fact, the silence during the delivery of the speech, and the lack of hearty demonstrations of approval immediately after its close, were taken by Mr. Lincoln as certain proof that it was not well received. In that opinion we all shared. If any person then present saw, or thought he saw, the marvellous beauties of that wonderful speech, as intelligent men in all lands now see and acknowledge them, his superabundant caution closed his lips and stayed his pen. Mr. Lincoln said to me after our return to Washington, "I tell you, Hill, that speech fell on the audience like a wet blanket. I am distressed about it. I ought to have prepared it with more care." Such continued to be his opinion of that most wonderful of all his platform addresses up to the time of his death.

I state it as a fact, and without fear of contradiction, that this famous Gettysburg speech was not regarded by the audience to whom it was addressed, or by the press and people of the United States, as a production of extraordinary merit, nor was it commented on as such until after the death of its author. Those who look thoughtfully into the history of the matter must own that Mr. Lincoln was, on that occasion, "wiser than he knew." He was wiser than his audience, wiser than the great scholars and orators who were associated with him in the events of that solemn day. He had unconsciously risen to a height above the level of even the "cultured thought" of that period.[6]

[6] Page 174, line 11, after the word "period."

The words of Clark E. Carr are entitled to credit, for no one present had more at heart than he the success of these ceremonies--he being one of the original commissioners comprising the board that purchased this, the first ground set apart for a national cemetery for our soldiers. He was on the platform from which Mr. Lincoln spoke. He says in his "Lincoln at

Gettysburg" that, "Before the great multitude of people could prepare themselves to listen intelligently, before their thoughts had become sufficiently centred upon the speaker to take up his line of thought and follow him, he had finished and returned to his seat. So short a time [only about three minutes] was Mr. Lincoln before them that the people could scarcely believe their eyes when he disappeared from their view. They could not possibly in so short a time mentally grasp the ideas that were conveyed. Many persons said to me that they would have supposed that on such a great occasion the President would have made a speech. Every one thought he made only a very few 'dedicatory remarks.' Mr. Carr further says that the general impression was that the remarks consisted of 'a dozen commonplace sentences scarcely one of which contained anything new, anything that when stated was not self-evident.'"

The marvellous perfection, the intrinsic excellence of the Gettysburg speech as a masterpiece of English composition, seem to have escaped the scrutiny of even the most scholarly critics of that day, on this side of the Atlantic. That discovery was made, it must be regretfully owned, by distinguished writers on the other side. The London "Spectator," the "Saturday Review," the "Edinburgh Review," and some other European journals were the first to discover, or at least to proclaim, the classical merits of the Gettysburg speech. It was then that we began to realize that it was indeed a masterpiece; and it dawned upon many minds that we had entertained an angel unawares, who had left us unappreciated. In no country and in no age of the world has the death of any man caused an outpouring of sorrow so universal. Every nation of the earth felt and expressed its sense of the loss to progressive civilization and popular government. In his life and death, thoughtful men in all lands found an inspiring theme. England's greatest thinker, John Stuart Mill, pronounced Abraham Lincoln to be "the greatest citizen, who has afforded a noble example of the qualities befitting the first magistrate of a free people." The London "Times" declared that the news of his death would be received throughout Europe "with sorrow as sincere and profound as it awoke in the United States," and that "Englishmen had learned to respect a man who showed the best characteristics of their race." The London "Spectator" spoke of him as "certainly the best, if not the ablest man ruling over any country in the civilized world."

For using in his Gettysburg speech the celebrated phrase, "the government of the people, by the people, and for the people," Mr. Lincoln has been subjected to the most brutal criticism as well as to the most groundless flattery. Some have been base enough to insinuate against that great and sincere man that he was guilty of the crime of wilful plagiarism; others have ascribed to him the honor of originating the phrase entire. There is injustice to him in either view of the case. I personally know that Mr. Lincoln made no pretence of originality in the matter; nor was he, on the other hand, conscious of having appropriated the thought, or even the exact words, of any other man. If he is subject to the charge of plagiarism, so is the great Webster, who used substantially the same phrase in his celebrated reply to Hayne. Both men may have acquired the peculiar form of expression (the thought itself being as old as the republican idea of government) by the process known as unconscious appropriation. Certain it is that neither Lincoln nor Webster originated the phrase. Let us see how the case stands.

In an address before the New England Antislavery Convention in Boston, May 29, 1850, Theodore Parker defined Democracy as "a government of all the people, by all the people, for all the people, of course," which language is identical with that employed by Mr. Lincoln in his Gettysburg speech. Substantially the same phrase was used by Judge Joel Parker in the Massachusetts Constitutional Convention in 1853. A distinguished diplomat has acquainted me with the singular fact that almost the identical phrase employed by Mr. Lincoln was used in another language by a person whose existence even was not probably known to Mr. Webster, the Parkers, or to Mr. Lincoln. On the thirty-first page of a work entitled "Geschichte der Schweizerischen Regeneration von 1830 bis 1848, von P. Feddersen," appears an account of a public meeting held at Olten, Switzerland, in May, 1830. On that occasion a speaker named Schinz used the following language, as translated by my friend just referred to: "All the governments of Switzerland [referring to the cantons] must acknowledge that they are simply from all the people, by all the people, and for all the people."

These extracts are enough to show that no American statesman or writer can lay claim to the origin or authorship of the phrase in question. No friend of Mr. Lincoln will pretend that it is the coinage of his fertile brain; nor will any fair-minded man censure him for using it as he did in his Gettysburg speech. As a phrase of singular compactness and force, it was employed by him, legitimately and properly, as a fitting conclusion to an address which the judgment of both hemispheres has declared will live as a model of classic oratory while free government shall continue to be known and revered among men.

"The world will little note, | "The speech will live when nor long remember, what we | the memory of the battle will say here; but it can never | be lost or only remembered forget what they did here." | because of the speech."

LINCOLN. SUMNER.

CHAPTER XII.

HIS UNSWERVING FIDELITY TO PURPOSE.

During the long series of defeats and disasters which culminated in the battles of Fredericksburg and of Chancellorsville, there arose in certain circles of the army and of the National Legislature a feeling of distrust and dissatisfaction, that reached its climax in an intrigue to displace Mr. Lincoln, if not from his position at least from the exercise of his prerogatives, by the appointment of a dictator. Such a measure would have been scarcely less revolutionary than many others which were openly avowed and advocated.

In this cabal were naturally included all those self-constituted advisers whose counsels had not been adopted in the conduct of the war; all those malcontents and grumblers who, conscious of their incapacity to become makers of pots and pitchers, are always so eager to exhibit their skill and ingenuity as menders of them. In this coalition of non-combatant guardian angels of the country and civilian warriors were to be found patriots of every shade and of every degree.

First, the political patriot, who recognized in a brilliant succession of Federal victories the only probable prospect of preserving the ascendency of his party and promoting his own personal fortunes.

Second, the commercial patriot, whose dominant passion was a love of--self; to whom the spoliation of the South and the swindling of his own government afforded the most fruitful expedient for feathering his nest.

Third, the religious patriot, whose love of country was subordinate to his hatred of slavery and of slaveholders; who having recanted his dictum that the Constitution of the United States was a "covenant with death and an agreement with hell," was now one of the most vindictive and unscrupulous advocates of a war of extermination. As is frequently the case where one class of persons is severely exercised over the iniquities of another, to a sentiment of philanthropy had succeeded the most violent animosity and intolerance, until sympathy for the slave degenerated into the most envenomed hostility toward his owner.

Among the most aggressive assailants of the President were thus comprised all those elements in his party, with whom the logic of the war might be summed up in the comprehensive formula, "Power, plunder, and extended rule." The evolution of events and his consistent policy, as foreshadowed and indicated on the close of hostilities, have clearly demonstrated that with such minds Mr. Lincoln could have little sympathy or fellowship. Conscientiously observant of his solemn oath to maintain the Constitution, he could not be persuaded to evade the obligations of his high trust by lending his authority to the accomplishment of their revolutionary and nefarious designs. Hinc ill?lachrym? hence, disappointed at the failure of their endeavor to shape his policy in obedience to the suggestions of their own ignoble designs, their open revolt.

No member of the cabal was better advised of its progress or of the parties concerned in it than Mr. Lincoln himself. He often talked with me on the subject. He did not fear it; he feared nothing except to commit an involuntary wrong or mistake of judgment in the administration of his high and responsible trust. He would willingly have resigned office and retired to the unobtrusive life and simple duties of a private citizen, if by so doing he could have restored the integrity of the Union, or in anywise have promoted the success of the Union cause. In this connection he would often say to me: "In God's name! if any one can do better in my place than I have done, or am endeavoring to do, let him try his hand at it, and no one will be better contented than myself."

One time I went to Mr. Lincoln's office at the White House and found the door locked. I went through a private room and through a side entrance into the office, where I found the President lying on a sofa, evidently greatly disturbed and much excited, manifestly displeased with the outlook. Jumping up from his reclining position he advanced, saying: "You know better than any man living that from my boyhood up my ambition was to be President. I am President of one part of this divided country at least; but look at me! I wish I had never been born! It is a white elephant on my hands, and hard to manage. With a fire in my front and rear; having to contend with the jealousies of the military commanders, and not receiving that cordial co-operation and support from Congress which could reasonably be expected; with an active and formidable enemy in the field threatening the very life-blood of the government,--my position is anything but a bed of roses."

I remarked to him: "It strikes me that you are somewhat in the position of the great Richelieu, of whom it was said that he was the first man in Europe but the second only in his own country."

"Oh, no! very far from it," he replied. "Richelieu never had a fire in his front and rear at the same time, but a united constituency, which it has never been my good fortune to have." Then brightening up, his whole nature seemed all at once to change. I could see a merry twinkle in his eye as he said: "If I can only keep my end of the animal pointed in the right direction, I will yet get him through this infernal jungle and get my end of him and his tail placed in their proper relative positions. I have never faltered in my faith of being ultimately able to suppress this rebellion and of reuniting this divided country; but this improvised vigilant committee to watch my movements and keep me straight, appointed by Congress and called the 'committee on the conduct of the war,' is a marplot, and its greatest purpose seems to be to hamper my action and obstruct the military operations."

Earnestly desirous of conciliating and harmonizing every element, with a view to the accomplishment of the one--the dearest--aspiration of his heart, a restoration of the Union, Mr. Lincoln had yielded until further concessions would have implied ductility or imbecility, until every sentiment of dignity and of self-respect would have uttered an indignant protest. He then well knew that he must assert himself, or be an unimportant factor in the body-politic in the struggle for the life and preservation of the nation; and rising at length to the full height of his matchless self-reliance and independence, he exclaimed: "This state of things shall continue no longer. I will show them at the other end of the Avenue whether I am President or not!"

From this moment he never again hesitated or wavered as to his course. From this moment he was recognized as the Executive Chief and Constitutional Commander of the Armies and Navy of the United States. His opponents and would-be masters were now, for the most part, silenced; but they hated him all the more cordially.

A short time before the fall of Vicksburg, great dissatisfaction became rife at General Grant's tardiness in moving on the enemy's works. There was a pretty general feeling in favor of relieving Grant from his command, and appointing some one who would make short work of that formidable stronghold of the enemy and relieve the people from their state of anxiety. Mr. Lincoln had great faith in General Grant. He was being constantly importuned and beset by the leading politicians to turn Grant out of the command. One day about this time he said to me, "I fear I have made Senator Wade, of Ohio, my enemy for life." "How?" I asked. "Wade was here just now urging me to dismiss Grant, and in response to something he said I remarked, 'Senator, that reminds me of a story.' 'Yes, yes!' Wade petulantly replied, 'it is with you, sir, all story, story! You are the father of every military blunder that has been made during the war. You are on your road to hell, sir, with this government, by your obstinacy; and you are not a mile off this minute.' I good-naturedly said to him: 'Senator, that is just about the distance from here to the Capitol, is it not?' He was very angry, and grabbed up his hat and cane and went away."

Lincoln then continued to say: "To show to what extent this sentiment prevails, even Washburne, who has always claimed Grant as his by right of discovery, has deserted him, and demands his removal; and I really believe I am the only friend Grant has left. Grant advises me [Mr. Lincoln had never seen General Grant up to that time] that he will take Vicksburg by the Fourth of July, and I believe he will do it; and he shall have the chance."

Had it not been for the stoic firmness of Mr. Lincoln in standing by Grant, which resulted in the speedy capture of Vicksburg, it is hard to predict what would have been the consequences. If nothing worse, certain it is that President Lincoln would have been deposed, and a dictator would have been placed in his stead as chief executive until peace could be restored to the nation by separation or otherwise. Mr. Lincoln thus expressed himself shortly before his death: "If I had done as my Washington friends, who fight battles with their tongues at a safe distance from the enemy, would have had me do, Grant, who proved himself so great a captain, would never have been heard of again."

That Mr. Lincoln sought to interfere as little as possible with the military affairs after General Grant took charge of the army will be shown by the following letter:--

EXECUTIVE MANSION, WASHINGTON, April 30, 1864.

LIEUTENANT-GENERAL GRANT,--Not expecting to see you before the spring campaign opens, I wish to express in this way my entire satisfaction with what you have done up to this time, so far as I understand it. The particulars of your plan I neither know nor seek to know. You are vigilant and self-reliant, and [I put no] restraints or constraints upon you. While I am very anxious that any great disaster or capture of any of our men in great numbers shall be avoided, I know that these points are less likely to escape your attention than they would be mine. If there be anything wanting which is within my power to give, do not fail to let me know it. And now with a brave army and a just cause, may God sustain you!

Yours very truly, (Signed) A. LINCOLN.

I am not aware that there was ever a serious discord or misunderstanding between Mr. Lincoln and General Grant except on a single occasion. From the commencement of the struggle, Lincoln's policy was to break the back-bone of the Confederacy by depriving it of its principal means of subsistence. Cotton was its vital aliment; deprive it of this, and the rebellion must necessarily collapse. The Hon. Elihu B. Washburne from the outset was opposed to any contraband traffic with the Confederates. Lincoln had given permits and passes through the lines to two persons,--Mr. Joseph Mattox, of Maryland, and General Singleton, of Illinois,--to enable them to bring cotton and other Southern products from Virginia. Washburne heard of it, called immediately on Mr. Lincoln, and after remonstrating with him on the impropriety of such a thing, threatened to have General Grant countermand the permits if they were not revoked. Naturally, both became excited. Lincoln declared that he did not believe General Grant would take upon himself the responsibility of such an act. "I will show you, sir, I will show you whether Grant will do it or not," responded Mr. Washburne as he abruptly withdrew.

By the next boat, subsequent to this interview, the Congressman left Washington for the headquarters of General Grant. He returned shortly afterward to the city, and so likewise did Mattox and Singleton. Grant had countermanded the permits.

The following important order relative to trade-permits was issued by Lieutenant-General Grant about this time:--

HEADQUARTERS ARMIES OF THE U. S. CITY POINT, VA., March 10, 1865.

Special Orders, No. 48.

1. The operations on all Treasury trade-permits, and all other trade-permits and licenses to trade, by whomsoever granted, within the State of Virginia, except that portion known as the Eastern Shore, and the States of North

Carolina and South Carolina, and that portion of the State of Georgia immediately bordering on the Atlantic, including the City of Savannah, are hereby suspended until further orders. All contracts and agreements made under or by virtue of any trade-permit or license within any of said States or parts of States, during the existence of this order, will be deemed void, and the subject of such contracts or agreements will be seized by the military authorities for the benefit of the government, whether the same is at the time of such contracts or agreements within their reach or at any time thereafter comes within their reach, either by the operations of war or the acts of the contracting parties or their agents. The delivery of all goods contracted for and not delivered before the publication of this order is prohibited.

Supplies of all kinds are prohibited from passing into any of said States or parts of States, except such as are absolutely necessary for the wants of those living within the lines of actual military occupation, and under no circumstances will military commanders allow them to pass beyond the lines they actually hold.

By command of Lieutenant-General Grant.

T. S. BOWERS, Assistant Adjutant-General.

Under all the circumstances it was a source of exultation to Mr. Washburne and his friends, and of corresponding surprise and mortification to the President. But he suppressed the resentment to which General Grant's conduct might naturally have given rise, and, with the equanimity and self-control that was habitual with him, merely remarked: "I wonder when General Grant changed his mind on this subject. He was the first man, after the commencement of the war, to grant a permit for the passage of cotton through the lines, and that to his own father." In referring afterwards to the subject, he said: "It made me feel my insignificance keenly at the moment; but if my friends Washburne, Henry Wilson, and others derive pleasure from so unworthy a victory over me, I leave them to its full enjoyment." This ripple on the otherwise unruffled current of their intercourse did not disturb the personal relations between Lincoln and Grant; but there was little cordiality between the President and Messrs. Washburne and Wilson afterwards.

Mr. Lincoln, when asked if he had seen the Wade-Davis manifesto, the Phillips speech[I] etc., replied: "No, I have not seen them, nor do I care to see them. I have seen enough to satisfy me that I am a failure, not only in the opinion of the people in rebellion, but of many distinguished politicians of my own party. But time will show whether I am right or they are right, and I am content to abide its decision. I have enough to look after without giving much of my time to the consideration of the subject of who shall be my successor in office. The position is not an easy one; and the occupant, whoever he may be, for the next four years, will have little leisure to pluck a thorn or plant a rose in his own pathway." It was urged that this opposition must be embarrassing to his Administration, as well as damaging to the party. He replied: "Yes, that is true; but our friends Wade, Davis, Phillips, and others are hard to please. I am not capable of doing so. I cannot please them without wantonly violating not only my oath, but the most vital principles upon which our government was founded. As to those who, like Wade and the rest, see fit to depreciate my policy and cavil at my official acts, I shall not complain of them. I accord them the utmost freedom of speech and liberty of the press, but shall not change the policy I have adopted in the full belief that I am right. I feel on this subject as an old Illinois farmer once expressed himself while eating cheese. He was interrupted in the midst of his repast by the entrance of his son, who exclaimed, 'Hold on, dad! there's skippers in that cheese you're eating!' 'Never mind, Tom,' said he, as he kept on munching his cheese, 'if they can stand it I can.'"

[I] In a speech at Cooper Institute in New York City, on the Presidential election (1864), Wendell Phillips said that for thirty years he had labored to break up the Union in the interest of justice, and now he labored to save it in the same interest. The same curse that he invoked on the old Union he would invoke on a new Union if it is not founded on justice to the negro. "Science must either demonstrate that the negro is not a man, or politics must accord to him equality at the ballot-box and in offices of trust." He judged Mr. Lincoln by his words and deeds, and so judging he was "unwilling to trust Abraham Lincoln with the future of the country. Let it be granted that Mr. Lincoln is pledged to Liberty and Union; but this pledge was wrung out of him by the Cleveland movement, and was a mere electioneering pledge. Mr. Lincoln is a politician. Politicians are like the bones of a horse's fore-shoulder,--not a straight one in it. A reformer is like a Doric column of iron,--straight, strong, and immovable. It is a momentous responsibility to trust Mr. Lincoln where we want a Doric column to stand stern and strong for the Nation.... I am an Abolitionist, but I am also a citizen watchful of constitutional Liberty; and I say if President Lincoln is inaugurated on the votes of Tennessee, Louisiana, and Arkansas, every citizen is bound to resist him. Are you willing to sacrifice the constitutional rights of seventy years for your fondness for an individual?"

Mr. Phillips then quoted some opinions from prominent men in the Republican party. "A man in the field said, 'The re-election of Abraham Lincoln will be a disaster.' Another said, 'The re-election of Abraham Lincoln will be national destruction.' Said another, 'There is no government at Washington,--nothing there.' Winter Davis of Maryland testifies to his [Lincoln's] inability. Said another, 'That proclamation will not stand a week before the Supreme Court; but I had rather trust it there than Abraham Lincoln to make the judges.' Mr. Lincoln has secured his success just as the South used to secure its success. He says to the radicals of the Republican party, 'I am going to nominate myself at Baltimore: risk a division of the party if you dare!' and the radicals submitted. Political Massachusetts submitted, and is silent; but Antislavery Massachusetts calls to the people to save their own cause." Mr. Phillips said he "wanted by free speech to let

Abraham Lincoln know that we are stronger than Abraham Lincoln, and that he is a servant to obey us. I distrust the man who uses whole despotism in Massachusetts and half despotism in South Carolina, and that man is Abraham Lincoln."

On another occasion Mr. Lincoln said to me: "If the unworthy ambition of politicians and the jealousy that exists in the army could be repressed, and all unite in a common aim and a common endeavor, the rebellion would soon be crushed." He conversed with me freely and repeatedly on the subject of the unfairness and intemperance of his opponents in Congress, of the project of a dictatorship, etc. The reverses at Fredericksburg and Chancellorsville Mr. Lincoln fully comprehended; and he believed them to have been caused by the absence of a proper support of Burnside and Hooker, prompted by the jealousies of other superior officers.

The appointment of a general to the supreme command of the Army of the Potomac, made vacant by the resignation of General Burnside, became a question of urgent import. General Rosecrans was the choice of the Secretary of War. The President regarded it as inexpedient to make the appointment outside the general officers serving in the Army of the Potomac. Having little preference in the selection of a successor to General Burnside, Mr. Lincoln, after advisement, adopted the views of the military department of the government, and offered the chief command to General Reynolds. The latter, however, declined to accept the trust, unless a wider latitude of action were granted him than had hitherto been accorded to officers occupying this high post.

The reverses in the field already referred to having occurred since General McClellan was relieved from the chief command of the Union forces, there now arose among his old companions-in-arms, and in the army generally, a clamor for his reinstatement as Commander of the Army of the Potomac. The propriety of such action was made the subject of a Cabinet consultation, which resulted in the rejection of an expedient so manifestly looking towards a dictatorship.

A strong influence was now exerted by the immediate friends of General Hooker in behalf of his appointment as Commander-in-Chief,--some of them being prompted by personal ambition, others by even less worthy motives. These partisans of a worthy and deserving officer, whose aspirations were known to be entirely within the sphere of military preferment, united their forces with a powerful political coterie, having for their chief object the elevation of Mr. Chase to the Presidency upon the expiration of Mr. Lincoln's first term. It was believed by this faction that Hooker, in the event of his bringing the war to a successful conclusion, being himself unambitious of office, might not be unwilling to lend his prestige and influence to a movement in favor of that distinguished statesman as the successor of Mr. Lincoln in the Presidency. Up to the present time the war had been conducted rather at the dictation of a political bureaucracy than in accordance purely with considerations of military strategy. Hooker was appointed by the President under a full knowledge of his political affinities.

In conversation with Mr. Lincoln one night about the time General Burnside was relieved, I was urging upon him the necessity of looking well to the fact that there was a scheme on foot to depose him, and to appoint a military dictator in his stead. He laughed, and said: "I think, for a man of accredited courage, you are the most panicky person I ever knew; you can see more dangers to me than all the other friends I have. You are all the time exercised about somebody taking my life,--murdering me; and now you have discovered a new danger: now you think the people of this great government are likely to turn me out of office. I do not fear this from the people any more than I fear assassination from an individual. Now, to show you my appreciation of what my French friends would call a coup, let me read you a letter I have written to General Hooker, whom I have just appointed to the command of the Army of the Potomac." He then opened the drawer of his table and took out and read the letter to General Hooker, which accompanied his commission as Commander of the Army of the Potomac, of which letter the following is a copy:--

(PRIVATE.)

EXECUTIVE MANSION, WASHINGTON, D. C., Jan. 26, 1863.

Major-General Hooker:

GENERAL,--I have placed you at the head of the Army of the Potomac. Of course I have done this upon what appears to me sufficient reasons; and yet I think it best for you to know that there are some things in regard to which I am not quite satisfied with you.

I believe you to be a brave and skilful soldier, which of course I like. I also believe you do not mix politics with your profession, in which you are right. You have confidence in yourself, which is a valuable, if not indispensable, quality. You are ambitious, which, within reasonable bounds, does good rather than harm. But I think that during General Burnside's command of the army you have taken counsel of your ambition solely, and thwarted him as much as you could; in which you did a great wrong to the country and to a most meritorious and honorable brother officer. I have heard, in such a way as to believe it, of your saying that both the country and the army needed a dictator. Of course it was not for this, but in spite of it, that I have given you the command. Only those generals who gain success can set themselves up as dictators. What I ask of you is military success, and I will risk the dictatorship. The government will support you to the utmost of its ability, which is neither more nor less than it has done and will do for all its commanders.

I much fear that the spirit which you have aided to infuse into the army, of criticising their commander and withholding confidence from him, will now turn upon you; and I shall assist you as far as I can to put it down. Neither you nor Napoleon, if he were alive again, could get any good out of an army while such a spirit prevails in it.

And now, beware of rashness, but with energy and sleepless vigilance go forward and give us victories.

Yours very truly, A. LINCOLN.

Some little time afterwards, in referring with much feeling to this letter, General Hooker declared: "It was just such a letter as a father might have addressed to his son. It was a great rebuke, however, to me at the time."

The question of a dictatorship had been everywhere ventilated. The President had heard a great deal about it; but he treated the whole subject as a pure vagary, not apprehending any serious danger from it. At first it may have given him some annoyance; but it soon ceased to disturb him, and ultimately it became the source of no little mirth and amusement to him. I was present upon one occasion when a party of the intimate friends of Mr. Lincoln were assembled at the White House, and the project of a dictatorship was the topic of conversation. The President gave full play to the exuberance of his humor and his sense of the ridiculous, entirely banishing the anxieties and apprehensions of such of his friends as were inclined to regard the question from a more serious point of view. "I will tell you," said he, "a story which I think illustrates the situation.

"Some years ago a couple of emigrants from the Emerald Isle were wending their way westward in search of employment as a means of subsistence. The shades of night had already closed in upon them as they found themselves in the vicinity of a large sheet of standing water, more vulgarly called a big pond. They were greeted upon their approach by a symphony of bull-frogs, which was the only manifestation of life in the darkness that surrounded them, literally 'making night hideous' with noise. This sort of harmony was altogether new to them, and for a moment they were greatly terrified at the diabolic din. Instinctively and resolutely grasping their shillalahs, under the impression that Beelzebub or some of his deputies was about to dispute their farther progress, they cautiously advanced toward the spot from whence the strange concert proceeded. The frogs, however, alarmed at their approaching footsteps, had beat a precipitate retreat, and taken refuge in their watery hiding-places, and all was as silent as the grave. After waiting for some seconds in breathless suspense for the appearance of the enemy, not a sound being audible, in great disappointment and disgust at the loss of so favorable an opportunity for a free fight, one of our heroes, seizing his companion by the coat-sleeve, whispered confidentially in his ear: 'Faith, Pat, and it's my deliberate opinion that it was nothing but a blasted noise!'"

Pursuing the topic in the same humorous vein, Mr. Lincoln again convulsed his auditors by relating the following story:--

"A benighted wayfarer having lost his way somewhere amidst the wilds of our Northwestern frontiers, the embarrassments of his position were increased by a furious tempest which suddenly burst upon him. To add to the discomforts of the situation his horse had given out, leaving him exposed to all the dangers of the pitiless storm. The peals of thunder were terrific, the frequent flashes of lightning affording the only guide to the route he was pursuing as he resolutely trudged onward leading his jaded steed. The earth seemed fairly to tremble beneath him in the war of elements. One bolt threw him suddenly upon his knees. Our traveller was not a prayerful man, but finding himself involuntarily brought to an attitude of devotion, he addressed himself to the Throne of Grace in the following prayer for his deliverance: O God! hear my prayer this time, for Thou knowest it is not often that I call upon Thee. And, O Lord! if it is all the same to Thee, give us a little more light and a little less noise!' I hope," said Mr. Lincoln, pointing the moral of the anecdote, "that we may have a much stronger disposition manifested hereafter, on the part of our civilian warriors, to unite in suppressing the rebellion, and a little less noise as to how and by whom the chief executive office shall be administered."

CHAPTER XIII.

HIS TRUE RELATIONS WITH McCLELLAN.

The character of no statesman in all the history of the world has been more generally or more completely misunderstood than that of Abraham Lincoln. Many writers describe him as a mere creature of circumstances floating like a piece of driftwood on the current of events; and about the only attribute of statesmanship they concede to him is a sort of instinctive divination of the popular feeling at a given period, and on a given subject. They do not thus dwarf Mr. Lincoln in set phrase or formal propositions, but that is the logic and effect of their narratives. Some of these writers go even further, and represent him as an almost unconscious instrument in the hands of the Almighty,--about as irresponsible as the cloud by day and the pillar of fire by night which went before the Israelites through the wilderness.

The truth is, that Mr. Lincoln was at once the ablest and the most adroit politician of modern times. In all the history of the world I can recall no example of a great leader, having to do with a people in any degree free, who himself shaped and guided events to the same extent, unless it was Julius Caesar. Mr. Lincoln was not the creature of circumstances. He made circumstances to suit the necessities of his own situation. He was less influenced by the inferior minds around him than was Washington, Jefferson, or Jackson. His policy was invariably formed by his own judgment, and it seldom took even the slightest color from the opinions of others, however decided. In this originality and independence of understanding he resembled somewhat the great William of Orange.

Mr. Lincoln was supposed at the outset of his Administration to have placed himself, as it were, under the tutelage of William H. Seward; and later he was generally believed to have abjectly endured the almost insulting domination of Edwin M. Stanton. But I say without the slightest fear of contradiction, that neither Mr. Seward nor Mr. Stanton, great men as they both were, ever succeeded either in leading or misleading Mr. Lincoln in a single instance. The Administration was not a week old when Mr. Seward had found his level, and the larger purposes, dangerous and revolutionary, with which Mr. Stanton entered the War Department, were baffled and defeated before he had time to fashion the instruments of usurpation. Consciously or unconsciously, Mr. Seward and Mr. Stanton, like others, wrought out the will of the great man who had called them to his side to be appropriately used in furtherance of plans far greater and more comprehensive than they themselves had conceived.

I shall not linger here to present instances of this subordination of high officials and party leaders to Mr. Lincoln; they may be gleaned without number from the published histories of the times. I shall content myself with recounting some of his relations with the illustrious, and at that time powerful, Democratic captain, George B. McClellan.

General McClellan was as bitterly disliked by the politicians of the country as he was cordially loved by the troops under his command. Whatever may be said by the enemies of this unsuccessful general, it must be remembered that he took command of the Army of the Potomac when it was composed of a mass of undisciplined and poorly armed men. Yet after fighting some of the hardest battles of the war, he left it, in less than eighteen months, a splendid military organization, well prepared for the accomplishment of the great achievements afterward attained by General Grant. At the time McClellan took command of that army, the South was powerful in all the elements of successful warfare. It had much changed when General Grant took command. Long strain had greatly weakened and exhausted the forces and resources of the South. There had come a change from the former buoyant bravery of hope to the desperate bravery of doubtful success; and it may well be questioned whether any commander could have crushed the rebellion in the time during which General McClellan was at the head of the army. That he lacked aggressiveness must be admitted by his most ardent admirers. His greatness as a defensive general precluded this quality.[7]

[7] Page 199, last line, after the word "quality."

While reading over some of the appealing telegrams sent to the War Department by General McClellan, Lincoln said, "It seems to me that McClellan has been wandering around and has got lost. He's been hollering for help ever since he went south--wants somebody to come to his deliverance and get him out of the place he's got into. He reminds me of the story of a man out in Illinois, who, in company with a number of friends, visited the state penitentiary. They wandered all through the institution and saw everything, but just about the time to depart, this man became separated from his friends and couldn't find his way out. At last he came across a convict who was looking out from between the bars of his cell door; he hastily asked: 'Say! How do you get out of this place?'"

At one time when things seemed at a standstill, and no aggressive movements could be induced by the anxious Washington authorities, Mr. Lincoln went to General McClellan's headquarters to have a talk with him; but for some reason he was unable to get an audience with the general. He returned to the White House much disturbed at his failure to see the commander of the Union forces, and immediately sent for two other general officers, to have a consultation. On their arrival, he told them he must have some one to talk to about the situation; and as he had failed to see General McClellan, he had sent for them to get their views as to the possibility or probability of soon commencing active operations with the Army of the Potomac. He said he desired an expression of their opinion about the matter, for his was, that, if something were not done and done soon, the bottom would fall out of the whole thing; and he intended, if General McClellan did not want to use the Army, to "borrow" it from him, provided he could see how it could be made to do something; for, said he, "If McClellan can't fish, he ought to cut bait at a time like this."

Mr. Lincoln never regarded General McClellan with personal or political jealousy. He never feared him. He once profoundly trusted him, and to the very last he hoped to employ his genius and his popularity in the deliverance of their common country. His unfailing sagacity saw in him a rising general, who should be at once Democratic and patriotic,--the readiest possible instrument of harmonizing the North, unifying the sentiment of the army, crushing the rebellion, and restoring the Union. Having, then, no thought of imparting to the war any other object or result than the restoration of the Union, pure and simple, and this being likewise McClellan's view, the harmony and confidence that obtained between them were plants of easy growth. The rise of discord, the political intrigues, Democratic and Republican, which steadily aimed to separate these noble characters, who were as steadily, of their own impulses, tending toward each other,--these are matters of public history. Through it all, Mr. Lincoln earnestly endeavored to support McClellan in the field; and the diversion of men and the failure of supplies were never in any degree due to a desire upon his part to cripple the Democratic general. The success of this Democratic general was the one thing necessary to enable the President to hold in check the aggressive leaders of his own party, to restore the Union with the fewest sacrifices, and to complete the triumph of his Administration without dependence upon interests and factions which he seriously and constantly dreaded.

One of the most striking instances of Mr. Lincoln's great moral courage and self-reliance occurred just after the second battle of Bull Run. The loss of this battle caused great consternation, not only in Washington, but throughout the whole country. Everything was thrown into confusion. All the Cabinet officers, except Secretary Welles and Secretary Seward (the latter being absent at the time), signed a protest denouncing the conduct of McClellan and demanding his immediate dismissal from the service,--which protest, however, was not delivered to the President. The feeling of indignation was very general throughout the country against McClellan, and it was greatly intensified by exaggerated reports of his supposed misconduct. Notwithstanding this deplorable state of things, McClellan was appointed in command of the forces at Washington. At a Cabinet meeting held three days after this battle, the members first learned of this appointment. They were thunderstruck at the announcement, and great regret was expressed. Mr. Stanton, with some excitement, remarked that no such order had issued from the War Department. The President then said with great calmness, but with some degree of emphasis, "No, Mr. Secretary, the order was mine; and I will be responsible for it to the country." By way of explanation, he said something had to be done; but there did not appear to be any one to do it, and he therefore took the responsibility on himself. He then continued to say that McClellan had the confidence of the troops beyond any other officer, and could, under the circumstances, more speedily and effectively reorganize them and put them into fighting trim than any other general. "This is what is now wanted most; and these," said the President, "were my reasons for placing him in command."

Mr. Lincoln well knew the danger, and was apprehensive of losing perhaps all except one of his Cabinet members by this action; but he felt at the same time deeper apprehension of danger to the whole country if the army were not immediately reorganized and fitted for instant action. He knew he could replace his Cabinet from the patriotic men of his acquaintance, but he feared he could not replace the army in statu quo unless he took the risk of losing them. He fully realized, as he said, that nearly all the trouble had grown out of military jealousies, and that it was time for some one to assert and exercise power. He caused personal considerations to be sacrificed for the public good, and in doing so he subdued his own personal feelings in the spirit of unselfish patriotism.[8]

[8] Page 203, line 14, after the word "patriotism."

Whether the act proved his wisdom or not, the result certainly sustained and justified his course; the proceeding at least exemplified his firmness and determination in desperate emergencies. There is perhaps no act recorded in our history that demanded greater courage or more heroic treatment.

In a conversation with me shortly after this Mr. Lincoln said, "Well, I suppose our victory at Antietam will condone my offence in reappointing McClellan. If the battle had gone against us poor McClellan (and I too) would be in a bad row of stumps."

Had not the tide of success and victory turned in our favor about this time, there is little doubt that Mr. Lincoln would have been deposed and a military dictatorship erected upon the ruins of his administration. The victory at Antietam was, without doubt, the turning point for fame or for downfall in the career of Mr. Lincoln.

Between Francis P. Blair and Mr. Lincoln there existed from first to last a confidential relationship as close as that maintained by Mr. Lincoln with any other man. To Mr. Blair he almost habitually revealed himself upon delicate and grave subjects more fully than to any other. When he had conceived an important but difficult plan, he was almost certain, before giving it practical form, to try it by the touchstone of Mr. Blair's fertile and acute mind. Mr. Blair understood Mr. Lincoln's conception of the importance of McClellan to the President and to the country, and, like the President himself, he realized that McClellan's usefulness, unless destroyed by some disaster in the field, could be abridged only by some needless misunderstanding between the two.

He knew the stubborn spirit of the Democratic party from long experience in it and with it; and he early foresaw the tremendous influence which would inevitably be brought to bear on McClellan to separate him from Lincoln. It was because he foresaw this that he desired to place nearest to General McClellan in the field some one who, having the complete confidence of both, would form a connecting link which could not be broken.

To this end, about the time General Pleasanton was appointed brigadier-general, and assigned to report to General McClellan, Mr. Blair sought a conference with him and said: "You are going to McClellan. You will have confidential relations with him. I like him, and I want him to succeed; but no general can succeed without proper relations with the Administration. Say to him from me that Frank P. Blair, Jr., can be of great service to him. I shall have access to the Administration, and can do much to keep McClellan right. Say to him that he ought to ask for the assignment of Blair to him, and to make him his chief of staff. Now, Pleasanton, when you get down in Virginia, say this to Mac, and telegraph me the result."

It was then agreed that the communication should be in cipher. If favorable, "The weather is fair;" if otherwise, "The weather is fair, but portends a storm." Mr. Blair's message was given to McClellan, and General Pleasanton saw that it made an impression; but General McClellan faltered, subject, no doubt, to some of the influences that Mr. Blair had foreseen. After three days' deliberation, the "bad weather" was indicated to Mr. Blair.

In the campaign for Presidential honors in 1864, General McClellan, in his letter of acceptance, repudiated the obvious meaning of the Democratic platform framed for his candidacy. The Convention demanded "a cessation of hostilities with a view of an ultimate convention of States." To this McClellan responded: "So soon as it is clear, or even probable, that our present adversaries are ready for peace on the basis of the Union, we should exhaust all the resources of statesmanship ... to secure such a peace." In this he stood precisely with Lincoln. The sentiments of the representatives of the Democratic party in Convention assembled seemed to be: Peace first, and Union would inevitably follow. The sentiments of the respective chosen party standard-bearers were: Union first, that peace might follow.

There was at no time during the campaign a reasonable doubt of the election of Mr. Lincoln over General McClellan. Early in this campaign, on going into Mr. Lincoln's office one night, I found him in a more gleeful humor than usual. He was alone, and said, "I am glad you have come in. Lamon, do you know that 'we have met the enemy, and they are ourn?' I think the cabal of obstructionists 'am busted!' I feel certain that if I live, I am going to be re-elected. Whether I deserve to be or not, it is not for me to say; but on the score even of remunerative chances for speculative service, I now am inspired with the hope that our disturbed country further requires the valuable services of your humble servant. 'Jordan has been a hard road to travel,' but I feel now that, notwithstanding the enemies I have made and the faults I have committed, I'll be dumped on the right side of that stream. I hope, however, that I may never have another four years of such anxiety, tribulation, and abuse. My only ambition is and has been to put down the rebellion and restore peace; after which I want to resign my office, go abroad, take some rest, study foreign governments, see something of foreign life, and in my old age die in peace with the good will of all of God's creatures."

About two weeks before the election, Mr. Lincoln began to consider how to make the result most decisive. He again recurred to McClellan, and again consulted Mr. Blair. It seemed that neither of these sagacious men could entirely free himself from the thought that in one way or another General McClellan, with the Democratic party at his back, was somehow to contribute a mighty blow toward the suppression of the rebellion and the pacification of the country. With the respect which they both entertained for General McClellan's intelligence, with the faith they both had in his patriotism, they did not doubt that, seeing as they did the utter impossibility

154

of his own election to the Presidency, he would be willing, if the way were graciously opened to him, to save his party from the humiliation of a crushing defeat, to use his remaining power to restore the Union without further unnecessary bloodshed, and to tranquilize the country without more needless and heedless political strife.

Mr. Lincoln said to Mr. Blair: "I shall be re-elected. No one can doubt it. I do not doubt it, nor do you. It is patent to all. General McClellan must see it as plainly as we do. Why should he not act upon it, and help me to give peace to this distracted country? Would it not be a glorious thing for the Union cause and the country, now that my re-election is certain, for him to decline to run, favor my election, and make certain a speedy termination of this bloody war? Don't you believe that such a course upon his part would unify public partisan sentiment, and give a decisive and fatal blow to all opposition to the re-establishment of peace in the country? I think he is man enough and patriot enough to do it. Do you? You have been his friend and mine. Will you try this last appeal to General McClellan's patriotism?"

Mr. Blair heartily assented; and, as the result of their consultation, Mr. Lincoln wrote a most remarkable autograph letter to his rival, suggesting that he retire from the canvass and allow Mr. Lincoln's election, then visibly impending, to be as nearly unanimous as might be. The compensations to General McClellan and his party for the timely relinquishment of a mere shadow were to be McClellan's immediate elevation to be General of the Army, the appointment of his father-in-law, Marcy, to be major-general, and the very substantial recognition of the Democracy which would necessarily have followed these arrangements.

This letter containing these distinct propositions was placed in Mr. Blair's hands, and by him delivered to General McClellan.[9] It was the attempted stroke of a master. Had it succeeded,--had the propositions contained in the letter been accepted,--Mr. Lincoln might have lived to prevent the follies and the crimes of reconstruction, and to bless his country with an era of peace and good-will,--thus preventing those long years of ferocious political contention over the results of the war which followed its conclusion and his murder.

[9] Page 208, line 3, after the word "McClellan."

WASHINGTON, April 13, 1888.

MY DEAR MARSHAL LAMON,--I received the proof sheet of your article enclosed in your note of the 8th. I have read it very carefully and I find the facts as stated are correct.

Mr. F. P. Blair, Senior, told me the incident of conveying in person President Lincoln's letter to McClellan.

I liked McClellan, but I have always believed he was politically slaughtered in the house of his alleged friends.

Yours truly, A. PLEASONTON.

What the great soldier might have done, if left alone to determine for himself the proper course of action in the premises, can never be known.

The letter was submitted by General McClellan to some of his party friends in New York, and its wise and statesmanlike propositions were declined. On the morning of the election he resigned his commission. His party was routed, and upon the death of Mr. Lincoln was opened the new Iliad of partisan conflict and reconstruction woes.

Mr. Lincoln fearlessly struck out and boldly pursued, in situations the most exacting, capital plans, of which none knew except those who might be absolutely necessary to their execution. If he failed in the patriotic objects which he proposed to accomplish by coalition with McClellan, and was ultimately compelled to achieve them by less Napoleonic and more tedious methods, the splendid conception and the daring attempt were his alone, and prove him one of the most masterful politicians of this or any recent age. The division of the Roman world between the members of the Triumvirate was not comparable to this proposal of his, because the Roman was a smaller world than the American, and it was partitioned among three, while this was only to be halved.

More than a quarter of a century has passed, and still the press teems with inquiries concerning the relations between Lincoln and McClellan, with accusation and defense by the literary partisans of each. Had the general seen fit to respond to the magnanimous tender of the President, their names would have been equally sacred in every American household, and their fame would have been united, like their parties and their country, by an act of patriotic statesmanship unparalleled in the history of this world.

CHAPTER XIV.

HIS MAGNANIMITY.

Mr. Lincoln regarded all public offices within his gift as a sacred trust, to be administered solely for the people, and as in no sense a fund upon which he could draw for the payment of private accounts. He was exempt from the frailties common to most men, and he cast aside the remembrance of all provocations for which he had cause to nourish resentment. Here is a notable instance: A rather distinguished man had been for years a respected acquaintance; his son, who was in the army, was convicted of a grave offence, the penalty of which might have been death. Lincoln, at the solicitation of the father, pardoned the son. Time passed on until the political campaign of 1864, when a secret military organization was formed in the

State of Illinois to oppose the re-election of Lincoln, and that father was at the head of this secret organization. Some time after the election, the filling of an important bureau office in the Treasury Department was under advisement. Among the applicants was an old acquaintance of Mr. Lincoln, who was strongly recommended by his friends. After a pause, Mr. Lincoln thoughtfully said, "Well, gentlemen, whatever you may think, I never thought Mr. ---- had any more than an average amount of ability when we were young men together,--I really didn't;" and then, after a short silence, he added: "But this is a matter of opinion, and I suppose he thought just the same about me; he had reason to, and--here I am! I guess we shall have to give him some good place, but not this one. This position requires a man of peculiar ability to fill it. I have been thinking seriously of giving it to a man who does not like me very well, and who sought to defeat my renomination. I can't afford to take notice of and punish every person who has seen fit to oppose my election. We want a competent man for this place. I know of no one who could perform the duties of this most responsible office better than ----," calling him by name. And this ingrate father got the appointment!

At another time there was an interview at the White House between a prominent politician of New York and Mr. Lincoln, in reference to the removal of an office-holder in New York. Every reason that could be thought of was urged in favor of the removal, and finally it was urged that this office-holder abused Mr. Lincoln personally. Mr. Lincoln at last got out of patience, and ended the interview as follows: "You cannot think ---- to be half as mean to me as I know him to be; but I cannot run this thing upon the theory that every office-holder must think I am the greatest man in the nation, and I will not." The man named, notwithstanding his meanness to Mr. Lincoln, remained in office as long as Mr. Lincoln was President.

So much of Mr. Lincoln's time was taken up with questions of office-seeking and office-holding, when he felt every moment should be devoted to plans to avert the perils then threatening the country, that he once compared himself to "a man so busy in letting rooms in one end of his house that he cannot stop to put out the fire that is burning the other."

Mr. Lincoln was an ambitious man, but he desired power less for the sake of prestige or authority than for the opportunities it presented of being useful and beneficent in its exercise. Eagerly as he sought the approval of his fellow-citizens where this could be attained without the sacrifice of principle, he was always generous in according to others whatever would lead to public approval. Immediately after the battle of Gettysburg, Mr. Lincoln sat down and wrote a peremptory order to General Meade to intercept Lee in his retreat, give him battle, and by this bold stroke crush the rebel army and end the rebellion. The order was accompanied by a friendly note, in which the great patriot said to Meade: "The order I inclose is not of record. If you succeed, you need not publish the order. If you fail, publish it. Then if you succeed, you will have all the credit of the movement. If not, I'll take the responsibility."

The manifestation of popular admiration and esteem as the people's choice for the highest position within their gift, Mr. Lincoln most highly valued, while his self-reliance and his amour propre led him at times to look upon favors bestowed upon him as a matter of personal right, as a consideration due to himself individually. With all this, his love of country was his paramount incentive. There was no period in the progress of the war at which he would not willingly have laid down his life, if by so doing he could have averted further bloodshed, and remanded his fellow-countrymen to the enjoyment of a restored tranquillity and renewed brotherhood. One instance in which this sentiment led him to propose an extraordinary act of self-immolation is deserving of special mention.

Mr. Lincoln ardently desired, on the return of peace, to exercise his functions as Chief Magistrate of a reunited country. This, with the reconstruction of the general government, was the darling aspiration of his heart, the dearest heritage which the advent of peace could bestow. But he subjected this ambition to the promptings of a Roman patriotism, and proposed upon certain conditions a frank, full, and honest renunciation of all claims to the Presidency for a second term; and in declining, under any circumstances, to be a candidate for re-election, he would cordially throw his entire influence, in so far as he could control it, in behalf of Horatio Seymour, then governor of New York, for President. The conditions were substantially as follows: Governor Seymour was to withdraw his opposition to the draft, use his authority and influence as governor in putting down the riots in New York, and co-operate in all reasonable ways with the Administration in the suppression of the Southern rebellion. This proposition was to be made through Mr. Thurlow Weed.

It so happened that at this time Mr. Weed was dissatisfied with the President for something he had either done or omitted to do, and had on several occasions refused to come to Washington when his presence was earnestly desired there. He must now be seen and advised with; he must personally effect the negotiation, for he could accomplish it more successfully than any other man. How to induce him to come to Washington was the question to be solved. "The tinkling of Mr. Seward's little bell" had struck terror to the souls of evil-doers in the North, and all his dispatches over the wires were narrowly watched. It was inexpedient for him to use telegraphic facilities of communication except upon the most commonplace subjects, since everything emanating from him was eagerly scanned and devoured by the quid nuncs throughout the country. A special messenger was therefore decided on, for affairs were now in a precarious condition, and daily, hourly growing worse, and time was important. The messenger started immediately for New York, but was recalled before reaching the train. He was thereupon directed to telegraph in his own name to Mr. Weed, and that gentleman arrived in Washington by the next succeeding train. After a lengthy interview with the President and Mr. Seward, Mr. Weed telegraphed to Governor Seymour requesting him to come to Washington on business of urgent importance. This the governor declined to do, adding, in his reply, that the distance to and from Washington and Albany was precisely the same, and that if they wanted to confer with him, to come to Albany, where he would be glad to meet them. Mr. Weed, upon this, left for that city, and after making a very brief stay there, returned to Washington and reported "Proposition declined."

This answer was not expected by Mr. Lincoln, especially in time of civil war, and from the governor of the great and influential State of New York; and it was with sincere and manifest chagrin that the President saw himself deterred from making the magnanimous self-sacrifice proposed.

Nothing that affected the interests of the government escaped Mr. Lincoln's vigilant thought and careful consideration. I recollect that on one occasion, just after the greenback currency got under full headway of circulation, I was in his office when the conversation turned on the condition of our finances, and on the greenback as a representative of money. He was in high spirits that day, and seemed to feel happier than I had seen him for a long time. I casually asked him if he knew how our currency was made.

"Yes," said he; "I think it is about--as the lawyers would say--in the following manner, to wit: the engraver strikes off the sheets, passes them over to the Register of the currency, who places his earmarks upon them, signs them, hands them over to Father Spinner, who then places his wonderful signature at the bottom, and turns them over to Mr. Chase, who, as Secretary of the United States Treasury, issues them to the public as money,--and may the good Lord help any fellow that doesn't take all he can honestly get of them!" Taking from his pocket a five dollar greenback, with a twinkle of his eye, he said: "Look at Spinner's signature! Was there ever anything like it on earth? Yet it is unmistakable; no one will ever be able to counterfeit it!"[J]

"But," I said, "you certainly don't suppose that Spinner actually wrote his name on that bill, do you?"

"Certainly I do; why not?"

I then asked, "How much of this currency have we afloat?"

He remained thoughtful for a moment, and then stated the amount.

I continued: "How many times do you think a man can write a signature like Spinner's in the course of twenty-four hours?"

The beam of hilarity left his countenance at once. He put the greenback into his vest pocket, and walked the floor; after awhile he stopped, heaved a long breath and said, "This thing frightens me!" He then rang for a messenger, and told him to ask the Secretary of the Treasury to please come over to see him. Mr. Chase soon put in an appearance. Mr. Lincoln stated the cause of his alarm, and asked Mr. Chase to explain in detail the modus operandi, the system of checks in his office, etc., and a lengthy discussion followed,--Lincoln contending that there were not sufficient checks to afford any degree of safety in the money-making department, and Mr. Chase insisting that all the guards for protection were afforded that he could devise. "In the nature of things," he said, "somebody must be trusted in this emergency. You have entrusted me, and Mr. Spinner is entrusted with untold millions, and we have to trust our subordinates." Words waxed warmer than I had ever known them to do between these distinguished gentlemen, when Mr. Lincoln feelingly apologized by saying,--

"Don't think that I am doubting or could doubt your integrity, or that of Mr. Spinner; nor am I finding fault with either of you; but it strikes me that this thing is all wrong, and dangerous. I and the country know you and Mr. Spinner, but we don't know your subordinates, who are great factors in making this money, and have the power to bankrupt the government in an hour. Yet there seems to be no protection against a duplicate issue of every bill struck, and I can see no way of detecting duplicity until we come to redeem the currency; and even then, the duplicate cannot be told from the original."

The result of this conversation was, that Lincoln became so impressed with danger from this source that he called the attention of Congress to the matter, and a joint committee was appointed. Senator Sprague of Rhode Island was its chairman; but the result of the investigation, like many others during the war, was never made public to my knowledge. Considering the crippled financial condition of our country, and the importance of first-class credit abroad during our war, as little publicity on the subject as possible was doubtless the best for us politically.

Apropos of greenbacks, Don Piatt gave a description in the "North American Review," a few years ago, of the first proposition to Mr. Lincoln to issue interest-bearing notes as currency, which was as follows:--

"Amasa Walker, a distinguished financier of New England, suggested that notes issued directly from the government to the people, as currency, should bear interest. This for the purpose, not only of making the notes popular, but for the purpose of preventing inflation, by inducing people to hoard the notes as an investment when the demands of trade would fail to call them into circulation as a currency.

"This idea struck David Taylor, of Ohio, with such force that he sought Mr. Lincoln and urged him to put the project into immediate execution. The President listened patiently, and at the end said, 'That is a good idea, Taylor; but you must go to Chase. He is running that end of the machine, and has time to consider your proposition.' Taylor sought the Secretary of the Treasury, and laid before him Amasa Walker's plan. Chase heard him through in a cold, unpleasant manner, and then said: 'That is all very well, Mr. Taylor; but there is one little obstacle in the way that makes the plan impracticable, and that is the Constitution.' Saying this, he turned to his desk, as if dismissing both Mr. Taylor and his proposition at the same moment.

"The poor enthusiast felt rebuked and humiliated. He returned to the President, however, and reported his defeat. Mr. Lincoln looked at the would-be financier with the expression at times so peculiar to his homely face, that left one in doubt whether he was jesting or in earnest. 'Taylor!' he exclaimed, 'go back to Chase and tell him not to bother himself about the Constitution. Say that I have that sacred instrument here at the White House, and I am guarding it with great care.' Taylor demurred to this, on the ground that Mr. Chase showed by his manner that he knew all about it, and didn't wish to be bored by any suggestion. 'We'll see about that,' said the President, and taking a card from the table he wrote upon it, 'The Secretary of the Treasury will please consider Mr. Taylor's proposition. We must have money, and I think this a good way to get it.--A. LINCOLN.'

"Armed with this, the real father of the greenbacks again sought the Secretary. He was received more politely than before, but was cut short in his advocacy of the measure by a proposition for both of them to see the President. They did so, and Mr. Chase made a long and elaborate constitutional argument against the proposed measure.

"'Chase,' said Mr. Lincoln, after the Secretary had concluded, 'down in Illinois I was held to be a pretty good lawyer, and I believe I could answer every point you have made; but I don't feel called upon to do it.... These rebels are violating the Constitution to destroy the Union; I will violate the Constitution, if necessary, to save the Union: and I suspect, Chase, that our Constitution is going to have a rough time of it before we get done with this row. Now, what I want to know is, whether, Constitution aside, this project of issuing interest-bearing notes is a good one?'

164

"'I must say,' responded Mr. Chase, 'that, with the exception you make, it is not only a good one, but the only one open to us to raise money. If you say so, I will do my best to put it into immediate and practical operation, and you will never hear from me any opposition on this subject.'"[10]

[10] Page 219, last line, after the word "subject."

At a cabinet meeting, the advisability of putting a motto on greenbacks similar to the "In God We Trust" on the silver coins was discussed and the President was asked what his view was. He replied, "if you are going to put a motto on the greenback, I would suggest that of Peter and John: 'Silver and gold we have not, but what we have we'll give you.'"

Mr. Lincoln acquired the name of "honest Abe Lincoln" by a kind of honesty much higher than that which restrains a man from the appropriation of his neighbor's goods. He did not feel at liberty to take every case that was offered him. He was once overheard saying to a man who was consulting him and earnestly urging his legal rights, "Yes, I can gain your suit. I can set a neighborhood at loggerheads. I can distress a widowed mother and six fatherless children, and get for you six hundred dollars, to which, for all I can see, she has as good a right as you have. But I will not do so. There are some legal rights which are moral wrongs."

Mr. Lincoln at no time in his life could tolerate anything like persecution; his whole nature appeared to rebel against any appearance of such a thing, and he never failed to act in the promptest manner when any such case was brought to his attention. One of the most celebrated cases ever tried by any court-martial during the war was that of Franklin W. Smith and his brother, charged with defrauding the government. These men bore a high character for integrity. At this time, however, courts-martial were seldom invoked for any other purpose than to convict the accused, regardless of the facts in the case, and the Smiths shared the usual fate of persons whose charges were submitted to such an arbitrament. They had been kept in prison, their papers seized, their business destroyed, and their reputation ruined, all which was followed by a conviction. After the judgment of the court, the matter was submitted to the President for his approval. The case was such a remarkable one, and was regarded as so monstrous in its unjust and unwarrantable conclusion, that Mr. Lincoln, after a full and careful investigation of it, annulled the whole proceeding. It is very remarkable that the record of the President's decision could never be found afterward in the Navy Department. No exact copy can be obtained of it. Some one in the office, however, familiar with the tenor and effect of it, furnished its wording as nearly as possible. The following embraces the sentiment, if not the exact words, of that remarkable document:--

"WHEREAS, Franklin W. Smith had transactions with the Navy Department to the amount of a million and a quarter of dollars; and Whereas, he had a chance to steal at least a quarter of a million and was only charged with stealing twenty-two hundred dollars, and the question now is about his stealing one hundred, I don't believe he stole anything at all. Therefore, the record and the findings are disapproved, declared null and void, and the defendants are fully discharged."

In 1862 Senator Sherman had prepared a very elaborate speech in which he devoted a good portion of it to prove that Mr. Lincoln was a failure and unless something was soon done by Congress, the war would be a failure. Someone told Mr. Lincoln that Senator Sherman intended to make such a speech. Lincoln said: "Well Sherman is a patriot and a statesman and is thoroughly for the Union; perhaps his opinion of me may be just. It may do good. I would not have him change a word." Lincoln's remarks that night were repeated to Sherman and they made such an impression on him that he omitted from his speech the criticism on Lincoln.

Colonel J. W. Forney relates a characteristic incident of Mr. Lincoln's generosity to an adversary. He says that one afternoon in February or March of 1865, he was startled by a visit from his old friend Washington McLean of the Cincinnati "Inquirer." "I have called," Mr. McLean said, "to ask you to do me a favor I shall never forget, and you must do it. I will not take no for an answer. You, and you alone can serve me."

"Well, old friend," said Colonel Forney, "you know I will serve you if I can; what is it?" "Now don't be alarmed when I tell you that Roger A. Pryor is in Fort Lafayette, having been captured within our lines, and that I want you to get him out."

"Roger A. Pryor, of Petersburg; Roger A. Pryor, who fired on Sumter; Roger A. Prior, the hot-spur of Congress?"

"Yes, and your old coadjutor of the Washington Union when you were both Democrats together. He went into the Rebellion, is now a prisoner, and I appeal to you to go with me to the President and ask his release." As there was no denying his impetuous friend, Colonel Forney got into his carriage and they were soon at the White House. Mr. McLean was introduced and it was soon found that Mr. Lincoln knew all about him and his paper. He told his story, which was patiently heard. Colonel Forney followed with a statement of his former relations with Mr. Pryor, and said that he thought an act of liberality to such a man, and on a request from a frank political opponent like Washington McLean would be worthy of the head of a great nation.

"Let me see," said Mr. Lincoln, as he fixed his spectacles and turned to a little drawer in the desk behind him, "I think I have a memorandum here that refers to some good thing done by General Pryor to a party of our Pennsylvania boys who were taken prisoners in an attack upon the Petersburg fortifications." And with that he took out from a small package a statement signed by the men who had enjoyed the hospitality of General Pryor on the occasion referred to.

He had, it appears, given them food from his larder at a time when his own family were in a most desperate condition for provisions. "The man who can do such kindness to an enemy," said the President, "cannot be cruel and revengeful;" then he wrote some lines on a card which he handed to Mr. McLean with the remark: "I think that will do; at any rate it is all that I can give you," and they took their leave. Going down stairs they looked with amazement at the writing on the card, which read thus: "To Colonel Burke, Commanding at Fort Lafayette, New York. Please release General Roger A. Pryor, who will report to Colonel Forney on Capitol Hill. A. Lincoln." "Report to Colonel Forney!" Colonel Forney who was "bubbling over with resentment against the Southern leaders who had hindered his advancement when Buchanan was elected President." But there was no changing the order, so Mr. McLean dashed off in the next train to New York, the happiest Democrat in the United States, and two days after he walked into Colonel Forney's office with the "prisoner." General Pryor took the upper rooms of Colonel Forney's lodgings and was his guest for more than a week, "during which time he was visited by all the chivalry, male and female, of the vicinage." The President enjoyed the fact that Colonel Forney had such good company, and Thaddeus Stephens, his neighbor, habitually accosted him in the morning with the grim salute: "How's your Democratic friend and brother this morning?" Colonel Forney had to admit that a more courteous gentleman he had never met than General Pryor, and did him the justice to say that he expressed the most fervent gratitude to Mr. Lincoln for his kindness.

CHAPTER XV.

CABINET COUNSELS.

In November, 1861, the public mind was wildly agitated by an episode of the war, which, although without military significance, at one time threatened to predetermine the final issue of the contest in favor of the independence of the Southern States, by the accession of a powerful ally and auxiliary to their cause. It not only seriously imperilled our existing relations of peace and amity with a foreign power, but came near converting its declared neutrality into an active sympathy and co-operation with the Confederacy. This incident, commonly known as the "Trent" affair, originated in the unauthorized and illegal arrest of the Confederate Commissioners, Messrs. Mason and Slidell, with their secretaries, on board a British mail packet, by Capt. Charles Wilkes of the United States Navy, and their forcible transfer from the protection of the British flag to the frigate "San Jacinto," under Wilkes's command.

This arbitrary proceeding, wholly unauthorized by the government and in flagrant violation of every principle of public law, was received with a universal outburst of joy and exultation throughout the entire country. The Confederates saw in this wanton aggression and outrage the realization of their cherished hopes of an imbroglio--possibly of a war--between England and the United States. The satisfaction evinced in the Northern States seemed less comprehensible, as the first outgoing blockade-runner could easily have supplied substitutes for the captured and imprisoned Commissioners. Yet for this act, which was acclaimed and sanctioned by a verdict of popular approval, indorsed by a special resolution of thanks in the National Legislature, Captain Wilkes was commended and congratulated in a letter from the chief of his Department. In fact, every one seemed to vie with every one else in weaving a civic chaplet to the commander of the "San Jacinto" for his lawless deed.

Amidst the wild excitement created by this international interlude, the President alone maintained an imperturbable calmness and composure. From the very first moment he regarded the capture of the Commissioners as unwise and inexpedient. He was heard to say repeatedly that it would lead to dangerous complications with England. "Unfortunately," said he, "we have played into the hands of that wily power, and placed in their grasp a whip with which to scourge us." He went on to say further that the "Trent" affair had occurred at the most inopportune and critical period of the war, and would greatly tend to its prolongation by creating a genuine bond of sympathy between England and the insurgent States.

When interrogated, on one occasion, as to whether it was not a great humiliation to him to surrender the captured Commissioners on the peremptory demand of John Bull, Mr. Lincoln replied, "Yes, it was the bitterest pill I have ever swallowed. There is, however, this counterbalancing consideration, that England's triumph will not have a long tenure of life. After our war is over, I trust and believe successfully to ourselves, we shall be powerful enough to call her to an account and settlement for the embarrassment and damage she has inflicted upon us in our hour of trouble; and this reminds me of a story which I think aptly illustrates the condition of things existing between their government and ours." He then related the following anecdote:

A sick man in Illinois, the hope of whose recovery was far from encouraging, was admonished by his friends present that as probably he had not many hours to live he should bear malice to none, and before closing his earthly account should make peace with all his enemies. Turning his face to the wall and drawing a long sigh, the invalid was lost for a few moments in deep reflection. Giving utterance to a deep groan as he mentally enumerated the long catalogue of enmities incurred, which would render the exertion of peace-making a somewhat prolonged one, he admitted in a feeble voice that he undoubtedly believed this to be the best course, and added: "The man whom I hate most cordially of all is Bill Johnson, and so I guess I'll begin with him." Johnson was summoned, and at once repaired to the bedside of his repentant friend. The latter extended to him his hand, saying with a meekness that would have done honor to Moses, that he wanted to die at peace with all the world, and to bury all his past enmity. Bill, who was much inclined to the melting mood, here burst into tears, making free use of his bandanna, and warmly returning the pressure of the dying man's hand, solemnly and impressively assured him of his forgiveness. As the now reconciled friends were about to separate, in the expectation of never again seeing each other on earth, "Stop," exclaimed the penitent invalid to his departing visitor, who had now reached the door; "the account is now square between us, Bill Johnson; but, see here, if I should happen to get well, that old grudge stands!"

In December, about one month after the arrest of the Confederate Commissioners, when Mr. Lincoln and his Cabinet were in a state of alarm, fearing a war with England, Mr. Chase one day came to the President and told him that Mr. Stanton, who had been attorney-general under Buchanan, had talked with him on the subject of this trouble with Great Britain, and had expressed the opinion that the action of the American government in arresting Mason and Slidell was legal and could be sustained by international law. The President told Mr. Chase that Stanton did not like him, and had treated him rudely on one occasion; but that if Mr. Chase thought Stanton would meet him, he would be glad to have him do so and give his views on the subject. In an hour Mr. Chase had Stanton in Mr. Lincoln's presence. Mr. Lincoln expressed his gratification at hearing of Mr. Stanton's views, and asked him to repeat them. When Mr. Stanton had finished the discussion of the case, and of the laws bearing thereon, Mr. Lincoln expressed his thanks, and asked Stanton to put his opinion in writing, which he promised to do by ten o'clock the next morning. The opinion was brought at the appointed time. Mr. Lincoln read it and filed it, and then said: "Mr. Stanton, this is a time of war, and you are as much interested in sustaining the government as myself or any other man. This is no time to consider mere party issues. The life of the nation is in danger. I need the best counsellors around me. I have every confidence in your judgment, and have concluded to ask you to become one of my counsellors. The office of the Secretary of War will be vacant, and I want you to accept the position. Will you do it?"

Stanton was amazed, and said: "Why, Mr. President, you take me by surprise! This is an embarrassing question, but if you will give me a day or two to consider, I will give you an answer." Two days later he called on the President and signified his intention to accept. On the 15th day of January, 1862, the portfolio of Secretary of War was placed in his hands.[K]

[K] DENVER, COL., May 23, 1885.

Hon. Wm. A. Wheeler, Malone, N. Y.

MY DEAR SIR,--A few days since I had the pleasure of reading your "Recollections of Lincoln" from the Malone (N. Y.) "Palladium," in which you say: "At the extra session of Congress in July, 1861, a law was passed authorizing the appointment of additional paymasters for the Army;" that the President assented to your request that your life-long friend, Major Sabin, should be one of the appointees; that, in September following, Mr. Lincoln wrote you saying he had sent the appointment of Mr. Sabin to the Secretary of War, who would notify him to appear for muster into the Service. October passed, and no notice came. Then, you say, a letter written to "Secretary Stanton" failed to bring a response; that the latter part of November you went to Washington to attend the regular session of Congress, taking Mr. Sabin with you. You then say: "The day after my arrival I waited upon Secretary Stanton," etc.; you then detail the conversation had with Mr. Lincoln, and the fact of his making a somewhat imperative order to the Secretary to make the appointment "at once." You say, "I called on Mr. Stanton the next morning, who on its [the letter's or order's] presentation was simply furious." And after this you speak of what was said and done by "Mr. Stanton, the Secretary of War."

Allow me, my dear sir, to assure you that I now entertain, and always have entertained, for you the most profound respect, and to express my sincere regret that you were not President instead of Vice-President of the United States. I therefore venture to hope that you will pardon me for saying that I am unable to reconcile the statements purporting to be made by you, alluded to above, with the historical fact that Mr. Stanton was not appointed Secretary of War until in January the year following,--namely, 1862. It occurs to me that there must be a mistake made in your paper, either of dates or of the name of the Secretary of War. I am certain this irreconcilable statement was not made by you as was the blunder made by Sir Walter Scott in his "Ivanhoe" (chap. i.). "The date of this story," as he says, "refers to a period towards the end of the reign of Richard I." Richard died in 1199; nevertheless, Sir Walter makes the disguised Wamba style himself "a poor brother of the Order of St. Francis," although the Order of St. Francis was not founded until 1210, and of course the saintship of the founder had still a later date.

If my recollection serves me correctly, Mr. Stanton, whose memory is now cherished by the great mass of the Republican party, at the dates you speak of and refer to was regarded as a Bourbon of the strictest sect. Up to the time of the capture of the "Trent," with Mason and Slidell aboard, on the 8th of November, 1861, if Mr. Stanton had conceived any "change of heart" and cessation of hostility to the Administration, it never was publicly manifested. It was something over a month after this capture that he was consulted by Mr. Lincoln, at the suggestion of Secretary Chase, as an international lawyer concerning the legality of the capture and arrest of Messrs. Mason and Slidell, which was the first interview that was had between Mr. Lincoln and Mr. Stanton since the commencement of the Administration. This interview led to Mr. Stanton's appointment as Secretary of War. Mr. Lincoln had occasion for regret about the "Trent" capture, but never for the capture of Mr. Stanton.

The immortal Shakespeare, like yourself and others, sometimes got his dates confused; for instance, in his "Coriolanus," he says of C. Marcius, "Thou wast a soldier even to Cato's will," when in fact Marcius Coriolanus was banished from Rome and died over two hundred years before Cato was born. Again, his reference in the same play, of Marcius sitting in state like Alexander: the latter was not born for a hundred and fifty years after Coriolanus's death. He also says in "Julius Caesar," "The clock strikes three," when in truth and in fact there were no striking clocks until more than eight hundred years after the death of Caesar. Another inaccuracy is to be found in "King Lear" in regard to spectacles. Spectacles were not worn until the thirteenth century. And still another in this immortal writer's statements in his play of "Macbeth," where he speaks of cannon: cannon were not invented until 1346, and Macbeth was killed in 1054.

You will pardon me these citations, for they are made in a spirit of playful illustration, to show how great minds often become confused about dates.

"What you have said I have considered; what you have to say I will with patience wait to hear."

I read your "Recollections of Lincoln" with great interest, as I do everything I see written about that most wonderful, interesting, and unique of all of our public men. I sincerely hope you will receive this in the same kindly spirit that it is written, prompted as it is by a curiosity to know how this variance about Mr. Stanton's official status during the first year of Mr. Lincoln's Administration can be reconciled. I will regard it as an esteemed favor if you will drop me a line explaining it.

Your interesting and graphic description of Mr. Lincoln's pardon of the soldier convicted and condemned for sleeping at his post interested me very much. I have a curiosity to know whether this soldier's name was not William Scott? If Scott was his name, I have a reason to believe he was the person whom Francis De Haes Janvier immortalized in verse.

I have the honor to be, very sincerely,

Your humble servant, WARD H. LAMON.

* * * * *

MALONE, N. Y., June 2, 1885.

Ward H. Lamon, Denver, Col.

MY DEAR SIR,--I thank you most sincerely for your letter of the 23d ultimo, and for the friendly feeling you evince for me.

I am simply mortified at my gross blunder, and can only plead in mitigation the lapse of more than twenty years since the affairs alluded to transpired, in which time, aside from having performed a large amount of hard public and private work, I have experienced an amount of trouble exceptional to ordinary men, having buried every one near to me,--father, mother, brothers, and sisters. I have no one left of nearer kin to me than cousins, and no one to care for my house except servants. For the last three years I have been an invalid, confined to my house and for a considerable portion of the time to my bed: what wonder that "the warder of the brain" should be sometimes at fault! The mistake must be one of time, for the actors in the transaction are too vividly impressed upon my memory ever to be forgotten until that faculty is wholly dethroned.

I may be mistaken in the fact that Sabin accompanied me when I went on for the regular session in December, 1861; but so sure was I of it that before your letter I would have sworn to it. You have furnished me with a needed caution. It is unpleasant to find out that years are telling upon us, but it is

175

healthful nevertheless. And so I may be mistaken as to the time intervening between the successive stages of the appointment. Sabin is somewhere in the West, and I will endeavor to find his whereabouts and get his statement of the facts. Brevet Brig.-Genl. Chauncey McKeever, now Assistant Adjutant-General of the Army, was at the time in Stanton's office in a confidential capacity, and I think will remember the transaction.

I do not remember the name of the pardoned soldier. One of Kellogg's sons lives in the southern part of the State; I will endeavor to get the name, and if successful will write you.

Now, my dear sir, mortified as I am, I feel almost compensated in having drawn from you such an admirable collection of anachronisms of famous literary men of the world. I am greatly interested in it, and shall take the liberty of showing it to my literary friends. In your readings have you ever encountered the "Deathless City," a beautiful poem written by Elizabeth A. Allen? I never saw but this single production from her pen. Who was or is she, and did she write other things?

My memories of Mr. Lincoln are a source of great pleasure to me. Many of them recall illustrations just a little "off color."

If you ever come east, I wish you would come across northern New York and drop in upon me. I should greatly delight to live over the days of the war with you.

Again thanking you for your letter, and fully reciprocating your good-will, I am

Very cordially yours, WM. A. WHEELER.

The appointment of Mr. Stanton in Mr. Lincoln's Cabinet was a great surprise to the country. Those who were acquainted with the relations existing between these two men when they were both practising lawyers were not only astonished at this appointment, but were apprehensive that there could not possibly be harmony of action and co-operation between them. There were perhaps seldom, if ever, two really great men who were as unlike in all respects as Mr. Lincoln and Mr. Stanton. They were dissimilar in their habits of life, disposition, taste, in fact in every particular of the general make-up of man. But Mr. Lincoln fully appreciated Mr. Stanton's great ability, both as a lawyer and as a Cabinet counsellor under Mr. Buchanan. The President needed the ablest counsel he could obtain, and allowed no personal consideration to influence him in selecting the right man for the service.

In order to make the history of this appointment complete in its personal element, it will be necessary to go back to the year 1858, when Abraham Lincoln was practising law in Springfield, Illinois, and Edwin M. Stanton was at the head of his profession in Cincinnati. The celebrated McCormick Reaper and Mower case was before the United States Court in Cincinnati. Mr. Stanton had been retained as counsel-in-chief on one side of the case, and to be associated with him were T. D. Lincoln of Cincinnati, and Abraham Lincoln of Illinois. When Mr. Lincoln arrived in Cincinnati to attend the trial, he called upon Mr. Stanton, who treated him in so impolite and rude a manner that he went to his client and informed him that he should have to withdraw as his counsel in the case and stated his reasons therefor. Mr. Lincoln was entreated to remain in the case, and Mr. Stanton was seen and was talked to about the matter. Mr. Lincoln happened to be in a room adjoining where this conversation occurred, and overheard Mr. Stanton say that he would not associate with such a d----, gawky, long-armed ape as that; if he could not have a man who was a gentleman in appearance associated with him in the case, he would himself abandon it. When the client returned, Mr. Lincoln refunded to him the five-hundred dollar retainer fee, peremptorily declining to keep it. He then returned to Urbana, Illinois, where court was in session, and, to explain his unexpected return, related the fact and his mortification to his associate members of the bar. After this event, Mr. Lincoln never met Mr. Stanton until the "Trent" affair brought them together; yet it is certain that Mr. Lincoln never forgot the gratuitous insult then cast upon him.

To this day there is a settled belief that at this time the Administration councils manifested a lack of hearty co-operation and unity of purpose and sentiment. This is a mistake, for throughout Mr. Lincoln's Administration as much harmony as could reasonably be expected existed between him and his Cabinet ministers. Differences arose between them at times in regard to minor considerations of policy, but never to the extent that the differences were not eventually harmonized, compromised, or accommodated. To be sure, many things occurred during the fearful war-struggle about which he and his Cabinet differed in their estimates and conclusions, and Mr. Lincoln thereby was often disappointed and grieved. As one instance of his disappointment, may be mentioned his abandonment of a message to Congress in deference to the opinion and counsel of his advisers. This occurred directly after his return from the conference he and Mr. Seward had with Messrs. Stephens, Campbell, and Hunter at City Point on the James River.

Notwithstanding his hatred of the institution of slavery, Mr. Lincoln believed that the holder of slaves had a right of property in them which the government had no right, legally or morally, to interfere with in the States unless forced thereto by the necessities of war. He gladly approved the action of Congress in providing for the payment of compensation for the slaves liberated in the District of Columbia. The message above referred to recommended an appropriation of three hundred million dollars to be apportioned among the several slave States, in proportion to slave population, as compensation to the owners of liberated slaves in the insurgent States, with the condition that the insurgents should lay down their arms, disband their troops, and return and renew their allegiance to the United States government. Mr. Seward at this time was not present, being confined to bed by injuries he had received by being thrown from his carriage. All the other members of the Cabinet were present, every one of whom opposed the message. Lincoln then asked: "How long will this war last?" No reply came. He then answered his own question, saying: "It will doubtless last one hundred days longer; we are now spending three million dollars a day, which rate will aggregate the amount I propose to appropriate in order to put an end to this terrible blood-shedding." Then with a deep sigh he said, "Since you are all opposed to me I will not send this message," and turning round he placed the paper in his drawer. It is rather a curious coincidence that the war did last just about a hundred days after Lincoln's remarkable interview with his Cabinet on this subject.

There is also a prevailing opinion that the Secretary of War (Stanton) at times arbitrarily refused to obey or carry out Mr. Lincoln's orders. This is also not true. This opinion is largely based upon Mr. Stanton's refusal of permits to persons desirous of going through the lines into insurgent districts. The persons who were disobliged in this respect were very severe in their comments on Mr. Stanton's course, which they considered harsh, disobliging, and sometimes cruel. On refusal of Mr. Stanton to accommodate in many such cases, Mr. Lincoln was appealed to, and his invariable reply was: "I cannot always know whether a permit ought to be granted, and I want to oblige everybody when I can; and Stanton and I have an understanding that if I send an order to him which cannot be consistently granted, he is to refuse it. This he sometimes does." This state of things caused him to say to a man who complained of Stanton, "I have not much influence with this Administration, but I expect to have more with the next."

Not long before the death of Mr. Lincoln, Mr. Stanton tendered his resignation as Secretary of War. His letter of resignation was couched in the kindest language, paying a heartfelt tribute to Mr. Lincoln's uniform and constant friendship, and his faithful devotion to the country. It stated that the writer had accepted the position of Secretary of War for the purpose of holding it only till the war should end, and that now he felt that his work was completed, and that it was his duty to resign. Mr. Lincoln was greatly moved by the tone of the letter, and said: "Mr. Stanton, you have been a faithful public officer, and it is not for you to say when you will be no longer needed here." At the President's earnest solicitation, the letter of resignation was withdrawn, and Mr. Stanton continued to occupy the War Office until after Mr. Lincoln's death.

When Mr. Lincoln submitted his Proclamation of Emancipation for the consideration of the Cabinet, he had not conferred with any one about the phraseology of the instrument. He read the document through, without a single interruption or comment. They all concurred in opinion that it was an admirable paper. Mr. Chase then said: "Mr. President, you have invoked the considerate judgment of mankind, but you have not invoked the blessing of Almighty God on your action in this matter. I believe He has something to do with this question." Mr. Lincoln then said: "You are right, Mr. Secretary. I most humbly thank you for that suggestion; it was an oversight of mine. Do me the favor of taking a pen and paper and adding what you would have in conclusion." Mr. Chase wrote seven words,--namely, "and the gracious favor of Almighty God." Mr. Lincoln then added them to the end of the last paragraph, which made it read as follows: "And upon this act, sincerely believed to be an act of justice, warranted by the Constitution upon military necessity, I invoke the considerate judgment of mankind and the gracious favor of Almighty God."[11]

[11] Page 235, line 25, after the word "God."

John W. Crisfield served in Congress with Mr. Lincoln in 1847 and was a warm friend of Lincoln. Being elected again as Representative in 1861, he was in Congress when the proposition was made for gradual emancipation in the border states by paying the loyal owners for their slaves. Mr. Crisfield was on the committee that was to draft the reply to this proposition. When he was at the White House one day in July, 1862, Mr. Lincoln said: "Well, Crisfield, how are you getting along with your report, have you written it yet?" Mr. Crisfield replied that he had not. Mr. Lincoln--knowing that the Emancipation Proclamation was coming, in fact was then only two months away--said, "You had better come to an agreement. Niggers will never be higher."

In referring to the differences of opinion entertained between Mr. Lincoln and the members of his Cabinet, it will be observed that in the matter of reconstruction of the State governments his policy was, according to his proclamation, that the persons who were authorized to re-establish such governments were to be "the qualified voters of the respective States before the acts of secession." Mr. Chase alone of all the Cabinet objected to this clause of the proclamation, and insisted that it should be changed so as to read, instead of "qualified voters," "citizens of the State." But the Attorney-General in the year 1862 had given an opinion that the colored men born in the United States were citizens of the United States; and if the phrase "one-tenth of the qualified voters required to re-organize" were changed to "one-tenth of the citizens," the organization might have been legally composed entirely of colored men. Mr. Lincoln was set in his purpose that the restored governments in the seceded States should be organized by the "qualified voters" of those States before secession was attempted, and Mr. Chase had to submit to the inevitable.

The great caution with which Mr. Lincoln approached the important subject of elective franchise may be shown in his letter to Governor Hahn:--

(PRIVATE.)

EXECUTIVE MANSION, WASHINGTON, March 13, 1864.

Hon. Michael Hahn:

MY DEAR SIR,--I congratulate you on having fixed your name in history as the first free-state Governor of Louisiana. Now, you are about to have a convention, which among other things will probably define the elective franchise. I barely suggest for your private consideration, whether some of the colored people may not be let in,--as, for instance, the very intelligent, and especially those who have fought gallantly in our ranks. They would probably help, in some trying time to come, to keep the jewel of liberty within the family of freedom. But this is only a suggestion,--not to the public, but to you alone.

Yours truly, (Signed) A. LINCOLN.

This would seem to show conclusively that Mr. Lincoln did not intend to force negro suffrage upon the people in the rebel States. Doubtless, he desired that the negroes should have the right of suffrage, but he expected and hoped that the people would confer the right of their own will. He knew that if this right were forced upon them, it could not or would not be exercised in peace. He realized in advance that the experiment of legislative equality was one fraught with difficulties and dangers, not only to the well-being of the negro, but to the peace of society. "While I am," said he, "in favor of freedom to all of God's human creatures, with equal political rights under prudential restrictions, I am not in favor of unlimited social equality. There are questions arising out of our complications that trouble me greatly. The question of universal suffrage to the freedman in his unprepared state is one of doubtful propriety. I do not oppose the justice of the measure; but I do think it is of doubtful political policy, and may rebound like a boomerang not only on the Republican party, but upon the freedman himself and our common country."

182

As the war approached its conclusion, and Mr. Lincoln foresaw the inevitable submission of the insurgents, his mind did not become less seriously affected by the contemplation of the new responsibilities which would devolve upon him as Chief Magistrate of the reorganized and reconstructed nation. His second Inaugural Address mirrored his frame of mind to a great extent. He was oppressed with great care, resulting from a consciousness that changes would occur in the near future which would impose upon him new and difficult duties, in which he might possibly find himself in conflict not only with the men in his own party who already persistently opposed him, but with many other public men who had supported his Administration throughout the existence of the war. There seemed to be no settled policy for the contemplated new state of things, and few men thought alike on the subject. There were almost as many theories as there were distinguished men to advance them. This state of things devolved the greater responsibility upon Mr. Lincoln, and he keenly felt the weight of it.

Upon no occasion, either public or private, did Mr. Lincoln hesitate to express freely his views and sentiments as to the conditions under which he would have liked the War of the Rebellion to terminate. All that he desired was that the enemy should cease fighting, lay down their arms, and return to their homes, their duties, and their allegiance to their country. He harbored no feeling of revenge, no thirst for the blood of his erring fellow-countrymen, his highest aspiration being peace and a restored Union. From what he has been repeatedly heard to declare, he would gladly have spared to his vanquished foes the humiliation of a public surrender if the war could otherwise have been brought to a close. He fondly hoped for a condition of things which would render reconstruction and love of country assured, fixed, and immutable. In discussing the question of reconstruction previous to the surrender of General Lee, I have more than once heard him say: "We cannot hang all these people, even if they were in our power; there are too many of them. Think of the consequences of such an act! Since this government was established, there have been comparatively few trials or executions for treason or offences against the State. This has been eminently a government of loyal citizens."

A distinguished gentleman, an earnest advocate for punishment of the rebels, once asked him what he intended to do when the moment arrived for him to act. "Do?" said he; "why, reconstruct the machinery of this government! This is all that I see I can properly do." The gentleman, with much asperity, exclaimed: "Mr. President, it does appear to some of your friends, myself included, as if you had taken final leave of your senses! As if it were intended that treason should henceforth not be regarded as odious, and the offenders, cut-throats, and authors of this war should not only go unpunished, but receive encouragement to repeat their outrages on the government with impunity! They should be hanged higher than Haman, sir!"

Mr. Lincoln here asked: "Mr. ----, suppose, when the moment has arrived, the hanging policy you recommend be adopted,--will you agree to be chief executioner? If so, let me know, and I will at once appoint you a brigadier-general and prospective public hangman of the United States. Will you serve, if so appointed?"

"Mr. Lincoln," responded his interlocutor, "I supposed you regarded me as a gentleman; at least you ought to know better than to ask me to do, or believe me capable of doing, such dirty work."

"You speak," said Mr. Lincoln, interrupting him, "of being a gentleman. In this free country of ours, when it comes to rights and duties, especially in time of war, the gentleman and the vagrant stand on exactly the same plane; their rights are equal, their duties the same. As a law-abiding citizen, you are no more exempt from the performance of what you call 'dirty work' than if you were not a gentleman."

His visitor here arose abruptly and left the room in great indignation, relieving himself of his pent-up wrath by a torrent of oaths and imprecations. He was a United States Senator, and I have not at all exaggerated his profanity or his deportment on the occasion here narrated. He did not, indeed, intermit his denunciations, which were, besides, embellished with the choicest specimens of billingsgate, until a casual rencontre on the Avenue with a member of the lower House afforded him the solace of exclaiming: "Lincoln is a damned idiot! He has no spirit, and is as weak as an old woman. He was never fitted for the position he holds. After this war is over, it would not at all surprise me if he were to fill the public offices with a horde of these infernal rebels, and choose for his constitutional advisers the damnable leaders of the rebellion themselves." I am not aware that this senator ever again visited the President.

After the capitulation of General Lee, what was to be done with the leaders of the rebellion became a most serious question. Persons who had been throughout the war the fiercest and most radical opponents of the rebels (such men as Horace Greeley and others) became suddenly most conservative; and the converse course was pursued by many of the most conservative persons, now urging relentless punishment of the offending leaders. General Grant asked for special instructions of Mr. Lincoln,--whether he should try to capture Jefferson Davis, or let him escape from the country if he wanted to do so. Mr. Lincoln replied by relating the story of an Irishman who had taken the pledge of Father Matthew, and having become terribly thirsty applied to a bar-tender for a lemonade; and while it was being prepared he whispered to the bar-tender, "And couldn't you put a little brandy in it all unbeknownst to myself?" Mr. Lincoln told the general he would like to let Jeff Davis escape all unbeknown to himself: he had no use for him.

On the day of the assassination, General Creswell came to Washington to see the President in the interest of an old friend who had been located in the

South, and had got into the rebel army, and had been captured by our troops and imprisoned. He drew an affidavit setting forth what he knew about the man, particularly mentioning extenuating circumstances which seemed to entitle him to the generosity or leniency of the government. General Creswell found the President very happy. The Confederacy had collapsed. The scene at Appomattox had just been enacted. He was greeted with: "Creswell, old fellow, everything is bright this morning. The war is over. It has been a tough time, but we have lived it out,--or some of us have," and he dropped his voice a little on the last clause of the sentence. "But it is over; we are going to have good times now, and a united country."

After a time, General Creswell told his story, read his affidavit, and said, "I know the man has acted like a fool, but he is my friend, and a good fellow; let him out, give him to me, and I will be responsible that he won't have anything more to do with the rebs."

"Creswell," said Mr. Lincoln, "you make me think of a lot of young folks who once started out Maying. To reach their destination, they had to cross a shallow stream, and did so by means of an old flatboat. When the time came to return, they found to their dismay that the old scow had disappeared. They were in sore trouble, and thought over all manner of devices for getting over the water, but without avail. After a time, one of the boys proposed that each fellow should pick up the girl he liked best and wade over with her. The masterly proposition was carried out, until all that were left upon the island was a little short chap and a great, long, gothic-built, elderly lady. Now, Creswell, you are trying to leave me in the same predicament. You fellows are all getting your own friends out of this scrape; and you will succeed in carrying off one after another, until nobody but Jeff Davis and myself will be left on the island, and then I won't know what to do. How should I feel? How should I look, lugging him over? I guess the way to avoid such an embarrassing situation is to let them all out at once."

A somewhat similar illustration he made at an informal Cabinet meeting, at which was being discussed the disposition of Jefferson Davis and other prominent Confederates. Each member of the Cabinet gave his opinion; most of them were for hanging the traitors, or for some severe punishment. Lincoln said nothing. Finally, Joshua F. Speed, his old and confidential friend, who had been invited to the meeting, said, "I have heard the opinion of your Ministers, and would like to hear yours."

"Well, Josh," replied Mr. Lincoln, "when I was a boy in Indiana, I went to a neighbor's house one morning and found a boy of my own size holding a coon by a string. I asked him what he had and what he was doing. He says, 'It's a coon. Dad cotched six last night, and killed all but this poor little cuss. Dad told me to hold him until he came back, and I'm afraid he's going to kill this one too; and oh, Abe, I do wish he would get away!' 'Well, why don't you let him loose?' 'That wouldn't be right; and if I let him go, Dad would give me hell. But if he would get away himself, it would be all right.' Now," said Mr. Lincoln, "if Jeff Davis and those other fellows will only get away, it will be all right. But if we should catch them, and I should let them go, 'Dad would give me hell.'"

The President of the Southern Confederacy was, however, afterwards captured and imprisoned at Fortress Monroe, charged with treason, etc., and at length admitted to bail,--Mr. Horace Greeley, the great Radical journalist, becoming one of his bondsmen. Mr. Davis was never brought to trial, and eventually the charges against him were ignored. He was a prisoner of State at Fortress Monroe for two years; in the year 1867 he was released on bail, went to Canada, but subsequently returned to the State of Mississippi, where he lived in retirement until his death.

On the night of the 3d of March, 1865, Mr. Lincoln, with several members of his Cabinet, was in attendance at the Capitol, awaiting the final passage of bills by Congress, in order that they might receive the Presidential signature.

In the intervals between the reading, considering, and approving of these bills, the military situation was freely discussed. Every one appeared to be happy at the prospect of the early re-establishment of peace, General Grant having just telegraphed a glowing account of his successes and his control of the situation, and expressing the hope that a very few days would find Richmond in the hands of the national forces and the army of General Lee disbanded or captured. While the members were felicitating one another on the approaching cessation of hostilities, a second dispatch from General Grant was handed to Mr. Stanton, who, having read it, handed it to the President and became absorbed in thought. The telegram advised the Secretary of the receipt of a letter from General Lee, requesting an immediate interview, with a view to the re-establishment of peace between the two sections. The dispatch having been read by others of the party, Mr. Lincoln's spirits rose to a height rarely witnessed since the outbreak of the war. All the better and kindlier impulses of his nature were aroused. The cry, "What is to be done with the rebels when this cruel war is over?" ceased to ring in his ears. He was unable to restrain himself from giving expression to the natural impulses of his heart, or from foreshadowing the magnanimity with which the Confederates were now to be treated. He did not hesitate to express himself as favorably disposed towards granting the most lenient and generous terms to a defeated foe.

Mr. Stanton could now no longer restrain himself; he was in a towering rage, and turning to the President, his eyes flashing fire, he exclaimed: "Mr. President, you are losing sight of the paramount consideration at this juncture, namely, how and by whom is this war to be closed? To-morrow is Inauguration Day; you will then enter upon your second term of office. Read again this dispatch: don't you appreciate its significance? If you are not to be President of an obedient, loyal, and united people, you ought not to take the oath of office,--you are not a proper person to be empowered with so high and responsible a trust. Your work is already achieved,--all but reconstruction. If any other authority than your own be for a moment recognized; or if terms of peace be agreed upon that do not emanate from yourself, and do not imply that you are the supreme head of the nation,--you are not needed. You should not consent to act in the humiliating capacity of a mere figure-head, to aid in the acquisition of that fame for others which rightfully belongs to yourself. By thus doing, you will scandalize every true friend you possess in the country."

It was now Mr. Lincoln's turn to become thoughtful. He sat at the table for a few minutes, absorbed in deep reflection, and then, addressing himself to the Secretary of War, said: "Stanton, you are right; this dispatch did not, at first sight, strike me as I now consider it." Upon this he took pen and paper and hurriedly wrote the following dispatch, handing it to Stanton, and requesting him to date, sign, and send it at once. The dispatch ran as follows:--

"The President directs me to say to you that he wishes you to have no conference with General Lee, unless it be for the capitulation of Lee's army, or on some minor and purely military matter. He instructs me to say that you are not to decide, discuss, or confer on any political questions; the President, holding the decision of these questions in his own hands, will submit them to no military conference or convention. In the mean time you are to press, to the utmost of your ability, your military advantage."

The above dispatch was read, signed, and sent by Mr. Stanton immediately, without one word of comment, and soon afterward the entire party left the Capitol for their respective homes, there to await further developments. At the same time, the Secretary of War sent the following telegram to General Grant:--

WASHINGTON, March 3, 1865.

LIEUTENANT-GENERAL GRANT,--I send you a telegram written by the

President himself, in answer to yours of this evening, which I have signed by his order. I will add that General Ord's conduct in holding intercourse with General Longstreet upon political questions not committed to his charge, is not approved. The same thing was done, in one instance, by Major Keys, when the army was commanded by General McClellan, and he was sent to meet Howell Cobb on the subject of exchanges; and it was in that instance, as in this, disapproved. You will please, in future, instruct officers appointed to meet rebel officers to confine themselves to the matters specially committed to them.

(Signed) EDWIN M. STANTON, Secretary of War.

On the succeeding day a dispatch was received from General Grant in cipher, of which the following is a translation:--

CITY POINT, March 4, 1865.

Hon. E. M. STANTON, Secretary of War:

Your dispatch of the 3d, midnight, received. I have a letter to General Lee, copy of which will be sent you by to-morrow's mail. I can assure you that no act of the enemy will prevent me pressing all advantages gained to the utmost of my ability. Neither will I, under any circumstances, exceed my authority, or in any way embarrass the government. It was because I had no right to meet General Lee on the subject proposed by him, that I referred the matter for instructions.

U. S. GRANT, Lieutenant-General.

CHAPTER XVI.

CONFLICT BETWEEN CIVIL AND MILITARY AUTHORITY.

The execution of the Fugitive Slave Law in the District of Columbia became a question much discussed in Congress, and was a frightful scandal to the Radical members. The law remained in force; and no attempt was made by Congress to repeal it, or to provide for the protection of the Executive officers whose duty it was to enforce it. The subject gave Mr. Lincoln great concern, but he could see no way out of the difficulty except to have the law executed. The District had become the asylum of the runaway slaves from the Border States, particularly from the rebel State of Virginia and the quasi-loyal State of Maryland. So far as the State of Virginia was concerned, she was still, according to the theory of the Administration, one of the United States; and all Congressional laws on the statute book were enforced in regard to her as well as to States not in rebellion, which made the question one of great embarrassment. The Confiscation Act, which gave liberty to all slaves that had been employed by the rebels for insurrectionary purposes, had gone into effect in the month of August, 1861. The military governor of the District assumed that by virtue of this law all slaves that came into the District from whatever section had been thus employed, and consequently were free, and it became his duty to give them military protection as free persons.

This state of things caused a fearful responsibility to rest upon the shoulders of the civil executive authorities. The President gave me private instructions to execute the laws until Congress modified or repealed them. "In doing this," Mr. Lincoln said, "you will receive much adverse criticism and a good deal of downright abuse from members of Congress. This is certain to come, but it will be not so much intended for you as for me; as our friend Senator Hale, the other day, said in the Senate, 'We must not strike too high nor too low, but we must strike between wind and water: the marshal is the man to hit.' And I say, we shall have to stand it whatever they send."

Martial law had not been declared; there was not even a temporary suspension of the civil authority, even in exceptional cases, in the District of Columbia. It was conceded by all, that in time of danger the temporary rule of military authority was virtually necessary to the preservation of the federal capital; but at this time there was no pretence of danger. The civil courts of the District being in full power for the adjudication of all cases arising within their jurisdiction, nothing but a pressing military necessity could give countenance or pretext for the suspension of the civil law. It was, therefore, only a question of time--and the time soon came--for a conflict to arise between civil and military authority.

The conflict grew out of an order of the military governor to take a female fugitive slave from the custody of the marshal and deliver her into the hands of the military. The deputies to whom the order was shown declined to obey the command, giving as a reason for their refusal that she was held under due process of law, and that they had no authority to give her up without the order of the court. Military officers, with a strong guard, then arrested the deputy marshals, seized the jail, released the slave, and left a military guard in charge of the captured jail.[L]

[L] WAR DEPARTMENT, WASHINGTON, D. C., May 22, 1862.

Captain Sherwood, or Officer in Command at Central Guard House:

SIR,--You will send a sentinel at once to the city jail, with orders to relieve the man now on duty there at the jail door, and give him orders to allow no person whatsoever to enter or leave the jail, without permission from General Wadsworth. This guard will be maintained until further orders.

By Command of Brigadier-General Wadsworth,

JOHN A. KRESS, A. D. C.

I was temporarily absent at the time of the seizure. When I returned I arrested the military guard, recaptured the jail, liberated the prisoners placed therein by the military, and held the military guard as prisoners. I was supported by the police and other civil authorities, and by the citizens of Washington; the military governor was supported by forces under his command, intended for the defence of the city. The matter was eventually laid before the President. He called to his aid his Attorney-General, who gave a prompt but decisive opinion that in the present state of things in the District of Columbia the civil authority outranked the military; and he gave the further opinion that the military governor's conduct had been misguided and unauthorized, however philanthropic might have been his purposes and intentions.

This decision on the subject of supremacy of authority by no means reconciled or put at rest the perturbed, aggressive spirit in Congress which opposed the President's policy. The enthusiastic adherents of this opposition made the District jail an objective point in the furtherance of their ends. They made personal visits to that institution, and examined all the inmates whose color was not of orthodox Albino-Anglo American tint. They would learn the story of their wrongs and injuries, then straightway proceed to the halls of Congress and make known their discoveries. Detectives were employed by them to make daily reports of the "cruelty" shown to colored inmates of the jail, which reports were soon dressed up in pathetic and classic language for the occasion. Professional and amateur demagogues made sensational speeches (sometimes written for them by department clerks and professional speech-writers), and "Rome was made to howl" in the halls of the American Congress. "Lincoln and his beastly negro catchers" were denounced in unmeasured terms.

The jail was now by the necessities of its surroundings made the receptacle for prisoners of all kinds,--civil, military, and State. Orders from the War Department were issued to the custodian of the jail to allow no person whatever to communicate with the military or State prisoners without an order from the War Department. The chairman of the District Committee in the Senate, and certain others of that Committee, claimed the right, by virtue of their position, to go into the jail and to examine all the prisoners, in the face of the orders of the Secretary of War; and this was repeated almost daily.

The situation became unbearable, and I sent in my resignation. This, however, was not accepted. The professional opinion of the Attorney-General was again invoked by the President, and he gave his views as to the duties of the custodian of the heterogeneous mass of prisoners in the jail,--which resulted in the request of the President to the Attorney-General to prepare such an order as was proper for the marshal to sign, giving notice of what would be required for admission of visitors to the jail. The paper was prepared in the Attorney-General's office, signed and sent forth; and before the close of the day on which it was signed, resolutions were passed in Congress declaring the marshal guilty of contempt of that body for having presumed to issue what it deemed a contemptuous restriction of its rights, and a committee was appointed to wait upon the President to demand the instant dismissal of that insolent officer. The President showed the committee my resignation already in his hands, and informed them that he would neither accept the resignation nor dismiss me from office, and gave his reasons for this action.

After this the opposition became more and more acrimonious and offensive toward Mr. Lincoln and his Administration. The leaders of the opposition now resorted to every means in their power to oppose him for his want of respect, and for his disobedience to the behests of the co-ordinate branch of the government,--forgetting that, Congress having made the offensive laws, it was the President's duty to execute them.

Soon the marshal's office was made the subject of legislation in Congress, to shear it of its power and reduce its emoluments. The custody of the jail and prisoners was soon given to a warden; and, shortly after, an Act was passed relieving the marshal from the duties of attending the Supreme Court of the United States, and providing a special marshal for that Court,--thus leaving the office still one of great responsibility, but without remuneration commensurate with its duties.

Before the appointment of the warden, the District court had sentenced three men to be hanged for murder, on a day subsequent to the change of custody. On the day set for the execution, I refused to act as the hangman. Congress again passed a resolution denouncing my conduct, and instituted an investigation into the facts. The facts were that the order of the court was that the marshal should hang the condemned men, but Congress had unconsciously relieved him from that painful duty! The warden had no order for their execution, and could not perform the service with any more propriety than the marshal. The result of this blundering legislation, superinduced by hasty, factious zeal to injure an object of their dislike, was that Congress had nullified the solemn acts of the United States District Court, and restored to life and liberty and immunity from punishment three miscreants whose lives had been forfeited and who should have been hanged! This legislative jail-delivery was a source of great annoyance and of some amusement to Mr. Lincoln. In speaking of certain members of Congress and the part they had taken in this and other petty acts, he said: "I have great sympathy for these men, because of their temper and their weakness; but I am thankful that the good Lord has given to the vicious ox short horns, for if their physical courage were equal to their vicious dispositions, some of us in this neck of the woods would get hurt."

The opposition was continued to the last, and Mr. Lincoln adhered to his policy to the end. But he was so outraged by the obloquy thrown upon his worthiest official acts, so stung by the disparagement with which his purest and most patriotic motives were impugned,--his existence, in a word, was rendered so unhappy by the personal as well as political attacks of those for whose sympathy and support he might naturally have urged the most logical and valid plea,--that life became almost a burden to him.

As illustrative of the amenities of language with which, at this epoch of his life, the Chief Magistrate of our Republic was habitually characterized, it will suffice to adduce such an expression as this,--"That hideous baboon at the other end of the Avenue, whom Barnum should exhibit as a zoological curiosity." Mr. Lincoln's existence was so cruelly embittered by these and other expressions quite as virulent, that I have often heard him declare, "I would rather be dead than, as President, thus abused in the house of my friends."

In the summer of 1861, shortly after the inglorious repulse of the Union army at Bull Run, Rev. Robert Collyer, the eminent divine, was on a visit to the federal capital. Participating in the prevailing sentiment in regard to the incapacity or inefficiency of the general government in the conduct of military affairs, he chanced to pass through the White House grounds on his way to the War Department. Casting a cursory glance at the Executive Mansion as he passed, his attention was suddenly arrested by the apparition of three pairs of feet, resting on the ledge of an open window, in one of the apartments of the second story, and plainly visible from below. The reverend gentleman paused, calmly surveyed the grotesque spectacle, and mentally addressed to himself the inquiry whether the feet, and boots belonging to them, were the property of officers of the Executive government,--at the same time thinking that if not, they would have proved sturdy pedestals to the bearers of muskets upon the recent battle-field. Resuming his walk, he accosted a rustic employee whom he found at work about the grounds, and pointing to the window, with its incongruous adjuncts, he requested of the man what that meant. "Why, you old fool," replied the rustic, "that's the Cabinet that is a settin'; and them thar big feet's old Abe's."

Some time after, in referring to this experience of his visit to the national capital in a lecture at Boston, the reverend gentleman commented on the imbecility of the government, and satirically added: "That's about all they are good for in Washington,--to project their feet out of windows and jabber away; but they go nowhere, and accomplish nothing." But he subsequently, on more than one occasion, rendered full justice to the President's able and zealous discharge of his high trust, saying: "I abused poor Lincoln, like the fool that the rustic called me, while his heart was even then breaking with the anxieties and responsibilities of his position."

CHAPTER XVII.

PLOTS AND ASSASSINATION.

The fact that we have in this country a literature of assassination, "voluminous and vast," suggests a melancholy reflection on the disordered spirit of the times through which we have passed, and on the woful perversity of human nature even under conditions most favorable to intellectual progress and Christian civilization. It is hurtful to our pride as Americans to confess that our history is marred by records so repugnant to the spirit of our liberal institutions, and to the good fellowship which ought to characterize both individual and national life in a free republic. But the appalling fact remains that two of our Chief Magistrates, within as many decades, were murdered in cold blood, and that bulky volumes have been filled with circumstantial accounts of plots and conspiracies by and against men born upon our soil and enjoying the full protection of our laws; and yet, voluminous and extensive as these records are, they are by no means complete.

One most daring attempt upon the life of Mr. Lincoln--the boldest of all attempts of that character, and one which approached shockingly near to a murderous success--was never made public. For prudential reasons details were withheld from the press; but as the motives which imposed silence respecting a strange freak of homicidal frenzy no longer exist, it is perhaps a matter of duty to make public the story, together with certain documents which show in what deadly peril Mr. Lincoln stood during the ceremonies attending his second inauguration at the Capitol in March, 1865. A glance at prior conspiracies will lead to a better understanding of the event to which these documents relate.

The first conspiracy, from motives of policy, had for its object the abduction of President Buchanan. There was intense disgust on the part of certain fiery and ferocious leaders in the secession movement with the conservative temper of the Executive and of the ruling members of his Cabinet. After fruitless attempts to bully the Administration into a change of policy in harmony with his revolutionary scheme, Mr. Wigfall, some time in the month of December, 1860, formed a plan for kidnapping Mr. Buchanan. A number of desperate men were banded together by him at Washington, and the details of the plot were discussed and agreed upon. The plan was to spirit Mr. Buchanan away, install Mr. Breckenridge in the White House, and hold the captive President as a hostage until terms of compromise could be proposed to conservative Democrats and Republicans in the North. Mr. Wigfall and other choice spirits had no doubt that their plan of accommodation could be enforced through the ad interim Executive. The scheme, however, could not be executed, in its first stage, without the concurrence and co-operation of Mr. Floyd, who threw Wigfall into a paroxysm of explosive wrath by flatly refusing to have anything to do with the enterprise. It was accordingly abandoned, so far as Mr. Buchanan was concerned.

When Mr. Lincoln was inaugurated, in March, 1861, the organization of plotters was still intact; but no plan of assassination had, as yet, received the sanction of the conspirators as a body. It was their purpose to kidnap Mr. Lincoln and hold him in captivity, without injury to his person, until such concessions were made to the Southern leaders as their plan of compromise rendered necessary. This second scheme of abduction, having proved as abortive as the first, was abandoned in favor of a more deadly purpose. Some of the more desperate among the conspirators, exasperated by repeated failures, resolved to dispose of Mr. Lincoln by the swifter and surer means afforded by the dagger or the bullet.

Circumstances, in a surprising way, seemed to favor their murderous designs. Against the protest of his friends, who by detective means had obtained from the plotters many of their secrets, Mr. Lincoln made the Soldiers' Home his summer residence. The conspirators thought that either abduction or assassination could be accomplished without difficulty. They resolved upon the latter. They would dispatch him during one of his lonely rides after nightfall from the White House to his summer retreat. The attempt was made.

In the spring and early summer of 1862 I persistently urged upon Mr. Lincoln the necessity of a military escort to accompany him to and from his residence and place of business, and he as persistently opposed my proposition, always saying, when the subject was referred to, that there was not the slightest occasion for such precaution. One morning, however, in the month of August he came riding up to the White House steps, where I met him, with a merry twinkle in his eye that presaged fun of some kind. Before he alighted he said, "I have something to tell you!" and after we had entered his office he locked the doors, sat down, and commenced his narration. (At this distance of time I will not pretend to give the exact words of this interview, but will state it according to my best recollection.) He said: "You know I have always told you I thought you an idiot that ought to be put in a strait jacket for your apprehensions of my personal danger from assassination. You also know that the way we skulked into this city, in the first place, has been a source of shame and regret to me, for it did look so cowardly!"

To all of which I simply assented, saying, "Yes, go on."

"Well," said he, "I don't now propose to make you my father-confessor and acknowledge a change of heart, yet I am free to admit that just now I don't know what to think: I am staggered. Understand me, I do not want to oppose my pride of opinion against light and reason, but I am in such a state of 'betweenity' in my conclusions that I can't say that the judgment of this court is prepared to proclaim a reliable 'decision upon the facts presented.'"

He paused; I requested him to go on, for I was in painful suspense. He then proceeded.

"Last night, about 11 o'clock, I went out to the Soldiers' Home alone, riding Old Abe, as you call him [a horse he delighted in riding], and when I arrived at the foot of the hill on the road leading to the entrance of the Home grounds, I was jogging along at a slow gait, immersed in deep thought, contemplating what was next to happen in the unsettled state of affairs, when suddenly I was aroused--I may say the arousement lifted me out of my saddle as well as out of my wits--by the report of a rifle, and seemingly the gunner was not fifty yards from where my contemplations ended and my accelerated transit began. My erratic namesake, with little warning, gave proof of decided dissatisfaction at the racket, and with one reckless bound he unceremoniously separated me from my eight-dollar plug-hat, with which I parted company without any assent, expressed or implied, upon my part. At a break-neck speed we soon arrived in a haven of safety. Meanwhile I was left in doubt whether death was more desirable from being thrown from a runaway federal horse, or as the tragic result of a rifle-ball fired by a disloyal bushwhacker in the middle of the night."

This was all told in a spirit of levity; he seemed unwilling, even in appearance, to attach that importance to the event which I was disposed to give to it. He seemed to want to believe it a joke. "Now," said he, "in the face of this testimony in favor of your theory of danger to me, personally, I can't bring myself to believe that any one has shot or will deliberately shoot at me with the purpose of killing me; although I must acknowledge that I heard this fellow's bullet whistle at an uncomfortably short distance from these headquarters of mine. I have about concluded that the shot was the result of accident. It may be that some one on his return from a day's hunt, regardless of the course of his discharge, fired off his gun as a precautionary measure of safety to his family after reaching his house." This was said with much seriousness.

He then playfully proceeded: "I tell you there is no time on record equal to that made by the two Old Abes on that occasion. The historic ride of John Gilpin, and Henry Wilson's memorable display of bareback equestrianship on the stray army mule from the scenes of the battle of Bull Run, a year ago, are nothing in comparison to mine, either in point of time made or in ludicrous pageantry. My only advantage over these worthies was in having no observers. I can truthfully say that one of the Abes was frightened on this occasion, but modesty forbids my mentioning which of us is entitled to that distinguished honor. This whole thing seems farcical. No good can result at this time from giving it publicity. It does seem to me that I am in more danger from the augmentation of imaginary peril than from a judicious silence, be the danger ever so great; and, moreover, I do not want it understood that I share your apprehensions. I never have."

At this time Mr. Lincoln was to me a study. It would seem that he was always prepared for the inevitable, and singularly indifferent as to his personal safety. He was then still suffering from his terrible domestic affliction, the death of his favorite son Willie. He doubtless at times acted an unnatural part in his endeavors to banish from his memory the disturbing recollections of his lost idol. I often recur with mingled feelings of admiration and sadness to the wonderful simplicity and perfect faith exemplified in his narration of the hazardous experience above described. He said: "I am determined to borrow no trouble. I believe in the right, and that it will ultimately prevail; and I believe it is the inalienable right of man, unimpaired even by this dreadful distraction of our country, to be happy or miserable at his own election, and I for one make choice of the former alternative."

"Yes," said I, "but it is a devil of a poor protection against a shot-gun in time of war; for that fellow on the road-side last night was just such a philosopher as yourself, although acting from a different standpoint. He exercised one of his supposed inalienable rights to make himself happy and the country miserable by attempting to kill you; and unless you are more careful and discreet, and will be governed by wiser counsels than you derive from your own obstinate persistency in recklessness, in less than a week you'll have neither inalienable nor any other rights, and we shall have no Lincoln. The time, I fear, may not be far distant when this republic will be minus a pretty respectable President."

It was impossible, however, to induce him to forego these lonely and dangerous journeys between the Executive Mansion and the Soldiers' Home. A stranger to fear, he often eluded our vigilance; and before his absence could be noted he would be well on his way to his summer residence, alone, and many times at night.

Another occasion when the vigilance and anxiety of his friends were exercised will appear in the following extract from a memorandum written by Robert Lamon, who was deputy marshal of the District of Columbia at the time:--

In the early part of the night my brother came to me and asked me to join him in the search for Mr. Lincoln. He was greatly disturbed. We drove rapidly to the Soldiers' Home, and as we neared the entrance to the grounds we met a carriage. Behind it we could see in the darkness a man on horseback. My brother, who seemed unusually suspicious, commanded the party to halt. His order was instantly obeyed. "Who are you?" he demanded, in the same peremptory tone. A voice from within the carriage responded, "Why do you ask?" The speakers recognized each other. The one in the carriage was Secretary Stanton, and the man behind it was one of his orderlies. "Where is Mr. Lincoln?" asked Stanton. "I have been to the Soldiers' Home and he is not there. I am exceedingly uneasy about him. He is not at the White House?" "No," said my brother, "he is not there. I have looked for him everywhere." We hurried back to the city. Arriving at the White House before Mr. Stanton, we found Mr. Lincoln walking across the lawn. My brother went with him to the War Department, and from there took him to his [Lamon's] house, where Mr. Lincoln slept that night and the three or four nights following, Mrs. Lincoln being at that time in New York.

(Signed) ROBT. LAMON.

My anxiety about Mr. Lincoln that evening grew out of a report of an alarming character made to me by one of my detectives. Stanton had threatening news also, and was therefore excited about Mr. Lincoln's safety. He told me that he never had so great a scare in his life as he had that night. The brusque Secretary thought the deputy marshal and I were assassins. The incident provoked much merriment among the parties concerned, no one enjoying the serio-comic part of it more than Mr. Lincoln himself.

Meanwhile the conspirators, becoming alarmed for their own safety, observed a stricter caution. Their movements were embarrassed by the escort of cavalry which Mr. Lincoln was finally induced to accept, after prolonged importunities by those who had certain knowledge of the dangers to which he was exposed. Lost opportunities, baffled hopes, exasperating defeats, served however only to heighten the deadly determination of the plotters; and so matters drifted on until the day of Mr. Lincoln's second inauguration.

A tragedy was planned for that day which has no parallel in the history of criminal audacity, if considered as nothing more than a crime intended.

Everybody knows what throngs assemble at the Capitol to witness the imposing ceremonies attending the inauguration of a President of the United States. It is amazing that any human being could have seriously entertained the thought of assassinating Mr. Lincoln in the presence of such a concourse of citizens. And yet there was such a man in the assemblage. He was there for the single purpose of murdering the illustrious leader who for the second time was about to assume the burden of the Presidency. That man was John Wilkes Booth. Proof of his identity, and a detailed account of his movements while attempting to reach the platform where Mr. Lincoln stood, will be found in many affidavits, of which the following is a specimen:--

DISTRICT OF COLUMBIA,} COUNTY OF WSHINGTON, } ss:

Robert Strong, a citizen of said County and District, being duly sworn, says that he was a policeman at the Capitol on the day of the second inauguration of President Lincoln, and was stationed at the east door of the rotunda, with Commissioner B. B. French, at the time the President, accompanied by the judges and others, passed out to the platform where the ceremonies of inauguration were about to begin, when a man in a very determined and excited manner broke through the line of policemen which had been formed to keep the crowd out. Lieutenant Westfall immediately seized the stranger, and a considerable scuffle ensued. The stranger seemed determined to get to the platform where the President and his party were, but Lieutenant Westfall called for assistance. The Commissioner closed the door, or had it closed, and the intruder was finally thrust from the passage leading to the platform which was reserved for the President's party. After the President was assassinated, the singular conduct of this stranger on that day was frequently talked of by the policemen who observed it. Lieutenant Westfall procured a photograph of the assassin Booth soon after the death of the President, and showed it to Commissioner French in my presence and in the presence of several other policemen, and asked him if he had ever met that man. The commissioner examined it attentively and said: "Yes, I would know that face among ten thousand. That is the man you had a scuffle with on inauguration day. That is the same man." Affiant also recognized the photograph. Lieutenant Westfall then said: "This is the picture of J. Wilkes Booth." Major French exclaimed: "My God! what a fearful risk we ran that day!"

ROBERT STRONG.

Sworn to and subscribed before me this 20th day of March, 1876.

JAMES A. TAIT, [SEAL] Notary Public.

From this sworn statement it will be seen that Booth's plan was one of phenomenal audacity. So frenzied was the homicide that he determined to take the President's life at the inevitable sacrifice of his own; for nothing can be more certain than that the murder of Mr. Lincoln on that public occasion, in the presence of a vast concourse of admiring citizens, would have been instantly avenged. The infuriated populace would have torn the assassin to pieces, and this the desperate man doubtless knew.

It is a curious fact, that, although Mr. Lincoln believed that his career would be cut short by violence, he was incorrigibly skeptical as to the agency in the expected tragedy, with one solitary exception. Elderly residents of Washington will remember one Gurowski, a Polish exile, as many believed. He was an accomplished linguist, a revolutionist by nature, restless, revengeful, and of a fiery and ungovernable temper. He had been employed in the State Department as a translator, I believe, but had quarrelled with Mr. Seward and was discharged. This caused him to pursue Lincoln, Seward, and Sumner with bitter hatred. The curious will find in a published diary of his a fantastic classification of his enemies. The President he rated as "third-class," according to his estimate of statesmanlike qualities.

From this man Gurowski, and from him alone, Mr. Lincoln really apprehended danger by a violent assault, although he knew not what the sense of fear was like. Mr. Lincoln more than once said to me: "So far as my personal safety is concerned, Gurowski is the only man who has given me a serious thought of a personal nature. From the known disposition of the man, he is dangerous wherever he may be. I have sometimes thought that he might try to take my life. It would be just like him to do such a thing."

The following letter was written one night when I was much annoyed at what seemed to me Mr. Lincoln's carelessness in this matter:--

WASHINGTON, D. C. Dec. 10, 1864, 1.30 o'clock, A. M.

Hon. A. Lincoln:

SIR,--I regret that you do not appreciate what I have repeatedly said to you in regard to the proper police arrangements connected with your household and your own personal safety. You are in danger. I have nothing to ask, and I flatter myself that you will at least believe that I am honest. If, however, you have been impressed differently, do me and the country the justice to dispose at once of all suspected officers, and accept my resignation of the marshalship, which is hereby tendered. I will give you further reasons which have impelled me to this course. To-night, as you have done on several previous occasions, you went unattended to the theatre. When I say unattended, I mean that you went alone with Charles Sumner and a foreign minister, neither of whom could defend himself against an assault from any able-bodied woman in this city. And you know, or ought to know, that your life is sought after, and will be taken unless you and your friends are cautious; for you have many enemies within our lines. You certainly know that I have provided men at your mansion to perform all necessary police duty, and I am always ready myself to perform any duty that will properly conduce to your interest or your safety.

God knows that I am unselfish in this matter; and I do think that I have played low comedy long enough, and at my time of life I think I ought at least to attempt to play star engagements.

I have the honor to be Your obedient servant, WARD H. LAMON.

Mr. Lincoln had in his great heart no place for uncharitableness or suspicion; which accounts for his singular indifference to the numberless cautions so earnestly and persistently pressed upon him by friends who knew the danger to which he was hourly exposed. He had a sublime faith in human nature; and in that faith he lived until the fatal moment when the nations of the earth were startled by a tragedy whose mournful consequences no man can measure.

An unwonted interest attaches to the assassination of Mr. Lincoln, not alone from the peculiarly dramatic incidents by which it was attended, but also from the controlling influence he would unquestionably have exerted, if his life had been spared, in modifying and facilitating the solution of perhaps the greatest social and political problem of modern times. This problem, after being committed to the solemn arbitrament of the sword, and passing through its ordeal, had now reached an ulterior stage of development which demanded, in the council chamber, the exercise of even higher administrative qualities than those which had hitherto directed its general conduct in the field. These attributes, it was generally recognized and conceded, were possessed by Mr. Lincoln in a pre-eminent degree. To a constancy of purpose and tenacity of will, of which conspicuous evidence had been presented in the final triumph of the Union cause, he united a conciliatory disposition, and the gentleness, sensibility, and simplicity of a child.

Frequent reference has already been made to the humane and generous promptings of Mr. Lincoln's great soul, in all the varied relations of his life, as well private as official, and to instances of patriotism and of self-sacrifice almost unparalleled in the annals of history.

With a more enlarged experience of the violence of party passion and of internecine strife, and of the excesses to which they sometimes unhappily lead, it seems almost incredible that the apprehensions of danger to Mr. Lincoln should have been shared by so few, when one thinks of the simplicity of his domestic habits, the facilities at all times afforded for a near approach to his presence, and the entire absence of all safeguards for the protection of his person, save the watchfulness of one or two of his most immediate friends; and this, too, at a period of such unprecedented party excitement and sectional strife and animosity. But the truth is, the crime of assassination was so abhorrent to the genius of Anglo-Saxon civilization, so foreign to the spirit and practice of our republican institutions, that little danger was apprehended of an outrage against society at large, the recollection of which even now suffices to tinge with a blush of shame the cheek of every true American, whether of Northern or of Southern birth.

In 1880, after the nomination of General Garfield for President, General Grant visited Boulder, Col., where I was at that time residing. We had a long conversation on the assassination of Mr. Lincoln; and he told me that about the period of the surrender of General Lee no subject gave him deeper concern than the personal safety of the President. He stated that while no special cause existed for this apprehension, as the war was manifestly and inevitably drawing to a conclusion, he had been harassed by almost constant fears and anxieties for Mr. Lincoln's life. "I learned," said he, "that your own apprehensions were excited from the very outbreak of the war; in fact, before war was declared. It seems unaccountable to me now, in reviewing the situation, that more persons were not so impressed. I was aware, during all the latter part of the war, of your own fears, and of what you had done and were doing for his safety and protection."

I read a communication addressed to the "St. Louis Democrat," in July, 1886, by Mr. R. C. Laverty, General Grant's telegraph operator, in which he states that at the time of the surrender, "General Grant reported every day regularly to Washington, and was in constant communication at that time with the capital, because he was extremely anxious about the personal safety of the President."

Upon the assassination of Mr. Lincoln being communicated to General Grant he exclaimed: "This is the darkest day of my life! I do not know what it means. Here was the Rebellion put down in the field, and it is reasserting itself in the gutter. We had fought it as war, we have now to fight it as murder." Continuing his observations he said: "I was busy sending off orders to stop recruiting and the purchase of supplies, and to muster out the army. Mr. Lincoln had promised to go to the theatre that evening and wanted me to accompany him. While I was with the President a note was received by me from Mrs. Grant, saying that she was desirous of leaving Washington on the same evening on a visit to her daughter at Burlington. Some incidents of a trivial character had influenced this determination, and she decided to leave by an evening train. I was not disinclined to meet her wishes, not caring particularly to go to the theatre. I therefore made my excuses to the President, and at the hour determined upon we left home for the railway station. As we were driving along Pennsylvania Avenue, a horseman rode rapidly past us at a gallop, and wheeling his horse, rode back, peering into our carriage as he again passed us. Mrs. Grant, with a perceptible shade of concern in her voice and manner, remarked to me: 'That is the very man who sat near us at lunch to-day with some others, and tried to overhear our conversation. He was so rude, you remember, as to cause us to leave the dining-room. Here he is again, riding after us!' For myself I thought it was only idle curiosity, but learned afterward that the horseman was Booth. It seemed that I was also to have been attacked, and Mrs. Grant's sudden determination to leave Washington deranged the plan. Only a few days afterwards I received an anonymous letter stating that the writer had been detailed to assassinate me; that he rode in my train as far as Havre de Grace, and as my car was locked he failed to get in. He now thanked God he had so failed. I remember very well that the conductor locked our car door; but how far the letter was genuine I am unable to say. I was advised of the assassination of Mr. Lincoln in passing through Philadelphia, and immediately returned to Washington by a special train."

When the dreadful tragedy occurred I was out of the city, having gone to Richmond two days before on business for Mr. Lincoln connected with the call of a convention for reconstruction, about which there had arisen some complications. I have preserved the pass Mr. Lincoln gave me to go through to Richmond, of which the following is a fac-simile:--[12]

[12] Page 275, line 5, after the word "fac-simile."

Apropos of passes to Richmond once when a man called upon the President and solicited a pass to Richmond. Mr. Lincoln said: "Well, I would be very happy to oblige, if my passes were respected; but the fact is, sir, I have, within the past two years, given passes to 250,000 men to go to Richmond and not one has got there yet."

A. Lincoln

April 11, 1865]

This was perhaps the last passport ever written or authorized by Abraham Lincoln.

On the eve of my departure I urged upon Mr. Usher, the Secretary of the

Interior, to persuade Mr. Lincoln to exercise extreme caution, and to go out as little as possible while I was absent. Mr. Usher went with me to see Mr. Lincoln; and when about to leave, I asked him if he would make me a promise. He asked what it was, and said that he thought he could venture to say he would. I wanted him to promise me that he would not go out after night while I was gone, particularly to the theatre. He turned to Mr. Usher and said:--

"Usher, this boy is a monomaniac on the subject of my safety. I can hear him or hear of his being around, at all times of the night, to prevent somebody from murdering me. He thinks I shall be killed; and we think he is going crazy." He then added: "What does any one want to assassinate me for? If any one wants to do so, he can do it any day or night, if he is ready to give his life for mine. It is nonsense."

Mr. Usher then said: "Mr. Lincoln, it is well to listen and give heed to Lamon. He is thrown among people that give him opportunities to know more about such matters than we can know."

I then renewed my request, standing with my hat in my hand, ready to start.

"Well," said Mr. Lincoln, "I promise to do the best I can towards it." He then shook me cordially by the hand, and said, "Good-bye. God bless you, Hill!"

This was the last time I ever saw my friend.

APRIL 14

Mr. Lincoln, accompanied by his wife, Miss Harris and Maj. Rathbone, of Albany, New York, was occupying a box at Ford's Theatre, in the city of Washington. The play was "Our American Cousin," with the elder Sothern in the principal role. Mr. Lincoln was enjoying it greatly. Lee had surrendered on the 9th; on the 13th the war was everywhere regarded as ended, and upon that day Secretary Stanton had telegraphed to Gen. Dix, Governor of New York, requesting him to stop the draft. Sothern as Lord Dundreary was at his best. Lincoln was delighted. The lines which care and responsibility had so deeply graven on his brow, were now scarcely visible. His people had just passed through the greatest civil war known in the history of nations and he had become well convinced that now, the cause of strife being destroyed, the government over which he was ruling would be made stronger, greater and better by the crucial test through which it has passed. Before leaving for the theatre he had pronounced it the happiest day of his life. He looked, indeed, as if he now fully realized the consummation of the long cherished and fondest aspiration of his heart. He was at length the undisputed Chief Magistrate of a confederation of States, constituting the freest and most powerful commonwealth of modern times.

At some part of the performance Sothern appeared on the stage with Miss Meridith, the heroine, on one arm and a wrap or shawl carelessly thrown over the other. The latter seats herself upon a garden lounge placed on the stage near the box occupied by the President on this occasion. Lord Dundreary retires a few paces distant from the rustic seat when Miss Meridith, glancing languidly at his lordship, exclaims: "Me lord, will you kindly throw my shawl over my shoulders--there appears to be a draught here." Sothern, at once complying with her request, advanced with the mincing step that immortalized him; and with a merry twinkle of the eye, and a significant glance directed at Mr. Lincoln, responded in the happy impromptu: "You are mistaken, Miss Mary, the draft has already been stopped by order of the President!" This sally caused Mr. Lincoln to laugh, as few except himself could laugh, and an outburst of merriment resounded from all parts of the house. It was Mr. Lincoln's last laugh!

NOTES.

APPENDIX.

LINCOLN IN A LAW CASE.

Mr. Lincoln believed that: "He who knows only his own side of a case knows little of that." The first illustration of his peculiar mental operations which led him always to study the opposite side of every disputed question more exhaustively than his own, was on his first appearance before the Supreme Court of Illinois when he actually opened his argument by telling the court that after diligent search he had not found a single decision in favor of his case but several against it, which he then cited, and submitted his case. This may have been what Mr. Lincoln alluded to when he told Thurlow Weed that the people used to say, without disturbing his self-respect, that he was not lawyer enough to hurt him.

The most important case Mr. Lincoln ever argued before the Supreme Court was the celebrated case of the Illinois Central Railroad Company vs. McLean County.

The case was argued twice before this tribunal; one brief of which is among the forty pages of legal manuscript written by Mr. Lincoln in the writer's possession. While its four pages may have more historic value than a will case argued in the Circuit Court of Sangamon County, still the latter is chosen to illustrate the period of Mr. Lincoln's mature practice and to show his analytical methods, his original reasoning, and his keen sense of justice.

The case is one wherein land has been left to three sons and a grandson and the personal estate to be divided among three daughters after the death of the widow. Mr. Lincoln is employed to defend the will against the three daughters and their husbands.

The brief consists of fifteen pages of legal cap paper only four of which are here given.

It is said that he wrote few papers, less perhaps than any other man at the bar; therefore this memorandum in his own hand is also valuable as an example of the notes he so rarely made.

1 General remarks on the law of Wills--

2. Answer the particular points and objections made by the other side--See notes taken while they were speaking--

3. Read from the authorities and settle on a +definition+ of "Sound mind and memory"--

4 Show that in this case, the Testator had such "+Sound mind and memory+" at the time of making the Will--

1 By his asking Dr Randall to write his Will.

2. His reply to Mrs Herron*, when she saw* he was too sick & weak to make Wills.

3. His saying his Will was already made, and getting roll of blank paper--

4 His getting the package of title papers--

5 His making first provision for his wife; and charge upon Sutcliff for her and his sisters--

6 His deciding correctly, as to the "+long-way+* of the land*

7 His providing that James should pay rent to his mother.

8 His decision as to what was to be done with the home place--

9 His reply when Correll proposed that all should leave the house--

10 His calling for Robert's widow; and +so+ +asking+ the land to be given to her children.

10-1/2 His recollection of his enmity to Correll & M. Lutiro*.

11 His objection that any of his own family should be Administrator.

12. His suggesting of Hamm* for Administrator

13 His asking Cyrus Correll & Samuel Havener to witness the Will--

Add to all this his long settled purpose to make, substantially, such a Will--Quote authorities--

His eagerness about it the night before, & on the day the Will was made--his being reminded of it the day +after+--and still remaining quiet till his death--

The Will is unquestionably as it would have been, if it had been made before his sickness.]

Then a copy of the will and the evidence of sixteen witnesses, after which the following page of authorities:--

Illustration: The declarations of the Testator long before his sickness, to make such a Will as he finally did make, are admissable, and weighty evidence in support of the Will

7 Ala. 55 5 Strob. 167 7 Humph. 320 7 Ala. 519 6 Geo. 324.

Where an influence is acquired+ over a testator, by kind offices, or persuasion, unconnected with fraud, the Will made under such influence, would not be set aside--

2 N. J. 117 5 Strob. 167 3 Strob. 44. 552. 6 Geo. 324. 3 Denis 37. 1 Rich. 80 . Cheve, 37. 2 J.J. Mav. 340. 3 SvR. 267 1 Hanrig* 454. 2 Do. 375

A lower degree of of intellect is requisite to make a Will than to make a contract.

21 Vt. 168 9 Iren. 99 6 Geo 324 7 B Mon. 655 3 Denis 37 9 Conn. 102. (over, on the start*)

On "+Sound mind and memory+" and also on "+opinions+" of witnesses, see.

Sowe vs Williamson 1 Green's Ch. 82 Stoan vs Maxwell 2 Green's Ch. 563. Hunt's heirs vs Hunt 3. B. Mon. 575 M. Daniel's Will 2. J.J. Mar 331

Note--Hunt's heirs vs Hunt, above cited, contains an excellent form of an instruction to be given to a jury, as to the weight and to the opinions of the witnesses--][M]

[M] This was evidently written twice by Mr. Lincoln for it seems to be the corrected page of one in the Collection of General Orendorff. This corrected page has not the first allegation found in the rough draft: "The widow of the testator is not a competent witness. II Hump. 565."

One of the opposing attorneys in the case was Mr. Lincoln's former law partner, Judge Stephen T. Logan, who was the acknowledged leader of the Illinois Bar for many years and from whom Mr. Lincoln derived more benefit than from any other.[N]

[N] Mr. Lincoln's first partner, John T. Stuart, enjoyed telling of his own arrival in Springfield in 1828 from Kentucky; how the next morning he was standing in front of the village store wondering how to introduce himself to the community, when a well-dressed old gentleman approached him, who, interesting himself in his welfare, inquired after his history and business. "I am from Kentucky," answered Mr. Stuart, "and my profession is that of a lawyer, sir. What is the prospect here?" Throwing back his head and closing his left eye the old gentleman reflected a moment, then replied: "Young man, d---- slim chance for that kind of a combination here."

That there was a chance for that combination in Springfield has been most conclusively proven. Lincoln's three law partners at that place as well as himself were all from Kentucky, to say nothing of other prominent members of the bar of Springfield who came from the Blue Grass state.

Wants the jury to watch me +very closely+.

Says some Judges decide one way, and some another, in Will cases--

Comments on what passed between Testator & Mrs Herron, the day +after+ the Will was made--

Jonathan M. Daniel--"how* sixteen feet high"--

Comments on what is "a sound memory"

Comments on the fact that the Will was not in strict conformity to his long expressed points* now*.

Comments on fact of several of the boys having died--

Jew's notion* that names* be perpetuated* on the land

Older* arguments of last term, as to new purpose to make all equal "to stand on judgment"--

Comments on the +real+ inequality of the distribution of the property.]

Was Mr. Lincoln's experience at the bar a mere episode in his wonderful career, or was it the foundation upon which rested the whole structure of that career? He said himself that "Law is the greatest science of man. It is the best profession to develop the logical faculty and the highest platform on which man can exhibit his powers of well trained manhood."

Chicago, March 28 1860

Hon. W. H. Lamon.

My dear Sir:

Yours about motion to quash an indictment, was received yesterday. I think I have* no authority but the Statute when I wrote the Indictment--In fact, I remember but little about it. I think yet there is no necessity for setting out the latter per +haec verba+. Our Statute, as I think, relaxes* the high degree of **** certainty formerly required--

I am so busy with our case on that heir, that I can not examine authorities near as freely as you can there--

If after all, the indictment shall be quashed, it will only prove that my forte is as a Statesman, rather than as a Prosecutor*

Yours, as ever A. Lincoln.]

MR. LINCOLN'S VIEWS OF THE AMERICAN OR KNOW-NOTHING PARTY.

That Mr. Lincoln found in the Declaration of Independence his perfect standard of political truth is perhaps in none of his utterances more conclusively shown than in a private letter to his old friend Joshua F. Speed, written in 1855, in which he says: "You enquire where I now stand. That is a disputed point. I think I am a Whig; but others say there are no Whigs, and that I am an Abolitionist. I am not a Know-Nothing! that is certain. How could I be? How can anyone who abhors the oppression of negroes be in favor of degrading classes of white people? Our progress in degeneracy appears to me to be pretty rapid. As a nation we began by declaring that 'All men are created equal.' We now practically read it, 'All men are created equal except negroes.' When the Know-Nothings get control it will read, 'All men are created equal, except negroes and foreigners and Catholics.' When it comes to this, I should prefer emigrating to some country where they make no pretence of loving liberty,--where despotism can be taken pure, and without the base alloy of hypocrisy."

ACCOUNT OF ARRANGEMENTS FOR COOPER INSTITUTE SPEECH.

NEW YORK, March 20, 1872.

MY DEAR SIR,--....I send you for such use as you may deem proper the following letter written by me when at "Old Orchard Beach" a few years ago, giving the "truth of history" in relation to the address of Mr. Lincoln at the

Cooper Institute in this City on the 27th of February, 1860....

... We, the world, and all the coming generation of mankind down the long line of ages, cannot know too much about Abraham Lincoln, our martyr President.

Yours truly, (Signed) JAMES A. BRIGGS.

MR. WARD H. LAMON, WASHINGTON, D. C.

"In October, 1859, Messrs. Joseph H. Richards, J. M. Pettingill, and S. W. Tubbs called on me at the office of the Ohio State Agency, 25 William Street, and requested me to write to the Hon. Thomas Corwin, of Ohio, and the Hon. Abraham Lincoln, of Illinois, and invite them to lecture in a course of lectures these young gentlemen proposed for the winter in Plymouth Church, Brooklyn.

"I wrote the letters as requested, and offered as compensation for each lecture, as I was authorized, the sum of two hundred dollars. The proposition to lecture was accepted by Messrs. Corwin and Lincoln. Mr. Corwin delivered his lecture in Plymouth Church as he was on his way to Washington to attend Congress. Mr. Lincoln could not lecture until late in the season, and a proposition was agreed to by the gentlemen named, and accepted by Mr. Lincoln, as the following letter will show:--

DANVILLE, ILL., November 13, 1859.

JAMES A. BRIGGS, Esq.:

DEAR SIR,--Yours of the 1st, closing with my proposition for compromise, was duly received. I will be on hand, and in due time will notify you of the exact day. I believe, after all, I shall make a political speech of it. You have no objection?

I would like to know in advance, whether I am also to speak or lecture in New York.

Very, very glad your election went right.

Yours truly, A. LINCOLN.

P. S. I am here at court, but my address is still at Springfield, Ill.

"In due time Mr. Lincoln wrote me that he would deliver the lecture, a political one, on the evening of the 27th of February, 1860. This was rather late in the season for a lecture, and the young gentlemen who were responsible were doubtful about its success, as the expenses were large. It was stipulated that the lecture was to be in Plymouth Church, Brooklyn. I requested and urged that the lecture should be delivered at the Cooper Institute. They were fearful it would not pay expenses--three hundred and fifty dollars. I thought it would.

"In order to relieve Messrs. Richards, Pettingill, and Tubbs of all responsibility, I called upon some of the officers of the 'Young Men's Republican Union' and proposed that they should take Mr. Lincoln, and that the lecture should be delivered under their auspices. They respectfully declined.

"I next called upon Mr. Simeon Draper, then President of 'The Draper Republican Union Club of New York,' and proposed to him that his 'Union' take Mr. Lincoln and the lecture, and assume the responsibility of the expenses. Mr. Draper and his friends declined, and Mr. Lincoln was left in the hands of 'the original Jacobs.'

"After considerable discussion, it was agreed on the part of the young gentlemen that the lecture should be delivered in the Cooper Institute, if I would agree to share the expenses, if the sale of tickets (twenty-five cents each) for the lecture did not meet the outlay. To this I assented, and the lecture was advertised to be delivered in the Cooper Institute on the evening of the 27th of February, 1860.

"Mr. Lincoln read the notice of the lecture in the papers and, without any knowledge of the arrangement, was somewhat surprised to learn that he was first to make his appearance before a New York instead of a 'Plymouth Church' audience. A notice of the proposed lecture appeared in the New York papers, and the 'Times' spoke of him 'as a lawyer who had some local reputation in Illinois.'

"At my personal solicitation Mr. William Cullen Bryant presided as chairman of the meeting, and introduced Mr. Lincoln for the first time to a New York audience.

"The lecture was over, all the expenses were paid, I was handed by the gentlemen interested the sum of $4.25 as my share of the profits, as they would have called on me if there had been a deficiency in the receipts to meet expenses."

[Mr. Briggs received as his share of the profits $4.25. What the country profited by this, Mr. Lincoln's first triumph outside of his own state, has never been computed.]

THE RAIL-SPLITTER.

It has been said that the term "rail-splitter" which became a leading feature of the campaign in 1860 originated at the Chicago convention when Mr. Deland of Ohio, who seconded the nomination of Mr. Lincoln, said: "I desire to second the nomination of a man who can split rails and maul Democrats."

Mr. Delano not only seconded the nomination, but "seconded" the campaign "cry."

Gov. Oglesby one week before at the State Convention at Decatur introduced into the assemblage John Hanks, who bore on his shoulder two small rails surmounted by a banner with this inscription: "Two rails from a lot made by Abraham Lincoln and John Hanks in the Sangamon Bottom in the year 1830."

For six months Rail-splitter was heard everywhere and rails were to be seen on nearly everything, even on stationery. One of the Lincoln delegates said: "These rails represent the issue between labor free and labor slave, between democracy and aristocracy."

The Democrats disliked to hear so much about "honest Old Abe," "the rail-splitter" the "flatboatman," "the pioneer." These cries had an ominous sound in their ears. Just after the State Convention which named Lincoln as first choice of the Republicans of Illinois, an old man, devoted to the principles of Democracy and much annoyed by the demonstration in progress, approached Mr. Lincoln and said, "So you're Abe Lincoln?"--"That's my name, sir," answered Mr. Lincoln. "They say you're a self-made man," said the Democrat. "Well, yes," said Lincoln, "what there is of me is self-made."--"Well, all I've got to say," observed the old man after a careful survey of the statesman before him, "is that it was a ---- bad job."

TEMPERANCE.

On the temperance question Mr. Lincoln has been quoted by the adherents of both sides. He had no taste for spirituous liquors and when he took them it was a punishment to him, not an indulgence. In a temperance lecture delivered in 1842 Mr. Lincoln said:--"In my judgment such of us as have never fallen victims have been spared more from the absence of appetite than from any mental or moral superiority over those who have. Indeed, I believe if we take habitual drunkards as a class their heads and their hearts will bear an advantageous comparison with those of any other class."

None of his nearest associates ever saw Mr. Lincoln voluntarily call for a drink but many times they saw him take whiskey with a little sugar in it to avoid the appearance of discountenancing it to his friends. If he could have avoided it without giving offence he would gladly have done so. He was a conformist to the conventionalities of the surroundings in which he was placed.

Whether Mr. Lincoln sold liquor by the dram over the counter of the grocery store kept by himself and Berry will forever remain an undetermined question. When Douglas revived the story in one of his debates, Mr. Lincoln replied that even if it were true, there was but little difference between them, for while he figured on one side of the counter Douglas figured on the other.

Mr. Lincoln disliked sumptuary laws and would not prescribe by statute what other men should eat or drink. When the temperance men ran to the Legislature to invoke the power of the state, his voice--the most eloquent among them--was silent. He did not oppose them, but quietly withdrew from the cause and left others to manage it.

In 1854 he was induced to join the order called Sons of Temperance, but never attended a single meeting after the one at which he was initiated.

Judge Douglas once undertook to ridicule Mr. Lincoln on not drinking. "What, are you a temperance man?" he inquired. "No," replied Lincoln, "I am not a temperance man but I am temperate in this, to wit: I don't drink."

He often used to say that drinking spirits was to him like thinking of spiritualism, he wanted to steer clear of both evils; by frequent indulgence he might acquire a dangerous taste for the spirit and land in a drunkard's grave; by frequent thought of spiritualism he might become a confirmed believer in it and land in a lunatic asylum.

In 1889 Miss Kate Field wrote W. H. Lamon saying:--

Will you kindly settle a dispute about Lincoln? Lately in Pennsylvania I quoted Lincoln to strengthen my argument against Prohibition, and now the W. C. T. U. quote him for the other side. What is the truth?

... As you are the best of authority on the subject of Abraham Lincoln, can you explain why he is quoted on the Prohibition side? Did he at any time make speeches that could be construed with total abstinence?

To this Lamon replied:--

You ask my recollection of Mr. Lincoln's views on the question of Temperance and Prohibition. I looked upon him as one of the safest temperance men I ever knew. He seemed on this subject, as he was on most others, unique in profession as well as in practice. He was neither what might be called a drinking man, a total abstainer, nor a Prohibitionist. My acquaintance with him commenced in 1847. He was then and afterwards a politician. He mixed much and well with the people. Believed what the people believed to be right was right.

Society in Illinois at that early day was as crude as the country was uncultivated. People then were tenacious of their natural as well as their acquired rights and this state of things existed until Mr. Lincoln left the State to assume the duties of President. The people of Illinois firmly believed it was one of their inalienable rights to manufacture, sell, and drink whiskey as it was the sacred right of the southern man to rear, work, and whip his own nigger,--and woe be unto him who attempted to interfere with these rights--(as the sequel afterwards showed when Mr. Lincoln and his friends tried to prevent the southern man from whipping his own nigger in the territories).

I heard Mr. Lincoln deliver several temperance lectures. One evening in Danville, Ill., he happened in at a temperance meeting, the "Old Washingtonian Society," I think, and was called on to make a speech. He got through it well, after which he and other members of the Bar who were present were invited to an entertainment at the house of Dr. Scott. Wine and cake were handed around. Mrs. Scott, in handing Mr. Lincoln a glass of homemade wine, said, "I hope you are not a teetotaler, Mr. Lincoln, if you are a temperance lecturer." "By no means, my dear madam," he replied; "for I do assure you (with a humorous smile) I am very fond of my 'Todd' (a play upon his wife's maiden name). I by no means oppose the use of wine. I only regret that it is not more in universal use. I firmly believe if our people were to habitually drink wine, there would be little drunkenness in the country." In the conversation which afterward became general, Judge David Davis, Hon. Leonard Swett, and others present joining in the discussion, I recollect his making this remark: "I am an apostle of temperance only to the extent of coercing moderate indulgence and prohibiting excesses by all the moral influences I can bring to bear."

LINCOLN'S SHREWDNESS.

Perhaps no act of Mr. Lincoln's administration showed his political shrewdness more clearly than the permission he gave for the rebel legislature of Virginia to meet for the purpose of recalling the state troops from General Lee's Army. This permission was given in a note to General Weitzel. Mr. Lincoln told Governor Francis H. Pierpont that "its composition occupied five hours of intense mental activity." Governor Pierpont says he was the loyal Governor of Virginia at the time, and Mr. Lincoln deemed it necessary to say something to him about so extraordinary a measure as permitting the rebel legislature to assemble when a loyal legislature with a loyal governor was in existence and was recognized by the federal government. Mr. Lincoln's note to General Weitzel read:--

"It has been intimated to me that the gentlemen who have acted as the legislature of Virginia in support of the rebellion may now desire to assemble at Richmond and take measures to withdraw the Virginia troops and other support from resistance to the general government. If they attempt it, give them permission and protection until, if at all, they attempt some action hostile to the United States, in which case you will notify them, give them reasonable time to leave, and at the end of which time arrest any who remain. Allow Judge Campbell to see this, but do not make it public."

To write this note occupied all Mr. Lincoln's time from 9 P. M. till 2 A. M.--"five hours of uninterrupted stillness."

Mr. Lincoln foresaw that an attempt would be made to construe his permission into a virtual recognition of the authority of the rebel legislature. He steered clear of this recognition by not speaking of them "as a legislature," but as, "the gentlemen who have acted as the legislature of Virginia in support of rebellion," and explained afterward when it was misconstrued, that he "did this on purpose to exclude the assumption that I was recognizing them as a rightful body. I dealt with them as men having power de facto to do a specific thing."

LETTERS.

FAIRFIELD, CONN., Jan. 9, 1861.

W. H. LAMON, Esq.:

DEAR SIR,--Yours of December 26th duly received. Connecticut is death on secession. I regard it the duty of the Government to uphold its authority in the courts as effectually south as it has done north if it can, and to hold its forts and public grounds at whatever cost and collect the revenue ditto. There is but one feeling here, I believe, though in the city of New York there are those who sustain her actions, that secession is disgraceful as well as ruinous on the part of South Carolina. I glory in Lincoln now for I feel that he is the most suitable man of our party for this terrible ordeal through which he has to pass. I rely with entire confidence upon his urbanity, gentleness, goodness, and ability to convince his enemies of his perfect uprightness as well as his firmness and courage. I do not expect him to be as warlike as Jackson, but I look for the calm courage befitting a Judge on the bench. With Lincoln as President and Scott as Lieutenant-General, I have no fears but the dignity of the Government will be sustained after the 4th of March. What is being done to protect Lincoln personally at Washington before and after Inauguration? Is there not a propriety in some of his friends making it their especial business to escort him without even his knowing it? You know these Southern men better than I do. If there is propriety in such a thing, or need for it, rather, I would meet you at Washington when he goes on and stay with you while it is needed.

Yours truly, BRONSON MURRAY.

NEWARK, OHIO, Feby. 14, 1861.

FRIEND LAMON,--I concluded to drop you this note, on learning that you in company with our mutual friend Judge Davis were with the President Elect on his tour to the Seat of Government. I was led to this through fear of the failure of some correspondence to reach your eye, the drift of it was to secure the appointment of postmaster at this city for your humble servant. Now if you have not been bored to death already by friends who are your humble servants, say a kind word for me. I have asked for the Post Office here for some good reasons. Poor enough to ask it and capable to fill it ... and have my second papers for being Black Republican. I might add that the Citizens would not look upon my appointment as an overt act against this City. I was removed from the Post Office Dept. in 1855 for opposition to Judge Douglas for removing the Missouri Compromise.... I would beg to be remembered to Messrs. Lincoln and Davis. Wishing you all a pleasant trip, safe arrival and a smooth sea in the future.

Yours very truly, JAS. H. SMITH.

The following letter may be of interest as showing the impression made at a time when opinions of Mr. Lincoln were in the formative state. New York City, as a whole, was unfriendly to Lincoln. Written when Lincoln was in New York on his way to Washington.

NEW YORK, Feby. 20, 1861.

DEAR LAMON,--I was glad today to recognize you; and drop you a line instead of a call when you must be so weary.

Just before we met, my father and old Ald^{n} Purdy (both wheel-horses in the Dem^{t} party here) were canvassing matters politic. Purdy said he had seen Lincoln and liked the man; said he was much better looking and a finer man than he expected to see; and that he kept aloof from old politicians here and seemed to have a mind of his own. Old Judge Benson too (who was with us) is a Democrat and was equally pleased with Lincoln. He says Lincoln has an eye that shows power of mind and will, and he thinks he will carry us safely.

I repeat these comments, because they came from behind the scenes of the popular apprehensions whence at present our friend Lincoln is excluded, and

I feel sure he will be pleased to know how favorable an impression he makes....

Tell Lincoln to use his own judgment and be bold and firm. The people of all parties here are prepared to sustain him. But he may beware of all old politicians of both parties.

Because he is a fresh man and an able one he was taken up. Let his freshness enter his policy also

Your friend, BRONSON MURRAY.

SPRINGFIELD, Feb. 22, 1861.

HILL,--This is Dick Gilmer of Pike--he is to that neck of Woods what you or Dick Oglesby are to this region of Country.... Do what you can consistently for him--and oblige

Your friend, O. M. HATCH.

BLOOMINGTON (ILL.), Feby. 25, 1861.

DEAR HILL,--Nothing of moment has occurred since your departure. Do write me immediately explaining the cause of your mysterious transit through Maryland.

Here let me say a word about Washington. It is the worst place in the world to judge correctly of anything. A ship might as well learn its bearings in the Norway Maelstrom, as for you people to undertake to judge anything correctly upon your arrival there.

You are the subject of every artful and selfish appliance. You breathe an air pregnant with panic. You have to decide before you can discover the secret springs of the action presented to you.

There is but one rule and that is to stand by and adopt the judgment you formed before you arrived there.

The atmosphere of Washington and the country are as unlike as the atmosphere of Greenland and the tropics.

The country is moved and moves by its judgment--Washington by its artificial life. The country really knows nothing of Washington and Washington knows nothing of the country. Washington is drunk, the Country is sober and the appeal from your judgment there to your home judgment is simply an appeal from Philip drunk to Philip sober.

Please give these ideas in better language than I have done to Mr. Lincoln. I know his sound home judgment, the only thing I fear is the bewilderment of that city of rumors. I do ache to have him do well.

Yours truly, LEONARD SWETT.

WASHINGTON, March 2, 1861.

DEAR SIR,--I have received your request and shall take great pleasure to do what you wish in respect to Delaware.

Very truly your friend, WINFIELD SCOTT.

WARD H. LAMON, Esq. DANVILLE, ILL., March 5, 1861.

DEAR HILL,--Have just read Lincoln's inaugural.--It is just right and pleases us much. Not a word too much or too little. He assumes the tone and temper of a statesman of the olden time. God bless him--and keep him safely to the end.--Are you coming home to see us ere you depart hence? You could unfold to us a chapter that would be spicy, rich and rare.

We were at first disposed to regret Lincoln's hasty trip from Harrisburgh. But the action of the crowd at Baltimore convinces us that it was the most prudent course to pursue....

O. F. HARMON.

ON BOARD STEAMER WARSAW, March 8, 1861.

DEAR LAMON,--I got home a week ago. I have heard a good many things said pro and con about the new administration, and as far as I have heard the mass of the people have confidence in Mr. Lincoln, and this applies to the people of the border slave states as well as the free states. But it is not worth while to disguise the fact that a large majority of the free states in the Northwest are opposed to Ultra measures and the people of the slave states are almost unanimous against coercion. Many appointments that have been made by the new administration were unfortunate. It must necessarily be so with all administrations, and Mr. Lincoln has had more than his share of trouble in making his selection. I fear that a majority of the Senators on our side care but little for his success further than it can contribute to their own glory, and they have had such men appointed to office as they felt would serve their own purpose without any reference to Mr. Lincoln and but little for the party....

As far as I could see when at Washington, to have been an original friend of Mr. Lincoln was an unpardonable offence with Members of Congress....

I have the utmost confidence in the success of Mr. Lincoln but I do not expect his support to come from the radical element of our party....

Your true friend, HAWKINS TAYLOR.

HON. W. H. LAMON.

STATE OF ILLINOIS, SECRETARY'S OFFICE, SPRINGFIELD, March, 18, 1861.

WARD H. LAMON:

DEAR HILL,--My brother is foolish enough to desire an office.--When you see him, and this, if he still insists that he has as good right to a place as anybody else, I want you to do for him, what you would for me. No more, no less--...

Your friend, O. M. HATCH.

March 19, 1861.

MY DEAR COLONEL,--When I left Washington I handed to Judge Davis a letter setting forth what I wished him to do for me in Washington if it met his views.

I desired to be detailed as acting Inspector General of the Army in place of Emory promoted Lieutenant-Colonel of the Cavalry. This appointment needs only an order of the Secretary of War. Mr. Cameron promised Judge Davis to attend to it at once, but I presume he has overlooked it. Will you do me the favor to see Cameron on the subject? He knows all about it and precisely what to do.

I hope you are having a good time in Washington. I presume you are as you seem to have very much enjoyed the excitement along the road and in

Washington. I shall always cherish a most pleasant remembrance of our journey and of the agreeable acquaintances and friends I made on the road. Among the last I have rated you and Judge Davis with peculiar satisfaction and I hope you will always believe that I shall cherish the warmest personal regard for you.

Very truly your friend, JOHN POPE.

MARCH 23, 1861.

DEAR HILL,--The public mind is prepared to hear of the evacuation of Sumter, but it is a great humiliation. Still if Mr. Lincoln gives the order you may swear that such is the public confidence in him it will be at once taken as a necessity of the situation.

W. H. HANNA.

BLOOMINGTON, ILL., March 30, 1861.

DEAR HILL,--I saw the "Telegraphic Announcement" of your prospective trip to Charleston before your kind and cordial letter was received. Yesterday, the "Telegraph" announced your return to Washington, which gratified us all. The papers represent you as quite a Lion. I have no doubt you bear your honors meekly....

I am anxious about the country. Are we to be divided as a nation? The thought is terrible. I never entertained a question of your success in getting to and from Charleston.

How do things look at Washington? Are the appointments satisfactory? No foreign appointments for the border slave states? Is this policy a wise one? Off here it does not look so to me.

Did Hawkins Taylor of Iowa get anything?...

Your friend, D. DAVIS.

URBANA, Apr. 6, 1861.

DEAR HILL,--The Judge and I are now attending Court at this place, the only wreck of that troupe which was once the life and soul of professional life in this country. I see Judge McLean has departed this life. The question is who shall succeed to the ermin so worthily worn by him. Why should not David Davis who was so instrumental in giving position to him who now holds the matter in the hollow of his hand? Dear Hill, if retribution, justice, and gratitude are to be respected, Lincoln can do nothing less than to tender the position to Judge Davis. I want you to suggest it to Lincoln.... Of course you will. I know your noble nature too well to believe that you would not think of a suggestion of this kind as soon as myself. Write me.

Yours, L. WELDON.

BLOOMINGTON, Apr. 7, 1861.

DEAR HILL,--Why don't you write. Tell us something.

By the way, since McLean's death the friends of Judge Davis think Lincoln ought to put him on Supreme Bench. Now I want you to find out when this appointment will be made. Also tell Lincoln that Judge Davis will be an applicant, so that he may not ignore the fact or act without that knowledge. I wish, too, you would without fail go immediately to Cameron, Caleb B. Smith, and Gov. Seward and tell them Davis will be an applicant. Tell Smith what I know, that it was through the Illinois fight and Judge Davis that Judd went out and he went in, and we think we ought to be remembered for it.

Now, Hill, I know you are bored to death, but our mutual regard for the Judge must make us doubly industrious and persistent in this case.

Write immediately what the chances are, how Lincoln feels about it, and what we ought to do.

Yours truly, LEONARD SWETT.

WASHINGTON, April 8, 1861.

HON. WARD H. LAMON:

MY DEAR SIR,--I cannot deny the request of the Reverend Mr. Wright, so far as to enclose the within letter. I do not know the person recommended personally; but the Reverend gentleman who writes the letter is a most estimable and worthy man, whom I should be delighted to gratify if I felt at liberty to recommend any one, which I do not under existing circumstances.

I am very respectfully your obedient servant, S. A. DOUGLAS.

ST. LOUIS, MO., April 11, 1861.

COL. WARD H. LAMON:

DEAR SIR,--On the 30th of July last I was assaulted by twenty-five outlaws in Texas--with but one fighting friend to stand by me. I gave an honorable compromise, and came forth from my stronghold, in the presence of my would-be hangmen, a daring Republican and a fearless Lincoln man. But it afterwards became necessary for me to leave Texas or be suspended. As I preferred dying in a horizontal position, I left, came to St. Louis and am now at the service of Mr. Lincoln and our country. If war is made I want a showing in Texas. There are many true and loyal men there. A few thousand soldiers thrown in there to form a nucleus around which the Houston Union men can rally will soon form a barrier to rebellion in the Southwest. When the "ball" opens I would like to be authorized to raise five hundred men to occupy a position on Red River at the mouth of Bogy Creek.

What can you do to assist me in doing something of the kind. I will look for a reply to this in a few days.

Yours truly, J. E. LEMON.

BLOOMINGTON, ILLINOIS, April 16, 1861.

COL. W. H. LAMON:

DEAR HILL,--I send you the result of a public meeting here last night. We are, thank God, all right....

Secession, disunion and even fault finding is done with in this City. We shall all stand firmly by the administration and fight it out.

On last Monday we had a few fights, for just at that time we could not and would not allow a single word of fault found with the administration; the result was that three Democrats got thrashed. Just then we were hearing the news of Fort Sumter, now we are all on one side.

I write this that you may know the exact truth about us. If there is any service I can render the government--count me always on hand to do it. Write me if you can get time.

Your friend, W. H. HANNA.

INDIANAPOLIS, INDIANA, April 19, 1861.

DEAR SIR,--Sufficient companies have been formed in Indiana or nearly so to fill the six Regiments of our state. They of course contain all classes of persons, but many of them are our best and dearest youths with whom it has cost many a sigh and burning tear to part. Thousands more will soon be made ready to join. We are now of course intensely anxious about the Commandants and suppose that the President will have the appointment of those officers, and my object in writing this is to request you without fail to see the President and General Cameron and say to them that we are all sensitive upon the appointments of the Brigadier General of this state, and say to them that the appointment of a mere civilian will give extreme dissatisfaction not only to the troops but to their friends.

I name no person of that character who is an aspirant but I regret to say that there are some of that character here. From the appointment of one of whom, may God in his infinite mercy save us.

I believe every man in our State will arm, and those who refuse will be hung and their property confiscated. There is a feeling all through the State of the most intense character, wholly indescribable. I can do nothing of business. I am now helping our 200 men off, encouraging and counselling them what I can. Unless some change in my feelings now strained to the utmost pitch, I shall not be far behind them.

Our boys are taking the oath in the Hall of the House, and the telegraph brings intelligence of the fighting at Baltimore and the burning of Harper's Ferry. The boys take the oath with a look of determination to do or die.

All our fears now are for Washington. May God preserve you until succor comes.

Ever yours, J. P. USHER.

I am so excited that I can scarcely write legibly, but say to the President that the entire power of Indiana with all its men, women and children, money and goods, will be sacrificed if necessary to sustain the government; the treachery of Virginia only intensifies the feeling.

J. P. U.

TERRE HAUTE, INDIANA, May 5, 1861.

W. H. LAMON, Esq.:

DEAR SIR,--Since I wrote to you on the 19th ult. I have been at Indianapolis endeavoring to aid the Governor in such way as I could. My desire has been to prevent rash counsels from being followed and from incurring unnecessary expense, and I think I have had some influence in keeping down extravagance. We are appalled every day by some new development of the dreadful conspiracy which has been formed for the entire overthrow of the Government. I hope its worst has now been realized and that whatever may occur hereafter will be for the better. Of one thing the President may rest perfectly satisfied, that the entire voice of Indiana is for the most vigorous prosecution of the War. I have no doubt but that 50,000 men could be raised in a month. All business has been suspended and the people do not expect to do anything until the war is ended. My desire is that it be pushed as fast as it possibly can, not rashly, but rapidly accompanied by such necessary severity as will be a terror to evil-doing. We have nothing to expect from Kentucky or Missouri, they remain partly quiet because of their proximity to the free states. My opinion is that they will not revolt now, or if they do, it will be in that partial way to avoid any entire destruction for the industrial interests of those states. However that may be, they refuse to answer to the call of the President for volunteers and I am totally opposed to their being suffered to remain in the attitude like cow-boys of the Revolution.

I am for suspending all trade with them, if they will not furnish their quota of troops.

If you please, and think it will not be deemed to be too impertinent in me, say to the President that my opinion is that the troops at Cairo should stop all boats of every kind passing down the river and that no provisions whatever should be permitted to be shipped to any state refusing to furnish their quota of troops. It will prevent violence here: throughout Indiana, Ohio, and Illinois most of the people think that trade of all kinds with the rebels should cease, and that can only be accomplished by the proclamation of the President. I hope he will make the proclamation. Our people want it, but his advisers there and his own wisdom, in which I have all confidence, will control. The people of the West expect him, nay all the civilized world expects him to press forward with undeviating firmness until the rebellion is crushed. We possess nothing too valuable for the sacrifice. Let us not be rash, but to the best advantage let us put the lives and worldly goods of us all upon the altar for the sacrifice, for the preservation of the government. Neither life nor goods will be valuable or worth preservation if the Constitution is to be overthrown. No villainy like this has ever occurred in the history of man, or one that deserves such terrible punishment. I believe it is said in history, though fabulous, that no spear of grass ever grew where Attila stepped his foot. I do most religiously hope that there will be a foot heavy enough to let down upon old Virginia to stop the growth of grass for a time. The evil must be met, and we were never in a better condition to test our patriotism.

Western Virginia has a Convention on the 14th; how will it do for Indiana to send a Commissioner? I think I could get Governor Morton to send R. W. Thompson. Suppose you ask Lincoln what he thinks of it. Thompson has been taking great interest in the war, making speeches and putting the people right. I have no doubt he will be much flattered at an appointment to the loyal Virginians, and if it is thought best at Washington, I think I can have it done. I shall be at Indianapolis for a day or two, when I shall return and be at the Charleston and Danville, Illinois, Courts for the next two weeks. Don't you wish you could be there?

Most truly yours, J. P. USHER.

BLOOMINGTON, ILL., May 6, 1861.

DEAR HILL,--Your anxious and harassing state at Washington during those perilous times has so occupied your time and attention that you have not had any leisure to write. I have not heard from you for three weeks. For the last three weeks I have been holding court in Lincoln. The excitement about enlisting nearly broke the court up for two weeks. I was at Springfield two days week before last and found everything astir. I need not say that you were missed at Lincoln by me and everybody else. Your absence was regretted by everyone and yet everyone thought you deserved your good fortune.

I found Trumbull very unpopular with the members of the Legislature and other parties at Springfield. Douglas is in the topmost wave. Douglas would beat Trumbull before this legislature. My course last summer in using my best endeavors to elect Trumbull does not meet with my own approbation.

This war and its dreadful consequences affects my spirits.... It is very lonely going round the circuit without you.

DAVID DAVIS.

DEAR HILL,--I have written you about every week since I left Urbana. Dan Voorhees has been here for two days. He is a devoted friend of yours. He feels badly about the state of the country but is for the maintenance of the Government....

Mr. [Joseph G.] Cannon the new Prosecutor is a pleasant, unassuming gentleman and will in time make a good Prosecutor.[O]

[O] This prophecy was certainly fulfilled.

I need not tell you that it is lonesome here--on account of your absence. This is my last court here and no lawyer is practising here who was practising here when I held my first court. This is emphatically a world of change.

Your friend as ever, DAVID DAVIS.

WASHINGTON, D. C., June 4, 1861.

COLONEL LAMON:

MY DEAR SIR,--I would be obliged to you to procure for me that Presidential interview as soon as practicable. I do not wish to trouble you, but I am in a considerable hurry. I wish to say some things to the President about matters in North Carolina. There are some Union men there yet.

Respectfully yours, CHAS. HENRY FOSTER.

BLOOMINGTON, ILLINOIS, August 25, 1861.

COL. WARD H. LAMON:

DEAR HILL,--We are making great preparations for war in this State, and will have twenty thousand men in camp, besides those already in Missouri, in a very short time. There is a universal demand for the removal of Mr. Cameron, and I think after all, the sooner it is done the better. Mr. Lincoln certainly has no idea of the universal disposition of the whole people on this subject. I feel that Cameron wants to render the war unpopular by mismanagement, for they all know that if this war is successfully prosecuted that all the scoundrels cannot keep Mr. Lincoln from being re-elected President.

Do tell Mr. Lincoln this thing, tell him also that he has the confidence of all parties, except the traitors....

I know Lincoln well enough to know that he will make no mistakes, if he will consult his own will and act up to it bravely and without hesitation. It is the best time in the world to be President, but he must be all President. Halfway measures will only now tend to our ruin and disgrace.

I fear Trumbull is a rascal,--the idea of his being unprepared in the Senate to vote for the resolution approving the act of the President, has killed him off. I will bet you a bottle of wine that he sees the day he will want to exchange that little speech....

I am perhaps too impatient, and I am besides under some personal obligations to Mr. Cameron, but in this fight I care nothing about obligations of friendship in opposition to the welfare of the country. No one man nor any number of men can in my estimation be allowed for one moment to stand in the way of good government.

Excuse me for all this and believe me in everything. I am,

Your friend, W. A. HANNA. The city is full of soldiers and we are all marching left foot foremost.

W. H. H.

WILLARD'S HOTEL, 7 P. M. Aug. 30, 1861.

DEAR SIR,--General Scott notified me that if I would make an arrangement with the President to receive the Fort Sumter Garrison at some definite time, he would be most happy to be present at the reception. My men are at leisure either to-morrow or Monday, or in fact any time during the next week. Will you have the kindness to arrange it and let me know the result? I will call at this hotel for your answer.

Yours very truly, A. DOUBLEDAY.

TO COL. WARD H. LAMON.

FORT LAFAYETTE, Oct. 24, 1861.

MY DEAR SIR,--It is nearly three months since I have been seized and held as a close prisoner by the Government of the United States. No charge ever has--none can be--preferred against me,--and yet I am robbed of my liberty--separated from my family and home, and have been subjected to irreparable pecuniary loss. Is it possible that your friend Mr. Lincoln can permit such acts to be done in his name and under his administration? It is not possible for me to give you in a brief letter a just view of my relations to the Government or of its conduct to me, but I ask you to get the President in company with yourself to examine my correspondence with the War and State Departments, commencing on the nineteenth of September. After their perusal I think you will agree with me, that no man has ever within the limits of the United States been more unjustly deprived of his liberty. In truth, the President and yourself will reach the conclusion that the honor and good faith of the Government demand my release.

Yours truly, CHAS. J. FAULKNER.

In 1862 Hawkins Taylor wrote:--

Thinking back to the Presidential Campaign I cannot help but think how strange things have turned. I was an original Lincoln man, worked for him before, at, and in the State Convention for the nomination of Delegates to the Chicago Convention. Grimes scouted the idea of such a country lawyer being President. When the Chicago Convention came off Colonel Warren, knowing that I was scarce of funds and knowing my anxiety for the nomination of Mr. Lincoln, sent me a ticket to Chicago and back. I pledged a watch that cost me $128 for money to pay expenses there and to our State Convention.

Colonel Warren also went to Chicago, and to my own certain knowledge, rendered most important services to Mr. Lincoln. At the State Convention he was put at the head of the electoral ticket, canvassed the entire state, made more than one hundred speeches, spent his money by the hundreds. While Grimes made two or three speeches, grumbled privately at the nomination, damned the President upon all occasions since he took his seat. Yet Grimes has controlled the entire patronage of the State of Iowa to the exclusion of Colonel Warren and all his friends. How can Mr. Lincoln expect friends in Iowa under this state of things?

ILLINOIS, Feb. 12, 1862.

... By the bye I do not care how soon you come back to Illinois provided always that I should hate for Hale Grimes & Co. to have their way in driving off every one who does not believe in negro stealing.... Yet I feel a good deal like they profess to feel. I should be glad to see the poor negroes free and provided for, but the abolition leaders seem to me to entertain more hatred to the owners than love for the negroes, and to be willing to sacrifice Whites, Negroes, Country and Constitution to the gratification of their ambition and malignity.

I feel very glad at the progress the war is now making as I do hope the present prospect of speedy success will enable Lincoln and other conservative Republicans and Democrats to set at defiance the ravings of the abolitionists and universal confiscation men. If their mouths can be stopped I have now good hope that the union can soon be restored and that a few months will bring daylight out of the troubles of the Country....

Yours respectfully, S. T. LOGAN.

OFFICE CHIEF QUARTER-MASTER DEPARTMENT OF THE GULF NEW ORLEANS, Dec. 8, 1862.

DEAR HILL,--I have given both our Representatives from here letters of introduction to you. Messrs. Flanders and Hahn. You will find Flanders old enough to take care of himself, but I desire that you be especially attentive to Hahn as I want him to defend Mr. Lincoln. He is very popular here and has very considerable influence and can do Mr. Lincoln a great deal of good. See that he falls into the right hands,--men who support the policy of the administration. Both men are now right and I depend on our friends to keep them right. Let me hear from you.

As ever your friend, J. WILSON SHAFFER.

Quietly say to Lincoln to cultivate these men as they both desire to find out what he wants and they will do it.

J. W. S.

12 NORTH A STREET, Feb. 26, 1863.

MY DEAR SIR,--Mr. J. N. Carpenter, who is a pay-master in the Navy, has always borne and does now bear the character of a truthfully upright and veracious man. I am requested to say this of him to you and I give my testimony accordingly without knowing what the object may be of getting it. He is a member of the true church which believes in the ancient gospel, and you are related by marriage to the same establishment. If you can do any good for Mr. C. you will recollect that it is done unto them of the household of faith and you will no doubt do it with the more alacrity when you remember that Satan also takes care of his own.

I am most respectfully yours, &c., HON. W. H. LAMON. J. S. BLACK.

DECATUR, ILL., March 24, 1863.

COLONEL WARD,--Received a letter yesterday from Judge Davis who informs me that you and Swett joined him heartily in efforts to secure my promotion, that this was all done without my knowledge or encouragement, from pure motives of personal attachment and kind old remembrances. Allow me, Sir, to thank you kindly for this disinterested and zealous effort to benefit and honor me. I did not deserve the honor. I will try to do my best, however, and save my friends and self from disgrace. I learn you are prospering and are unchangeably the same. I hope some day to meet you again when our Country will allow us all once more to feel happy and at rest.

I go to the field to-day, although I am far from well....

Do not forget to remember me to the President cordially. May God spare his life many years yet. I hope he never despairs or falters under his heavy burden.

Most respectfully Your friend, R. J. OGLESBY.

WARD H. LAMON, Marshal of D. C.

NASHVILLE, January 10, 1865.

TO WARD H. LAMON:

DEAR SIR,--I am anxious to have a young Philadelphia lawyer made captain of the regular army, and I know of no one so likely to present the matter directly to Mr. Stanton or the President as yourself. Will you oblige me by attending to the matter? I am suffering from a fall and unable to get to Washington.

Most respectfully your obedient servant, J. CATRON.

KENTUCKY, January 23, 1865.

WARD H. LAMON, Esq.:

MY DEAR SIR,--....Please remember me to Mr. Lincoln and thank him for his great kindness shown me during my last visit to your city. I do hope and pray that he may stand firm to the end of this wicked Rebellion, and while he administers mercy so freely that he will not forget justice. I am in favor of mercy, but never at the expense of justice_. I know he is magnanimous. He is too much so sometimes, I fear. But I had rather trust him in this great crisis than any other man living. May God give him wisdom to direct, mercy to temper, and justice to balance the mighty interests of humanity that tremble in the balance!

I should be happy to hear from you at an early date.

With kindest wishes for your health and prosperity,

I am, dear Sir, Your most obedient servant, D. P. HENDERSON.

CHICAGO, February 10, 1865.

DEAR SIR,--Enclosed is a letter which I wish you to place in the hands of President Lincoln in person.

I fear it will not get to him until action is had.

I am very sorry to trouble him, but my friends demand it of me. I told them that you would put it in his hands yourself.

Your obedient servant, JNO. WENTWORTH.

BLOOMINGTON, ILL., April 4, 1865.[P]

[P] Only ten days before the Assassination.

COL. WARD H. LAMON:

DEAR HILL,--....I am going with Governor Oglesby to visit the armies of Grant and Sherman, and shall call on you in passing.

We have glorious news, and am feeling happy over it.

I hope the President will keep out of danger; the chivalry are a greater set of scoundrels than he thinks them to be.

Mr. Lincoln's personal safety is of such vast importance to the country at this time, that his friends feel more or less solicitous when they read of his "going to the front." But he has made a glorious trip this time.

Your friend, W. H. HANNA.

RELIGION.

January 31, 1874.

REV. HENRY WARD BEECHER:

MY DEAR SIR,--My attention has been directed to a "Review of the Life of Lincoln" which appeared in the "Christian Union." This paper was by many attributed to your pen; it certainly must have received your editorial sanction.

I do not conceal the fact that some of its criticisms touched me sharply; but I determined, after no little deliberation, that it was better to submit in silence to whatever might be said or written of that biography. It happens, however, that certain lectures delivered by Mr. Herndon of Illinois have renewed the discussion of Mr. Lincoln's unbelief, and incident to that discussion some of the bitterest enemies of my own have taken occasion to renew their assaults upon me for what my honest duty as a biographer made it necessary for me to record in regard to so important an element in Mr. Lincoln's character.

Many of these self-appointed critics I know, and have long known. Their motives need no interpretation. Their hostility to me is very great, but it fails to equal the treachery with which they betrayed Mr. Lincoln while living, or the hypocrisy with which they chant his eulogies when dead.

Their malignment of the lamented President during the most anxious and trying period of his administration was so outrageous and vindictive that if Booth had wrapped his bullet in a shred of their correspondence he might have lodged a vindication of his crime in the brain of his victim. But these men could have no connection with this letter were it not that in this assault upon my character they have claimed the authority of the "Union" to sustain one of their unjust charges. I trust you will pardon the earnestness with which I protest against your conclusions as to myself, both because of their intrinsic injustice, and the sanction they have since given to the expression of others who can know nothing of the dignity and impartiality which belongs to honest criticism.

When the life of Lincoln was written it was my honest purpose to give to the world a candid, truthful statement of all facts and incidents of his life of which I was possessed, or could, by diligent investigation, procure, so as to give a true history of that wonderful man. I was well aware from the first that by pursuing such a course I would give offence to some; for who that ever had courage enough to write or utter great truths, since the commencement of the Christian era to the present time, has not been held up to public scorn and derision for his independence? Knowing this and yet believing that I knew Mr. Lincoln as well, and knew as much about him as any man living, I undertook to furnish biography, facts, truth, history--not eulogy--believing then, as I believe now, that the whole truth might be told of him and yet he would appear a purer, better, and greater man than there is left living. But he was human, composed of flesh and blood, and to him, as to others, belonged amiable weaknesses and some of the small sins incident to men. He was not perfect as a man, yet with all his humanity he was better than any other man I ever knew or expect to know. He was not a Christian in the orthodox sense of the term, yet he was as conscientiously religious as any man. I think I am justified in saying that had Mr. Lincoln been called upon to indicate in what manner the biography of him should be written, he would have preferred that no incident or event of his life should be omitted; that every incident and event of his history and every characteristic of his nature should be presented with photographic accuracy. He would have been content that the veil of obscurity should be withdrawn from his early life. All that was rude in it could detract nothing from the career which he afterwards so wonderfully accomplished. The higher elements of his character, as they were developed and wrought their effect, could have lost nothing in the world's judgment by a contrast, however strong, with the weaker and cruder elements of his nature. His life was a type of the society in which he lived, and with the progress and development of that society, advanced and expanded with a civilization which changed the unpeopled West to a land of churches and cities, wealth and civilization.

In your comment upon that part of the biography which treats of Mr. Lincoln's religion you say:--"A certain doubt is cast upon his argument by the heartlessness of it. We cannot avoid an impression that an anti-Christian animus inspires him." And you further say, "He does not know what Lincoln was, nor what religion is." That I did not know what Mr. Lincoln was, I must take leave to contradict with some emphasis; that I do not know what religion is, in the presence of so many illustrious failures to comprehend its true character, I may be permitted to doubt. Speaking of Mr. Lincoln in reference to this feature of his character, I express the decided opinion that he was an eminently moral man. Regarding him as a moral man, with my views upon the relations existing between the two characteristics, I have no difficulty in believing him a religious man! Yet he was not a Christian. He possessed, it is true, a system of faith and worship, but it was one which Orthodox Christianity stigmatizes as a false religion.

It surely cannot be a difficult matter to determine whether a man who lived so recently and so famously was a Christian or not. If he was a Christian he must have been sincere, for sincerity is one of the first of Christian virtues, and if sincere he must have availed himself of the promises of our Lord by a public profession of His faith, baptism in His name and membership of His church. Did Mr. Lincoln do this? No one pretends that he did, and those who maintain that he was nevertheless a Christian must hold that he may follow Jesus and yet deny Him; that he may be ashamed to own his Redeemer and yet claim His intercession; that he may serve Him acceptably, forsaking nothing, acknowledging nothing, repenting nothing.

When it is established by the testimony of the Christian Ministry that sinners may enter Heaven by a broad back gate like this, few will think it worth while to continue in the straight and narrow path prescribed by the Word of God. They who would canonize Mr. Lincoln as a saint should pause and reflect a brief moment upon the incalculable injury they do the cause which most of them profess to love. It would certainly have been pleasant to me to have closed without touching upon his religious opinions; but such an omission would have violated the fundamental principle upon which every line of the book is traced. Had it been possible to have truthfully asserted that he was a member of the Church of Christ or that he believed in the teachings of the New Testament, the facts would have been proclaimed with a glow of earnest and unfeigned satisfaction.

In conclusion I may say that my friendship for Mr. Lincoln was of no recent hot-house growth. Unlike that of many who have made me the subject of hostile criticism, it antedates the beginning of his presidential term and the dawn of his political triumphs. I had the good fortune to be in intimate association with his private life when it was humble and obscure, and I was near him too in the darkest hour of his executive responsibility, until, indeed, the first rays of God-given peace broke upon the land. I can say, with truth that none can assail, that I retained his confidence unshaken as he retained my affections unbroken until his life was offered up as a crowning sacrifice to domestic discord at the very threshold of his and the nation's triumph. Is it, therefore, likely that words of mine, written or spoken, should do purposed injustice to his memory? With the most profound respect, I am

Very truly your obedient servant, WARD H. LAMON.

www.ingramcontent.com/pod-product-compliance
Lightning Source LLC
Chambersburg PA
CBHW060755100426
42813CB00004B/832